FUNDAMENTALS OF INTERNET PROGRAMMING

Mir Shehzad Ahmad

Toronto Academic Press

Fundamentals of Internet Programming

Mir Shehzad Ahmad

Toronto Academic Press
224 Shoreacres Road
Burlington, ON L7L 2H2
Canada
www.tap-books.com
Email: orders@arclereducation.com

ISBN: 978-1-77469-762-7

ABOUT THE AUTHOR

Mir Shahzad Ahmad is an accomplished information security expert with over seven years of experience in the field. With a passion for cybersecurity and a drive to keep individuals and businesses safe from cyber threats, Mir has become a respected authority in his field. Mir's expertise lies in understanding the ever-changing landscape of cyber threats and developing effective strategies to mitigate risks. He has worked with a wide range of clients, from small businesses to multinational corporations, helping them to safeguard their data and systems. Throughout his career, Mir has developed a reputation for his ability to communicate complex cybersecurity concepts in a clear and concise manner. He has authored numerous articles on the subject and is a sought-after speaker at conferences and events. Mir is also an experienced educator, having trained a number of individuals and organizations on best practices in cybersecurity. He holds several certifications in the field, including CISSP, CEH, and CISM. Mir is dedicated to helping businesses and individuals stay ahead of the curve when it comes to cybersecurity. His insights and expertise make him a valuable resource for anyone looking to protect themselves from cyber threats.

Contents

List of Figures

List of Tables

List of Abbreviations

ACID	Atomic, Consistent, Isolated, and Durable
AJAX	Asynchronous JavaScript and XML
API	Application Programming Interface
ASP	Active Server Pages
BER	Bit Error Rate
BSBR	Best Sensor-Best-untrusted Relay
CE	Channel Estimation
CGI	Common Gateway Interface
CRM	Customer Relationship Management
CRUD	Create, Read, Update, Delete
CSS	Cascading Style Sheets
DBMS	Database Management System
DNS	Domain Name System
DoS	Denial-of-Service
DRL	Deep Reinforcement Learning
EH	Energy Harvesting
FQL	Facebook Query Language
GSPN	Generalized Stochastic Petri Net
GUI	Graphical User Interface
HD	Half-Duplex
HL	Hexagonal Lattice
HTML	Hypertext Markup Language
HTTP	Hyper Text Transport Protocol

IEEE	Institute of Electrical and Electronics Engineers
IETF	Internet Engineering Task Force
ISO	International Organization for Standardization
LQI	Link Quality Indicator
MCL	Maximum Coupling Loss
NOMA	Non-Orthogonal Multiple Access
ODL	Open Daylight
ODM	Object-Document Mapping
OGM	Object-Graph Mapping
OOP	Object-Oriented Programming
ORM	Object-Relational Mapping
OTA	Over-the-Air
PEFM	Policy Enforcement Fog Module
PS	Power Splitting
RACH	Random-Access Channel
RAW	Restricted Access Window
REST	Representational State Transfer
RSSI	Received Signal Strength Indicator
RTS	Radiating Two-Stage
SDN	Software-Defined Networking
SISO	Single-Input Single-Output
SL	Square Lattice
SNR	Signal-to-Noise to Noise Ratio
SNs	Sensor Nodes
SOAP	Simple Object Access Protocol
SoC	System-on-Chip
SOP	Secrecy Outage Probability
SQL	Structured Query Language
SSRs	Spectrum-Sensing Results
ST	Secrecy Throughput

TLS	Transport Layer Security
TRP	Tagged Response Probability
UAV	Unmanned Aerial Vehicle
URIs	Uniform Resource Identifiers
URL	Uniform Resource Locator
W3C	World Wide Web Consortium
WSN	Wireless Sensor Networks
WWW	World Wide Web
XHTML	Extensible Hypertext Markup Language
XML	eXtensible Markup Language

PREFACE

Internet programming is the process of designing, creating, and maintaining software applications that can be accessed and used over the internet. One of the core fundamentals of internet programming is the use of web standards and technologies, such as HTML, CSS, and JavaScript. These technologies allow developers to create web pages and applications that are easily accessible and can be viewed on a wide range of devices, including desktops, laptops, tablets, and mobile phones. HTML provides the structure and content of web pages, CSS is used to style and format the visual appearance of web pages, and JavaScript is used to create interactive and dynamic web content.

Fundamentals of Internet Programming is a comprehensive guide that provides readers with a thorough understanding of the essential principles and practices of internet programming. The book covers the client-server architecture, the role of web servers and web browsers, and the different types of websites and tools used in web development. It also provides readers with insights into HTML, CSS, JavaScript, and object-oriented programming (OOP), as well as the importance of database integration and web application security. The book is suitable for beginners and intermediate-level learners seeking to gain a deeper understanding of internet programming concepts and best practices.

Chapter one sets the stage for the book, introducing readers to the basics of internet programming and the key concepts involved in designing and building web-based applications. Chapter two delves into the World Wide Web (WWW) and website development, providing an in-depth understanding of the technology that underpins the internet and how it has evolved over time.

Chapter three explores the building blocks of the web, HTML and CSS, and how they are used to create visually appealing and responsive web pages. Chapter four focuses on JavaScript, the language of the web, and its importance in creating dynamic and interactive web pages.

Chapter five introduces readers to object-oriented programming, a powerful programming paradigm that is widely used in modern web development. Chapter six delves into database integration, examining the benefits and limitations of using SQL and NoSQL databases in web applications.

Chapter seven addresses the critical issue of web application security, providing insights into the various threats that web applications face and how to protect against them. Finally, chapter eight explores performance methodologies in internet programming, providing guidance on how to optimize web applications for speed, scalability, and user experience.

This book is suitable for beginners and intermediate-level learners seeking to gain a deeper understanding of internet programming concepts and best practices. It is also an excellent resource for professionals and students seeking to refresh their knowledge and stay up-to-date with the latest trends and techniques in the field.

–Author

CHAPTER 1

INTRODUCTION TO INTERNET PROGRAMMING

UNIT INTRODUCTION

Introduction to Internet programming is a broad topic that covers a wide range of technologies and concepts used for creating web-based applications and services. It involves understanding how web applications work, how they interact with web servers, databases, and clients, and how to program them using different programming languages, frameworks, and tools. Internet programming is a crucial skill for web developers, software engineers, and IT professionals, as it allows them to create powerful, dynamic, and interactive web applications that can run on any device connected to the internet. The fundamentals of internet programming include client-server architecture, protocols and standards, internet communication models, web browsers and servers, URLs and DNS. Web development involves programming in HTML, CSS, JavaScript, and web frameworks such as React, Angular, and Vue.js. Server-side programming involves programming languages such as PHP, Java, and Python, and using databases like MySQL or PostgreSQL to store data (Pallen, 1995).

Web services are another essential aspect of internet programming, and they enable different applications to communicate with each other over the internet using standard protocols such as REST and SOAP. Mobile web development involves creating web applications that can run on mobile devices, while security and privacy are critical aspects that need to be considered while developing web applications. Overall, Introduction to Internet programming is an exciting and constantly evolving field that provides a range of opportunities for developers to create innovative, powerful, and dynamic web applications and services that can be accessed by millions of users worldwide (Wetherall et al., 1998).

Learning Objectives

At the end of this chapter, readers will be able to:

- Define the scope and importance of Internet programming.
- Understand the evolution and applications of Internet programming.
- Identify the fundamentals of Internet programming, including client-server architecture, protocols and standards, internet communication models, web browsers and servers, URLs and DNS.
- Gain an introduction to web development, including HTML basics, CSS basics, JavaScript basics, and web frameworks.
- Understand server-side programming and its importance in web development.
- Learn about server-side programming languages, the common gateway interface (CGI), and an introduction to PHP.
- Gain an introduction to databases and their connectivity with server-side code, including SQL basics and an introduction to MySQL.

Key Terms

- Applications
- CGI
- Client-Server Architecture
- Communication Models
- CSS
- Databases
- DNS
- Evolution
- HTML
- Internet Programming
- JavaScript
- Languages
- MySQL
- PHP
- Protocols
- Servers
- Server-Side Programming

- SQL
- Standards
- URLs
- Web Browsers
- Web Development
- Web Frameworks

1.1. OVERVIEW OF INTERNET PROGRAMMING

Internet programming is the process of developing web applications and services that can be accessed over the internet. It involves understanding the principles of client-server architecture, internet communication models, web browsers and servers, and protocols and standards. Internet programming includes web development, server-side programming, database connectivity, web services, client-side programming, mobile web development, and security and privacy. The goal of internet programming is to create powerful, dynamic, and interactive web applications that can be accessed by users worldwide (McKnight & Bailey, 1995) (Figure 1.1).

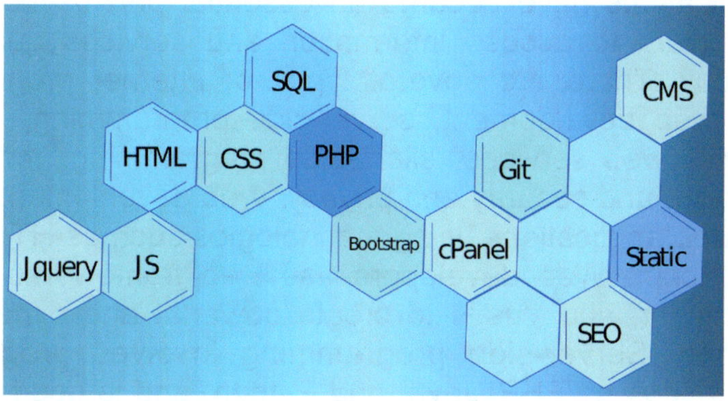

Figure 1.1. Illustration of various concepts in internet programming.

Source: Wachemo University, creative commons license.

1.2. DEFINITION AND SCOPE OF INTERNET PROGRAMMING

Internet programming refers to the creation of web-based applications and services that can be accessed over the internet. It involves a range of technologies, programming languages, and frameworks that allow developers to create dynamic and interactive web applications.

1.2.1. Definition of Internet Programming

Internet programming is the process of creating web-based applications and services that can be accessed by users over the internet. It involves using various programming languages, frameworks, and tools to create dynamic and interactive web applications that can run on any device with an internet connection (Khera et al., 1993). Internet programming involves several key concepts and terms, including client-server architecture, protocols and standards, internet communication models, web browsers and servers, URLs, DNS, HTML, CSS, JavaScript, and web frameworks. Internet programming differs from other types of programming, such as desktop programming or mobile app development, because it focuses on creating applications that can be accessed over the internet. This requires a unique set of skills and knowledge, including an understanding of web technologies, server-side programming languages, and database connectivity.

1.2.2. Scope of Internet Programming

Internet programming has a wide range of applications, including e-commerce, social media, online banking, gaming, and education. Web applications have become an essential part of modern life, enabling users to access information and services quickly and conveniently. There are several types of internet programming, including web development, server-side programming, database connectivity, web services, client-side programming, mobile web development, and security and privacy. Web development involves creating web applications using technologies such as HTML, CSS, and JavaScript. Web developers use web frameworks such as React, Angular, and Vue.js to create powerful and dynamic web applications. Server-side programming involves programming languages such as PHP, Java, and Python, and is used to create server-side logic that interacts with databases and other systems (Golpira et al., 2021) (Figure 1.2).

Figure 1.2. Web applications development in internet programming using technologies such as HTML, CSS, and Java etc.

Database connectivity involves connecting web applications to databases such as MySQL or PostgreSQL. This enables web applications to store and retrieve data from databases. Web services enable different applications to communicate with each other over the internet using standard protocols such as REST and SOAP. Client-side programming involves using JavaScript frameworks such as React or Angular to create interactive and dynamic web applications that run on the client-side.

Mobile web development involves creating web applications that can run on mobile devices. Developers use technologies such as responsive web design and mobile web development frameworks such as Ionic or Framework. Security and privacy are critical aspects of internet programming. Developers must consider security threats and attacks and follow best practices to ensure the security and privacy of users' data and information (Srinath, 2017).

1.3. EVOLUTION OF INTERNET PROGRAMMING

Internet programming has evolved significantly since the inception of the internet. In the early days, web pages were static, and internet programming was limited to basic HTML and CSS. Over time, web technologies advanced, and developers began to use more sophisticated programming languages and frameworks to create dynamic and interactive web applications (Kahn et al., 1997).

1.3.1. Early days of Internet Programming

1.3.1.1. Origins of the Internet

The internet was first created in the late 1960s as a way for researchers to share information and resources. In the early days, the internet was used primarily for academic and research purposes.

1.3.1.2. Early Web Technologies

The first web page was created in 1991, and it consisted of basic HTML and CSS. In the early days of internet programming, web pages were static, and there was little interactivity or dynamic content.

1.3.1.3. Static Web Pages

Static web pages were the norm in the early days of internet programming. They consisted of basic HTML and CSS and did not have any dynamic or interactive content (Leiner et al., 2009).

1.3.2. Emergence of Dynamic Web Applications

1.3.2.1. Introduction of JavaScript

JavaScript was introduced in 1995 and quickly became a popular programming language for creating dynamic and interactive web applications. JavaScript enabled developers to create dynamic user interfaces and add interactivity to web pages.

1.3.2.2. Use of CGI

Remember

The use of Common Gateway Interface (CGI) enables web servers to interact with other programs and execute complex tasks to produce dynamic web content.

Common Gateway Interface (CGI) was introduced in 1993 and allowed web servers to execute programs on the server-side in response to client requests. This enabled developers to create dynamic web pages that could be customized based on user input.

1.3.2.3. ASP and PHP

Active Server Pages (ASP) and PHP were introduced in the late 1990s and early 2000s and became popular server-side programming languages for creating dynamic web applications. ASP and PHP enabled developers to create server-side logic and dynamically generate HTML pages (Schiavone & Paterno, 2015) (Figure 1.3).

Figure 1.3. Comparison of security in PHP and ASP.

Source: Sudeep Srivastava, creative commons lincese.

1.3.3. Web 2.0 and Beyond

Asynchronous JavaScript and XML (AJAX) was introduced in the early 2000s and enabled developers to create dynamic web applications that could update content without refreshing the entire page. This made web applications more responsive and interactive (Figure 1.14).

Figure 1.4. Illustration of web 2.0 and its components.

Source: Markus Angermeier, creative commons license.

1.3.3.1. Web Services and APIs

Web services and APIs became popular in the mid-2000s and enabled developers to create web applications that could communicate with other applications and services over the internet. This enabled the creation of powerful and complex web applications.

1.3.3.2. Mobile Web Development

Mobile web development became essential in the late 2000s and early 2010s as mobile devices became more prevalent. Developers began to use responsive web design and mobile web development frameworks to create web applications that could run on mobile devices.

The evolution of internet programming has been significant, from the early days of static web pages to the emergence of dynamic web applications, web services, and mobile web development. The advancements in web technologies have enabled developers to create powerful, dynamic, and interactive web applications that can be accessed by users worldwide (Zhang et al., 2011).

1.4. APPLICATIONS OF INTERNET PROGRAMMING

Internet programming has a wide range of applications in various industries, including e-commerce, social media, online banking, gaming, and education. With the increasing number of internet users worldwide, web applications have become an essential part of modern life, enabling users to access information and services quickly and conveniently.

1.4.1. E-commerce

E-commerce is one of the most popular applications of internet programming. E-commerce websites enable users to buy and sell goods and services online. Developers use web technologies such as HTML, CSS, and JavaScript to create user-friendly and secure e-commerce websites. The e-commerce industry has experienced significant growth over the years, and internet programming has played a crucial role in enabling businesses to reach a global audience (Vladimir, 1996).

1.4.2. Social Media

Social media is another popular application of internet programming. Social media platforms enable users to connect with friends and family, share content, and communicate with each other online. Developers use web technologies such as React and Angular to create dynamic and interactive social media platforms. The social media industry has also experienced significant growth over the years, and internet programming has played a vital role in enabling users to connect with each other online (Kaplan & Haenlein, 2010).

Did you Know?

As of April 2021, there were over 3.8 billion active social media users worldwide, which accounts for more than 49% of the world's population?

1.4.3. Online Banking

Online banking is a critical application of internet programming. Online banking platforms enable users to access their accounts, transfer funds, and pay bills online. Developers use web technologies such as PHP and Java to create secure and user-friendly online banking platforms. The online banking industry has experienced significant growth over the years, and internet programming has played a crucial role in enabling users to access their financial information and services online (Chong et al., 2010) (Figure 1.5).

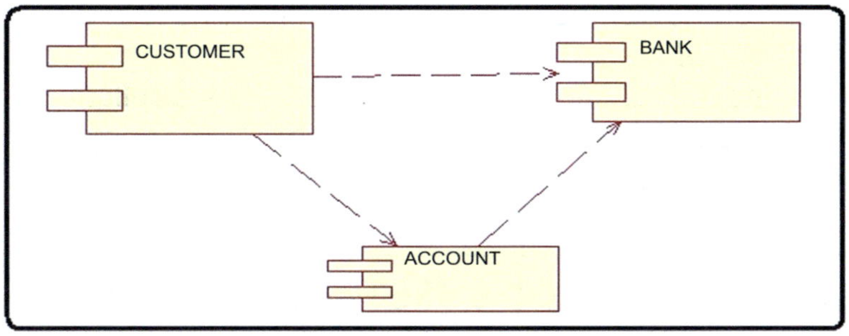

Figure 1.5. Class Diagram: Online banking system.

Source: Learning Tutorial, creative commons license.

1.4.4. Gaming

Gaming is another popular application of internet programming. Online gaming platforms enable users to play games online and connect with other players from around the world. Developers use web technologies such as JavaScript and HTML5 to create dynamic and interactive gaming platforms. The gaming industry has experienced significant growth over the years, and internet programming has played a vital role in enabling users to play games online and connect with other players (Wang et al., 2008).

1.4.5. Education

Education is an essential application of internet programming. Online education platforms enable users to access educational content and courses online. Developers use web technologies such as Moodle and Canvas to create user-friendly and interactive online education platforms. The online education industry has experienced significant growth over the years, and internet programming has played a crucial role in enabling users to access educational resources and courses online (Dillenbourg, 2016; Williamson, 2016). Web applications have revolutionized education by providing online learning platforms that offer flexibility in accessing course materials. These platforms enable collaboration and interaction among students and teachers, fostering a sense of community in virtual classrooms. Additionally, web-based assessment tools streamline the evaluation process, providing timely feedback and automated grading. Access to a wide range of educational resources, including e-books and multimedia content, enhances the learning experience. Web applications make education more accessible, overcoming geographical limitations and accommodating diverse schedules. They promote engagement and participation, creating inclusive learning environments. These applications empower self-directed learning and support lifelong learning opportunities. With personalized learning experiences tailored to individual needs, educational web applications have transformed teaching and learning methods, offering enhanced accessibility, collaboration, and resource availability.

1.5. IMPORTANCE OF INTERNET PROGRAMMING

The internet has revolutionized the way we communicate, access information, and conduct business. The increasing reliance on the internet has made internet programming an essential skill in today's technological landscape. Internet programming is the process of designing, creating, and maintaining applications and websites that operate on the internet. In this article, we will discuss the importance of internet programming in detail (Ritterband et al., 2003).

1.5.1. Global Reach

The internet has a global reach, making it possible for businesses and individuals to connect with people from different parts of the world. With internet programming, businesses can create websites and applications that are accessible to people across the globe. This makes it possible for businesses to expand their reach and attract a broader audience.

1.5.2. Interactive Web Applications

Internet programming has made it possible to create interactive web applications that can engage users in ways that were not possible before. For instance, social media platforms such as Facebook and Instagram have been made possible by internet programming.

Figure 1.6. Schematic of interactive web apps.

Source: Calvin Hendryx-Parker, creative commons license.

These platforms allow users to interact with each other, share photos, videos, and messages, among other things (Balasubramanian et al., 2008) (Figure 1.6).

1.5.3. E-commerce

E-commerce has become a vital part of the global economy, and internet programming has played a crucial role in making it possible. Internet programming has made it possible for businesses to create online stores that are accessible to customers worldwide. This has helped businesses to expand their reach and increase their revenue.

1.5.4. Mobile-Friendly Applications

The rise of mobile devices has made it essential for businesses to create mobile-friendly applications. Internet programming has made it possible to create applications that are compatible with different mobile devices. This has made it possible for businesses to reach customers who prefer to use mobile devices to access the internet (Islam et al., 2010).

1.5.5. Speed and Efficiency

Internet programming has made it possible to create websites and applications that are fast and efficient. This is crucial because users tend to abandon websites and applications that take too long to load. Internet programming has made it possible to optimize websites and applications for speed and efficiency, which has helped businesses to retain their customers (Trott & Oslon, 2010).

1.5.6. Cost-Effective

Internet programming has made it possible for businesses to create websites and applications without incurring high costs. This is because internet programming allows businesses to leverage open-source tools and platforms that are available for free. Additionally, internet programming allows businesses to create scalable solutions that can grow as their needs evolve (Tate et al., 2009).

1.6. BASIC CONCEPTS IN INTERNET PROGRAMMING

1.6.1. Client-Server Architecture

Client-server architecture is a widely used model in computer networking that describes the relationship between two software applications: (Cao et al., 2018) a client and a server. In this architecture, the client is the software that requests services or resources from the server, and the server is the software that provides those services or resources. This model has several key features that make it an effective way to build scalable and reliable distributed applications. In this article, we will discuss the main features and advantages of the client-server architecture (Cao et al., 2018) (Figure 1.7).

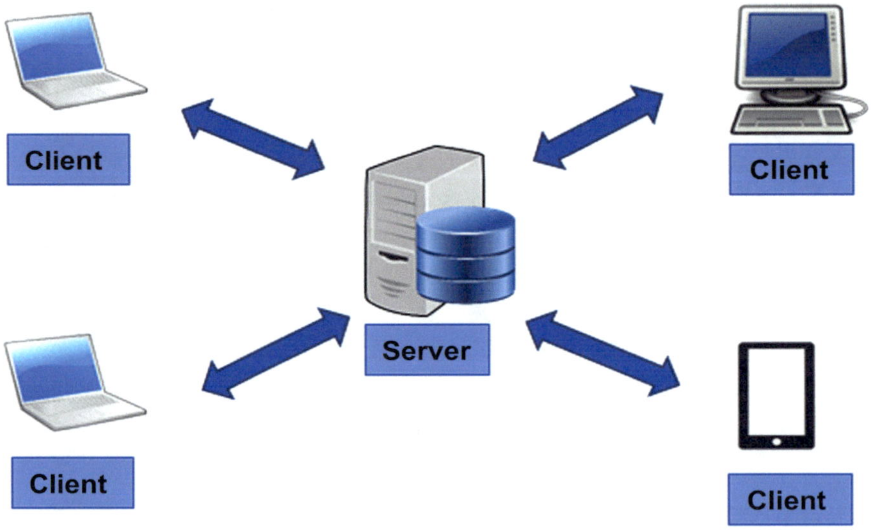

Figure 1.7. Illustration of a client -server architecture.

Source: Matthew MacFarquhar, creative commons license.

The client and server are two separate software components that communicate with each other over a network. The client component runs on a user's computer or device, while the server component runs on a remote computer or device. The client initiates the communication by sending a request to the server, and the server responds to the request by sending back the requested data or performing the requested operation (Ivkovic & Milanov, 2010).

1.6.1.1. Communication Protocol

The communication between the client and server is governed by a communication protocol. The protocol defines the rules for how the data is exchanged between the client and server. There are several widely used communication protocols, including HTTP, FTP, SMTP, and TCP/IP. Each protocol has its own rules and features that are optimized for specific types of applications and use cases.

1.6.1.2. Scalability

One of the key benefits of the client-server architecture is its scalability. The server can handle requests from multiple clients simultaneously, which makes it possible to build applications that can serve large numbers of users. This scalability is achieved by using a pool of resources that are shared among the clients. For example, a web server can handle thousands of requests per second by using a pool of worker processes that handle incoming requests (Castagnos & Boyer, 2006).

1.6.1.3. Reliability

Another advantage of the client-server architecture is its reliability. The server can provide redundancy and fault tolerance by using multiple servers in a cluster or using load balancing to distribute the workload across multiple servers. This ensures that if one server fails, the other servers in the cluster can take over and continue to serve the clients. This approach also makes it possible to perform maintenance or upgrades on one server while the other servers in the cluster continue to handle requests (Cardinal & Aitken, 2010).

1.6.1.4. Security

The client-server architecture can also provide security by controlling access to the server and its resources. The server can authenticate clients using a variety of mechanisms, such as username and password, digital certificates, or biometric authentication. This ensures that only authorized clients can access the server and its resources. Additionally, the server can use encryption to protect the data that is exchanged between the client and server (Zissis & Lekkas, 2012).

1.6.2. Protocols and Standards

Protocols and standards are essential components of the internet and computer networking. They provide a common language and framework for communication between different devices and software applications. In this article, we will discuss what protocols and standards are and why they are important in computer networking.

1.6.2.1. Protocols

A protocol is a set of rules that governs how data is transmitted and received between two or more devices. Protocols are used in all aspects of computer networking, including communication between computers, between devices in a network, and between applications on different devices. Protocols define the format of the data, the order in which it is transmitted, and the actions that should be taken in response to certain events. Some examples of commonly used protocols include TCP/IP, HTTP, FTP, SMTP, and DNS (Yao, 1982) (Figure 1.8).

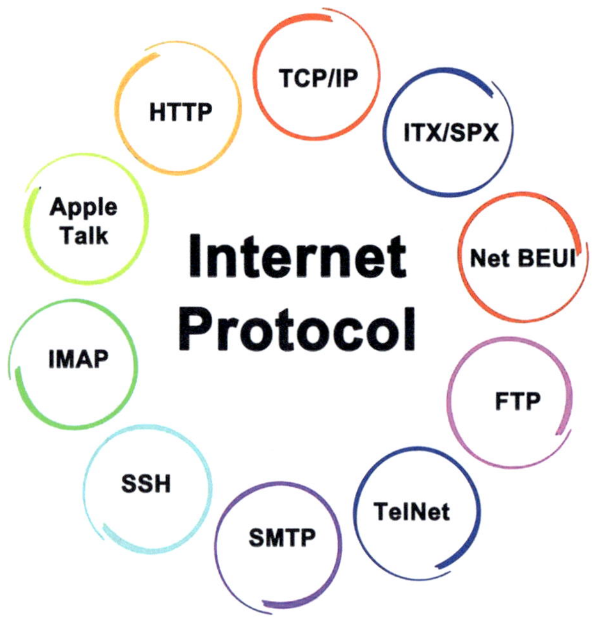

Figure 1.8. Schematic of the internet protocol and its components.

Source: Vaeenma, creative commons license.

1.6.2.2. Standards

A standard is a set of specifications that defines how a particular technology or process should be implemented. Standards are developed and maintained by organizations such as the International Organization for Standardization (ISO), the Institute of Electrical and Electronics Engineers (IEEE), and the Internet Engineering Task Force (IETF). Standards provide a common language and framework for developers to follow when creating products or applications. This ensures that products from different vendors can work together seamlessly and that applications can be easily deployed across different platforms (Severance, 1995).

1.6.2.3. Importance of Protocols and Standards

Protocols and standards are essential for computer networking for several reasons:

1. **Interoperability:** Protocols and standards ensure that different devices and software applications can communicate with each other, regardless of the manufacturer or operating system. This allows for greater interoperability between devices and applications, which is essential for building complex systems.
2. **Reliability:** Protocols and standards provide a consistent and reliable way of transmitting and receiving data. This helps to ensure that data is transmitted accurately and efficiently, reducing the likelihood of errors or data loss (Salman & Jain, 2017).
3. **Security:** Protocols and standards provide a framework for securing data and networks. For example, encryption protocols ensure that data is transmitted securely over the internet, while security standards provide guidelines for securing networks and devices.
4. **Innovation:** Protocols and standards encourage innovation by providing a common language and framework for developers to work within. This enables developers to focus on creating new applications and services without having to worry about compatibility issues (Tanenbaum, 1981).

1.6.3. Internet Communication Models

Internet communication models are crucial for understanding how information is exchanged between different devices and applications over the internet. In this article, we will discuss different internet communication models and their significance in the digital age.

1.6.3.1. Peer-to-Peer Communication Model

The peer-to-peer communication model is a decentralized model that allows devices to communicate directly with each other without the need for a central server. This model is often used in file-sharing applications, where users can share files directly with other users without having to go through a central server. The peer-to-peer model can be highly efficient, as it does not rely on a single point of failure, but it can also be more challenging to secure (Fawkes & Gregory, 2001).

1.6.3.2. Client-Server Communication Model

The client-server communication model is the most common internet communication model. In this model, a client device sends a request to a server device, and the server responds with the requested information or resource. This model is used for a wide range of applications, including web browsing, email, and online gaming. The client-server model is highly scalable and reliable, making it ideal for applications that need to handle large amounts of traffic (Hsieh & Sivakumar, 2004).

1.6.3.3. Publish-Subscribe Communication Model

The publish-subscribe communication model is a messaging model in which publishers send messages to subscribers who have expressed an interest in receiving those messages. This model is often used in real-time applications such as instant messaging and stock market updates. The publish-subscribe model can be highly efficient, as it only sends messages to subscribers who have expressed interest in receiving them (Oluwatosin, 2014).

1.6.4. Web Browsers and Servers

Web browsers and servers are two essential components of the internet that work together to enable users to access and view websites. In this article, we will explore the functions of web browsers and servers, and their roles in facilitating internet communication (Figure 1.9).

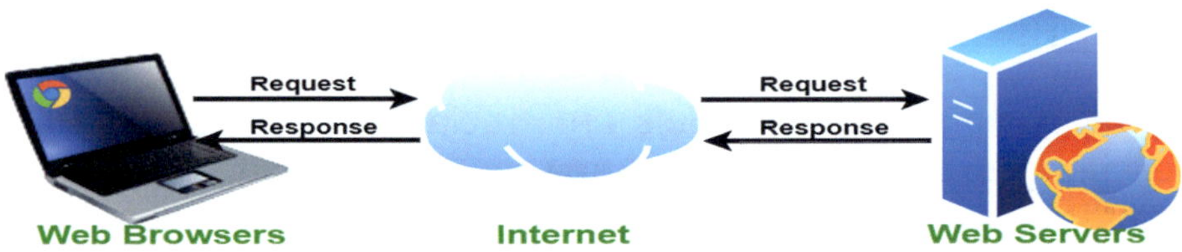

Figure 1.9. Schematic of web browsers and web servers.

Source: Nanduri Balajee, creative commons license.

1.6.4.1. Web Browsers

A web browser is software that allows users to access and view websites. It interprets HTML, CSS, and JavaScript code to display web pages and content. Web browsers provide an interface for users to interact with websites and enable users to navigate between pages, click on links, and submit forms. Web browsers have evolved over time, and currently, the most popular browsers are Google Chrome, Mozilla Firefox, Microsoft Edge, and Apple Safari. Each browser has its unique features and capabilities, but they all perform the essential function of rendering web pages (Eugster et al., 2003).

1.6.4.2. Web Servers

Web servers are software applications that run on remote computers and respond to requests from web browsers. They store and serve web pages, images, and other resources, and handle incoming requests from web browsers. When a user requests a web page, the browser sends a request to the server that hosts the website. The server then responds with the requested page and any associated resources, such as images or scripts. Web servers use protocols like HTTP or HTTPS to communicate with browsers and ensure the secure transmission of data.

Web servers can be either dedicated or shared. A dedicated server is a single computer that hosts one or more websites, while a shared server hosts multiple websites on the same computer (Eckersley, 2010).

1.6.5. URLs and DNS

URLs and DNS are two important components of the internet that are essential for accessing websites and web resources. In this article, we will explore the functions of URLs and DNS, and their roles in facilitating internet communication (Bohrer et al., 2002).

1.6.5.1. URLs

A Uniform Resource Locator (URL) is a string of characters that identifies the location of a web page or web resource on the internet. URLs contain several parts, including the protocol (http or https), domain name (such as google.com), and path to the resource on the server.

URLs can also contain query parameters that specify additional information or parameters for the server. URLs provide a way for users to access web pages and resources by simply clicking on links or entering the URL into a web browser. They are also used by web developers to create hyperlinks between web pages and to reference resources like images or scripts (Jiang et al., 2018).

1.6.5.2. DNS

Domain Name System (DNS) is a system that translates domain names into IP addresses. Every computer on the internet has a unique IP address, which is used to identify the computer on the network. However, domain names are easier for humans to remember and use than IP addresses. When a user enters a domain name into a web browser, the browser sends a request to a DNS server to resolve the domain name into an IP address. The DNS server then returns the IP address to the browser, which uses it to connect to the server hosting the website. DNS is critical for the functioning of the internet as it enables users to access web pages and resources using domain names, which are easier to remember and use than IP addresses.

URLs and DNS are essential components of the internet that enable users to access and view web pages and resources. URLs provide a way for users to identify the location of web pages and resources on the internet, while DNS translates domain names into IP addresses, making it easier for users to remember and use domain names. Understanding how URLs and DNS work together is crucial for web developers and designers to create websites that can be accessed and viewed by users worldwide (Shaikh et al., 2001).

1.7. INTRODUCTION TO WEB DEVELOPMENT

Introduction to web development is a course that teaches the basics of building websites and web applications. The course covers the essential technologies and tools used in web development, including HTML, CSS, JavaScript, and web frameworks like React or Angular. Students learn how to create and design websites, develop interactive web pages, and manage data on the web. The course may also cover topics like web security, version control, and web hosting. By the end of the course, students will have a solid foundation in web development and be able to create basic websites and web applications (Gottschalk et al., 2002).

1.7.1. HTML Basics

Hypertext Markup Language (HTML) is the foundation of web development and is used to structure content on the web. It provides a framework for organizing content, defining its structure, and presenting it to users in a readable and understandable format. HTML consists of a series of tags and elements that define the structure and content of a web page.

TIPS

Understanding the basic structure and syntax of HTML, such as using appropriate tags and attributes, is essential for creating well-structured and visually appealing web pages.

Each tag specifies how the content should be formatted and displayed on the page. The basic structure of an HTML document includes the <!DOCTYPE> declaration, the <html> tag, the <head> tag, and the <body> tag.

The <!DOCTYPE> declaration tells the web browser which version of HTML the page is written in, while the <html> tag defines the start and end of the HTML document. The <head> tag contains metadata about the page, such as the title, keywords, and character encoding, while the <body> tag contains the main content of the page (MacBeth & MacBeth, 2004).

HTML tags can be used to format text, add images, create links, and more. Text can be formatted using tags such as <h1> for headings, <p> for paragraphs, and <em> for emphasis. Images can be added to a web page using the <img> tag, which specifies the location of the image file. Links can be created using the <a> tag, which can link to other web pages, email addresses, or files on the web server. Forms can be created using the <form> tag, which allows users to enter information, such as their name, email address, and other details, and submit it to the web server.

HTML tags can be nested inside one another, allowing for more complex page layouts. For example, a <div> tag can be used to group elements together, and then styled with CSS to create a layout for the page. In addition to structural tags, HTML also includes tags for creating tables, lists, and other elements that can make web pages more interactive and engaging.

Understanding HTML is essential for web development, as it forms the basis for all web content. HTML provides a standard format for web pages, allowing them to be viewed on any device with a web browser. It is the first step in creating a website or web application, and is essential for web designers and developers to master (Casario et al., 2012).

1.7.2. CSS Basics

Cascading Style Sheets (CSS) is a style sheet language used to describe the presentation of a document written in HTML or XML. CSS provides a way to style web pages and control the visual appearance of elements on a web page. CSS allows web developers to separate the content of a web page from its presentation, making it easier to maintain and update the site. CSS consists of a series of rules that define the styling properties of elements on the page.

Each rule consists of a selector, which specifies the element to be styled, and a set of styling properties, which define how the element should look. CSS can be used to style text, fonts, colors, backgrounds, borders, and more.

Text can be styled using properties such as font-size, font-family, and font-weight. Colors can be applied to text, backgrounds, and borders using the color property.

Backgrounds can be styled using the background-color and background-image properties, which allow images to be used as backgrounds. Borders can be styled using properties such as border-color, border-width, and border-style.

CSS also includes a box model, which defines the layout of elements on the page. The box model consists of four components: the content, padding, border, and margin. The content is the actual content of the element, while the padding is the space between the content and the border. The border is the line around the element, and the margin is the space between the border and other elements on the page..

CSS can be applied to web pages in several ways, including inline styles, embedded styles, and external stylesheets. Inline styles are applied directly to individual elements using the style attribute. Embedded styles are placed in the head section of the HTML document using the <style> tag. External stylesheets are stored in separate files and linked to the HTML document using the <link> tag. Understanding CSS is essential for web development, as it provides a way to style web pages and control their visual appearance. CSS allows web developers to create visually appealing and responsive web pages that can be viewed on any device with a web browser. By separating the content of a web page from its presentation, CSS makes it easier to maintain and update the site (Meyer & Meyer, 2010).

1.7.3. JavaScript Basics

JavaScript is a programming language that allows web developers to create dynamic and interactive web pages. It is used to add interactivity and functionality to web pages and is one of the core technologies of web development. JavaScript is a client-side scripting language, which means that it is executed by the web browser on the client-side, rather than on the server-side. JavaScript can be used to perform a wide range of tasks, including manipulating the HTML and CSS of a web page, responding to user input, validating forms, and creating animations and effects.

JavaScript code is executed in the browser and can be embedded directly into an HTML document using the <script> tag (Freeman & Freeman, 2018). JavaScript includes a variety of built-in objects and functions, which can be used to perform common tasks, such as manipulating strings and arrays, creating and manipulating HTML elements, and working with dates and times. JavaScript also includes a number of control structures, such as if/else statements, loops, and switch statements, which allow developers to control the flow of their code.

JavaScript can also interact with other technologies on the web, such as AJAX, which allows web pages to load and update content dynamically without requiring a page refresh. JavaScript frameworks, such as React, Angular, and Vue.js, provide pre-built libraries and components that make it easier to build complex web applications.

Understanding JavaScript is essential for web development, as it allows web developers to create interactive and responsive web pages and applications. It is a versatile and powerful language that can be used to perform a wide range of tasks and is an essential tool for building modern web applications (Theisen, 2019).

1.7.4. Web Frameworks

Web frameworks are software libraries that provide a pre-built structure and set of tools for web developers to build web applications. Web frameworks provide a way to streamline the development process and reduce the amount of time and effort required to build a web application. They typically include a variety of components and features, such as templates, routing, database integration, security, and more. Web frameworks are available in a variety of programming languages, including JavaScript, Python, Ruby, PHP, and more. Some of the most popular web frameworks include React, Angular, Vue.js, Django, Ruby on Rails, and Laravel (Brady et al., 2002).

Web frameworks are designed to simplify the process of building web applications, allowing developers to focus on the application logic rather than the underlying infrastructure. They provide a consistent and standardized approach to building web applications, making it easier for developers to collaborate and maintain code. Web frameworks also provide a way to handle common web development tasks, such as form validation, authentication, and database integration. They often include pre-built components and modules that can be easily integrated into a web application, saving time and effort.

Web frameworks are essential tools for web developers, as they provide a pre-built structure and set of tools for building web applications. They simplify the development process, reduce the amount of time and effort required to build a web application, and provide a consistent and standardized approach to web development. By using web frameworks, developers can focus on the application logic rather than the underlying infrastructure, making it easier to build and maintain web applications (Curie et al., 2019).

1.8. SERVER-SIDE PROGRAMMING

Server-side programming is a type of programming that runs on the server-side of a web application. It involves writing code that processes user requests and generates dynamic web pages on the server before sending them to the client-side for display.

Server-side programming allows web developers to create interactive and dynamic web pages that can respond to user input and provide personalized content. Server-side programming can be done using a variety of programming languages, including PHP, Python, Ruby, Java, and more. Each language has its own strengths and weaknesses, and choosing the right language for a web application depends on various factors, such as the complexity of the application, the required performance, and the developer's familiarity with the language (Schmidt, 2000) (Figure 1.10).

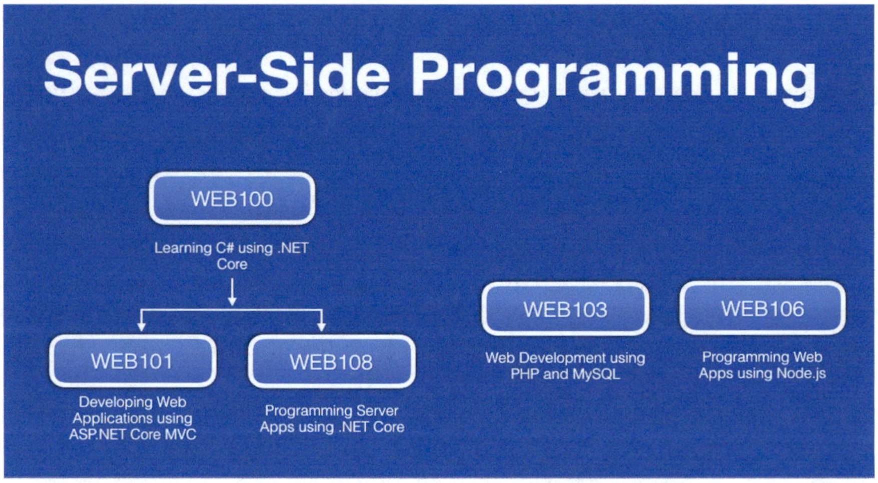

Figure 1.10. Illustration of the server side programming.

Source: Enaviya information technology, creative commons license.

The CGI is a protocol that allows web servers to communicate with external programs running on the server-side. CGI programs can be written in any programming language, and they receive data from the web server in the form of HTTP requests and respond with HTTP responses. CGI programs can be used for a wide range of tasks, including processing form data, generating dynamic web pages, and accessing databases. PHP is a popular server-side programming language that is widely used for web development. PHP is an open-source language that is easy to learn and has a large community of developers. It is designed specifically for web development and has a range of built-in functions and libraries that make it easy to create dynamic and interactive web pages. Server-side programming is an essential component of web development, as it allows developers to create dynamic and interactive web pages that can respond to user input and provide personalized content. There are many programming languages that can be used for server-side programming, and choosing the right language depends on various factors, such as the complexity of the application and the developer's familiarity with the language. The CGI is a protocol that allows web servers to communicate with external programs, and PHP is a popular server-side programming language that is widely used for web development (Zhu et al., 2015).

1.9. DATABASE CONNECTIVITY

Database connectivity is a critical component of web development, as it allows web applications to store and manage large amounts of data. In this section, we will explore the basics of databases, SQL, and connecting to databases from server-side code. A database is a collection of data that is organized and structured in a specific way to allow for efficient storage and retrieval. Databases are used to store information for web applications, such as user data, product information, and more. Databases can be relational or non-relational, and they are typically managed by a database management system (DBMS), such as MySQL, Oracle, or MongoDB.

Structured Query Language (SQL) is a programming language used to communicate with relational databases. SQL allows developers to create, modify, and query data in a database. SQL is used to create tables and define their structure, insert data into tables, retrieve data from tables, and update and delete data in tables. Connecting to databases from server-side code involves establishing a connection to the database from the server-side code, executing SQL queries to retrieve or modify data, and handling any errors that may occur. The process of connecting to a database depends on the programming language being used and the DBMS being used (Sud & Sud, 2020).

Database connectivity is an essential component of web development, as it allows web applications to store and manage large amounts of data. Databases are typically managed by a DBMS, and SQL is used to communicate with relational databases. Connecting to databases from server-side code involves establishing a connection to the database, executing SQL queries, and handling errors. Understanding database connectivity is crucial for web developers to create scalable and robust web applications.

1.10. WEB SERVICES

Web services are a way for web applications to communicate and exchange data over the internet. They allow for interoperability between different systems and applications, and they are typically built using standard web technologies, such as HTTP and XML (Ferris & Farrell, 2003).

The Representational State Transfer (REST) architecture is a popular approach to building web services. REST is based on a set of principles and constraints that define how web services should be designed and implemented. RESTful web services use HTTP methods to perform Create, Read, Update, Delete (CRUD) operations on resources, which are identified by unique Uniform Resource Identifiers (URIs). RESTful web services are scalable and flexible, and they can be easily integrated with other systems. Simple Object Access Protocol (SOAP) is another approach to building web services. SOAP is a messaging protocol that uses XML to encode messages and HTTP to transport them over the internet. SOAP web services provide a standardized way for applications to exchange data, and they are typically used in enterprise environments where security and reliability are critical. Web service security is an important consideration when building web services. Web services can be vulnerable to attacks, such as injection attacks, cross-site scripting (XSS) attacks, and denial-of-service (DoS) attacks. Web service security involves implementing measures to protect against these attacks, such as using secure communication protocols like HTTPS, implementing access control measures, and validating user input.

Web services are an essential component of web development, as they allow for interoperability between different systems and applications. RESTful web services and SOAP web services are two popular approaches to building web services, each with its own strengths and weaknesses. Web service security is an important consideration when building web services, and developers should implement measures to protect against common attacks (Roy & Ramanujan, 2001).

ACTIVITY 1.1:

You are working on a team to develop a social media platform. What are some key concepts and technologies you would need to understand in order to successfully build and deploy a scalable and secure web application?

SUMMARY

The chapter "Introduction to Internet Programming" provides an overview of the fundamental concepts and principles of internet programming. It covers the definition and scope of internet programming, its evolution over time, and its applications. The chapter discusses the client-server architecture, protocols, and standards used in internet communication, and the models used to establish internet communication. It also covers web browsers and servers, URLs, and DNS. Furthermore, the chapter introduces the basics of web development, including HTML, CSS, JavaScript, and web frameworks. It also covers server-side programming, including server-side programming languages, CGI, and PHP. The chapter concludes with an introduction to databases and database connectivity, including SQL basics, connecting to databases from server-side code, and an introduction to MySQL. Overall, this chapter provides a foundational understanding of internet programming and the various tools and technologies involved in developing web-based applications. It is useful for anyone interested in learning about internet programming and its applications.

REVIEW QUESTIONS

1. What is internet programming and why is it important?
2. Explain the evolution of internet programming.
3. What is the client-server architecture and how does it work?
4. What are the basic components of web development?
5. Explain the concept of server-side programming and its importance.
6. What is the purpose of databases in internet programming?
7. How does SQL enable connectivity to databases in internet programming?

MULTIPLE CHOICE QUESTIONS

1. What is the purpose of internet programming?

a. Maximizing sales
b. Realizing a particular market share
c. Maximizing profit
d. All of the above

2. Which architecture is used in internet programming?

a. Client-server architecture
b. Peer-to-peer architecture
c. Centralized architecture
d. Decentralized architecture

3. **What are the basic components of web development?**
   a. HTML, CSS, JavaScript, and web frameworks
   b. Protocols and standards
   c. Client-server architecture
   d. SQL basics
4. **Which programming language is commonly used for server-side programming?**
   a. HTML
   b. CSS
   c. JavaScript
   d. PHP
5. **What is the purpose of SQL in internet programming?**
   a. To create web pages
   b. To connect to databases
   c. To establish internet communication
   d. To define protocols and standards
6. **What is the purpose of CGI?**
   a. To create web pages
   b. To connect to databases
   c. To establish internet communication
   d. To facilitate server-side programming
7. **What is the purpose of DNS?**
   a. To create web pages
   b. To connect to databases
   c. To translate URLs to IP addresses
   d. To establish internet communication

Answers to Multiple Choice Questions

1. (d) **2.** (a) **3.** (a) **4.** (d);
5. (b); **6.** (d); **7.** (c)

REFERENCES

1. Al-Masri, E., & Mahmoud, Q. H., (2008). Investigating web services on the world wide web. In: Proceedings of the 17th International Conference on World Wide Web (Vol. 1, No. 1, pp. 795–804).

2. Balasubramanian, A., Levine, B. N., & Venkataramani, A., (2008). Enhancing interactive web applications in hybrid networks. In: Proceedings of the 14th ACM International Conference on Mobile Computing and Networking, 1(1), 70–80.
3. Bohrer, P., Elnozahy, E. N., Keller, T., Kistler, M., Lefurgy, C., McDowell, C., & Rajamony, R., (2002). The case for power management in web servers. Power Aware Computing, 261–289.
4. Brady, A., McDowell, R. C., & Schultz, K., (2002). JavaScript programming basics: A laboratory series for beginning programmers. Journal on Educational Resources in Computing (JERIC), 2(2), 1–20.
5. Cao, Y., Li, Q., Tan, Y., Li, Y., Chen, Y., Shao, X., & Zou, Y., (2018). A comprehensive review of energy internet: Basic concept, operation and planning methods, and research prospects. Journal of Modern Power Systems and Clean Energy, 6(3), 399–411.
6. Carbonaro, A., & Ravaioli, M., (2017). Peer assessment to promote deep learning and to reduce a gender gap in the traditional introductory programming course. Journal of e-Learning and Knowledge Society, 13(3).
7. Cardinal, R. N., & Aitken, M. R., (2010). Whisker: A client—Server high-performance multimedia research control system. Behavior Research Methods, 42(4), 1059–1071.
8. Casario, M., Wormser, N., Saltzman, D., Bradford, A., Reid, J., Improta, F., & Congleton, A., (2012). CSS basics. CSS3 Solutions: Essential Techniques for CSS3 Developers, 1(1), 1–24.
9. Castagnos, S., & Boyer, A., (2006). A client/server user-based collaborative filtering algorithm: Model and implementation. In: 17th European Conference on Artificial Intelligence (ECAI 2006), 1(1), 617–621.
10. Chong, A. Y. L., Ooi, K. B., Lin, B., & Tan, B. I., (2010). Online banking adoption: An empirical analysis. International Journal of Bank Marketing, 28(4), 267–287.
11. Curie, D. H., Jaison, J., Yadav, J., & Fiona, J. R., (2019). Analysis on web frameworks. In: Journal of Physics: Conference Series (Vol. 1362, No. 1, p. 012114). IOP Publishing.
12. De Raadt, M., (2010). Introductory programming in a web context. In: Conferences in Research and Practice in Information Technology (CRPIT) (Vol. 103, pp. 79–86).
13. Dillenbourg, P., (2016). The evolution of research on digital education. International Journal of Artificial Intelligence in Education, 26, 544–560.
14. Dustdar, S., & Schreiner, W., (2005). A survey on web services composition. International Journal of Web and Grid Services, 1(1), 1–30.
15. Eckersley, P., (2010). How unique is your web browser? In: Privacy Enhancing Technologies: 10th International Symposium, PETS 2010, Berlin, Germany, July 21–23, 2010; Proceedings 10 (pp. 1–18).
16. Eugster, P. T., Felber, P. A., Guerraoui, R., & Kermarrec, A. M., (2003). The many faces of publish/subscribe. ACM Computing Surveys (CSUR), 35(2), 114–131.
17. Fawkes, J., & Gregory, A., (2001). Applying communication theories to the internet. Journal of Communication Management, 5(2), 109–124.

18. Ferris, C., & Farrell, J., (2003). What are web services? Communications of the ACM, 46(6), 31.
19. Freeman, A., & Freeman, A., (2018). An HTML and CSS primer. Pro. Angular, 6, 43–61.
20. Golpîra, H., Khan, S. A. R., & Safaeipour, S., (2021). A review of logistics internet-of-things: Current trends and scope for future research. Journal of Industrial Information Integration, 22, 100194.
21. Gottschalk, K., Graham, S., Kreger, H., & Snell, J., (2002). Introduction to web services architecture. IBM Systems Journal, 41(2), 170–177.
22. Hsieh, H. Y., & Sivakumar, R., (2004). On using peer-to-peer communication in cellular wireless data networks. IEEE Transactions on Mobile Computing, 3(1), 57–72.
23. Islam, R., Islam, R., & Mazumder, T., (2010). Mobile application and its global impact. International Journal of Engineering & Technology, 10(6), 72–78.
24. Ivkovic, M., & Milanov, D., (2010). Affiliate internet marketing: Concept and application analysis. In: 2010 International Conference on Education and Management Technology, 1(1), 319–323.
25. Jiang, J., Chen, J., Choo, K. K. R., Liu, C., Liu, K., Yu, M., & Wang, Y., (2018). A deep learning based online malicious URL and DNS detection scheme. In: Security and Privacy in Communication Networks: 13th International Conference, SecureComm 2017, Niagara Falls, ON, Canada, October 22–25, 2017, Proceedings, Springer International Publishing (Vol. 13, pp. 438–448).
26. Kahn, R., Leiner, B. M., Cerf, V. G., Clark, D. D., Kleinrock, L., Lynch, D. C., & Wolff, S., (1997). The evolution of the internet as a global information system. The International Information & Library Review, 29(2), 129–151.
27. Kaplan, A. M., & Haenlein, M., (2010). Users of the world, unite! The challenges and opportunities of social media. Business Horizons, 53(1), 59–68.
28. Khera, V., Astrachan, O., & Kotz, D., (1993). The internet programming contest: A report and philosophy. ACM SIGCSE Bulletin, 25(1), 48–52.
29. Leiner, B. M., Cerf, V. G., Clark, D. D., Kahn, R. E., Kleinrock, L., Lynch, D. C., & Wolff, S., (2009). A brief history of the internet. ACM SIGCOMM Computer Communication Review, 39(5), 22–31.
30. MacBeth, G. S., & MacBeth, G. S., (2004). HTML basics. C# Programmer's Handbook, 1(1), 441–463.
31. Mahmoud, Q. H., (2011). A mobile web-based approach to introductory programming. In: Proceedings of the 16th Annual Joint Conference on Innovation and Technology in Computer Science Education, 1(1), 334.
32. Malik, S. I., Mathew, R., Al-Nuaimi, R., Al-Sideiri, A., & Coldwell-Neilson, J., (2019). Learning problem solving skills: Comparison of E-learning and M-learning in an introductory programming course. Education and Information Technologies, 24(5), 2779–2796.

33. McKnight, L. W., & Bailey, J. P., (1995). An introduction to internet economics. Journal of Electronic Publishing, 1(1, 2), 1–20.
34. Meyer, J., & Meyer, J., (2010). The basics. The Essential Guide to HTML5: Using Games to Learn HTML5 and JavaScript, 1(1), 1–19.
35. O'Kearney, R., Gibson, M., Christensen, H., & Griffiths, K. M., (2006). Effects of a cognitive-behavioral internet program on depression, vulnerability to depression and stigma in adolescent males: A school-based controlled trial. Cognitive Behavior Therapy, 35(1), 43–54.
36. Oluwatosin, H. S., (2014). Client-server model. IOSR Journal of Computer Engineering, 16(1), 67–71.
37. Pallen, M., (1995). Guide to the internet: Introducing the internet. BMJ, 311(7017), 1422–1424.
38. Ritterband, L. M., Gonder-Frederick, L. A., Cox, D. J., Clifton, A. D., West, R. W., & Borowitz, S. M., (2003). Internet interventions: In review, in use, and into the future. Professional Psychology: Research and Practice, 34(5), 527.
39. Roy, J., & Ramanujan, A., (2001). Understanding web services. IT Professional, 3(6), 69–73.
40. Salman, T., & Jain, R., (2017). Networking protocols and standards for internet of things. Internet of Things and Data Analytics Handbook, 1(1), 215–238.
41. Schiavone, A. G., & Paternò, F., (2015). An extensible environment for guideline-based accessibility evaluation of dynamic web applications. Universal Access in the Information Society, 14(1), 111–132.
42. Schmidt, W. C., (2000). The server side of psychology web experiments. In: Psychological Experiments on the Internet (Vol. 1, No. 1, pp. 285–310). Academic Press
43. Severance, C., (1995). The value of the formal standards process. Computer, 28(8), 82, 83.
44. Shaikh, A., Tewari, R., & Agrawal, M., (2001). On the effectiveness of DNS-based server selection. In: Proceedings IEEE INFOCOM 2001; Conference on Computer Communications. Twentieth Annual Joint Conference of the IEEE Computer and Communications Society (Cat. No. 01CH37213) (Vol. 3, pp. 1801–1810).
45. Srinath, K. R., (2017). Python–the fastest growing programming language. International Research Journal of Engineering and Technology, 4(12), 354–357.
46. Sud, K., & Sud, K., (2020). Database connectivity. Practical Hapi: Build Your Own Hapi Apps and Learn from Industry Case Studies, 1(1), 63–84.
47. Tanenbaum, A. S., (1981). Network protocols. ACM Computing Surveys (CSUR), 13(4), 453–489.
48. Tate, D. F., Finkelstein, E. A., Khavjou, O., & Gustafson, A., (2009). Cost effectiveness of internet interventions: Review and recommendations. Annals of Behavioral Medicine, 38(1), 40–45.

49. Theisen, K. J., (2019). Programming languages in chemistry: A review of HTML5/ JavaScript. Journal of Cheminformatics, 11(1), 11.
50. Trott, O., & Olson, A. J., (2010). AutoDock Vina: Improving the speed and accuracy of docking with a new scoring function, efficient optimization, and multithreading. Journal of Computational Chemistry, 31(2), 455–461.
51. Vladimir, Z., (1996). Electronic commerce: Structures and issues. International Journal of Electronic Commerce, 1(1), 3–23.
52. Wang, C. K. J., Khoo, A., Liu, W. C., & Divaharan, S., (2008). Passion and intrinsic motivation in digital gaming. Cyber Psychology & Behavior, 11(1), 39–45.
53. Ward, R., & Smith, M., (1998). JavaScript as a first programming language for multimedia students. In: Proceedings of the 6th Annual Conference on the Teaching of Computing and the 3rd Annual Conference on Integrating Technology into Computer Science Education: Changing the Delivery of Computer Science Education (Vol. 1, No. 1, 249–253).
54. Wetherall, D., Legedza, D., & Guttag, J., (1998). Introducing new internet services: Why and how. IEEE Network, 12(3), 12–19.
55. Williamson, B., (2016). Digital education governance: An introduction. European Educational Research Journal, 15(1), 3–13.
56. Yao, A. C., (1982). Protocols for secure computations. In: 23rd Annual Symposium on Foundations of Computer Science (SFCS 1982) (pp. 160–164). IEEE.
57. Zhang, D., Guo, B., & Yu, Z., (2011). The emergence of social and community intelligence. Computer, 44(7), 21–28.
58. Zhu, Y., Richins, D., Halpern, M., & Reddi, V. J., (2015). Microarchitectural implications of event-driven server-side web applications. In: Proceedings of the 48th International Symposium on Microarchitecture (Vol. 1, No. 1, pp. 762–774).
59. Zissis, D., & Lekkas, D., (2012). Addressing cloud computing security issues. Future Generation Computer Systems, 28(3), 583–592.

CHAPTER 2

WORLD WIDE WEB AND WEBSITE DEVELOPMENT

UNIT INTRODUCTION

The web can be described as the exchange of resources, files, and data between people across the web (Aghaei et al., 2012). Information is linked to collect through hyperlinks that include text, photos, voice, and video (Choudhury, 2014). It also functions as a tunnel to obtain storing data on the server and show it to a customer by browser thru the internet. The initial web was composed of a group of HTML-formatted text-based websites kept on servers. In contrast, Tim Berners-Lee, a British physicist, created the web in the1989s, when it was still in its infancy. The web was initially developed to satisfy the demand for data exchanges among researchers at universities and research institutions around the globe. Berners-Lee spoke with the CERN director about the Mesh system, which referred to ENQUIRE, in March 1989 (Berners, 1998). Web 1.0 was created as the initial web paradigm, where users could view content without posting (Nath et al., 2014).

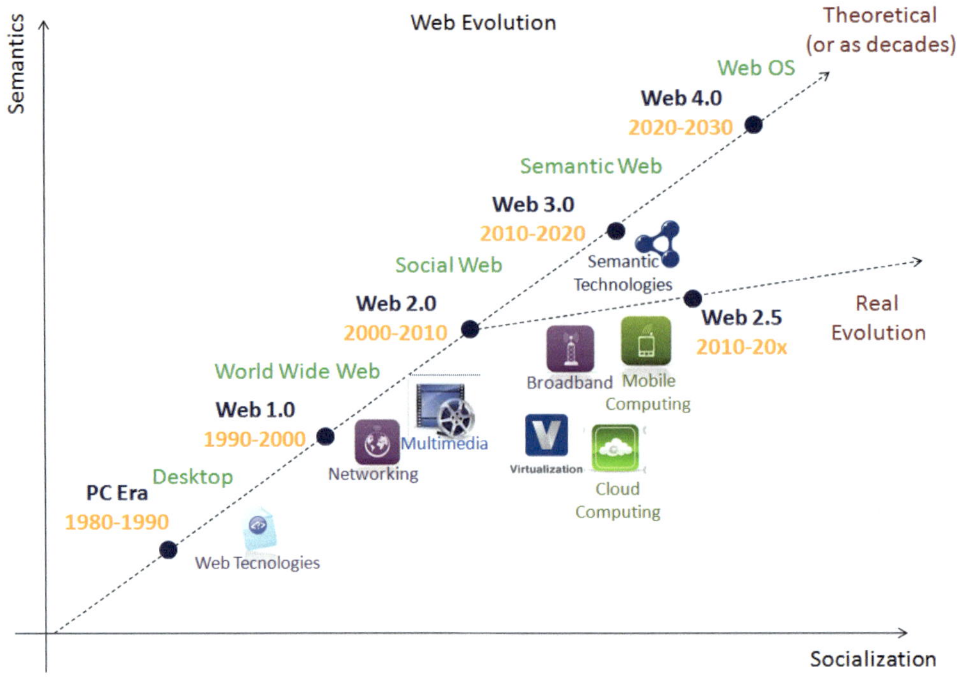

Figure 2.1. Graph of history of the web.

Source: Vivek Madurai, creative commons license.

Darcy DiNucci chose to unveil Web 2.0 in 1999, which then became prominent in 2004. It is a read-write system application where users may exchange and communicate with one another. It is also known as the Participative and Social Web. In 2015, Web 3.0 was established as a semantic web and became popular, sometimes referred to as "The Internet of Things." (Aghaei et al., 2012). Figure 2.1 depicts the web stage. In this chapter, the history of the internet is discussed in-depth, along with an evaluation of every version.

Learning Objectives

At the end of this chapter, readers will be able to learn the following:

- World wide web and its development.
- Different types of web.
- The web technology stack.
- Development of web pages, websites, and web browsers.

Key Terms

- Portals
- Search Engines

- Web 1.0
- Web 2.0
- Web 3.0
- Web Browser
- Web Page
- Web Site
- World Wide Web (WWW)

2.1. WORLD WIDE WEB AND ITS DEVELOPMENT

The abbreviation WWW stands for the World Wide Web (WWW), a hypertext-based data recovery tool. The WWW is a group of electronic content stored on servers. Information is structured so that the viewer may determine the sequence in which it is delivered.

The web functions as a worldwide database through which users can exchange information via internet-connected devices (Du, 2009). Numerous resources describe the evolution phases of Web technology. Whenever the technology becomes simpler for consumers, it becomes more complicated for developers. The web contains both simple and advanced architecture. The web was developed half a century ago, with Web 1.0 being the initial version and the Semantic web being the latest update (Berners, 1998).

2.1.1. Web 1.0

It is merely a viewable site with primary data from the WWW, and Tim Berners-Lee developed it. It is the fundamental building block of the internet and was utilized as recently as 2003. The user can only search for content and view it through the browser; he cannot contribute or give feedback on the site. To put it another way, knowledge is unchanging and unchanging through time (King, 2008). Compared to the enormous number of users who do not necessarily need information regarding how the webpages are constructed, only a few people could produce and modify webpages in web 1.0. These few individuals required information on how web pages are built. In the Web 1.0 strategy, some businesses develop applications that enable users to download content from the web. Still, the consumers are prevented from viewing the process by which the applications function. HTML, HTTP, and URI are the techniques utilized in Web 1.0 (Choudhury, 2014).

Figure 2.2.
Image of web 1.0.

Source: Nazmi Dincer, creative commons license.

Web 1.0 utilized other standards such as CSS, XML, and XHTML. Several coupled technologies exist among servers and clients, including ASP, JSP, PHP, and PERL. On the client end, the server side uses JavaScript, VBScript, and Flash. Web 1.0 is highly sluggish, requiring visitors to reload the page when new content is uploaded. The web 1.0 issue only functions in one direction. To put it another way, the user cannot add to or change the website (Aghaei et al., 2012). Figure 2.2 depicts Web 1.0.

2.1.2. Web 2.0

It is the 2nd web version. In 2004, vice president of O'Reilly Media Dale Dougherty released it officially. It is also known as the read-and-write web and represents a novel way to utilize the existing internet technology; the web might become bidirectional. Web 1.0 allows the user to load and retrieve from a website as a provider, but with little control. In other words, real user interactivity enables simple upload and retrieval. Web 2.0 consumers have greater engagement but need more authority. The technology backbone of web 2.0 consists of rules like RSS, Atom, and RDF, which designers utilize to create web 2.0 services. Web 2.0 also employs Ajax-based internet technologies like JavaScript and XML, CSS, DOM, REST, and XML. Web 2.0 enables users to create and engage in social interactions and communication. However, since a user's confidentiality and personal details can be compromised, these features also address privacy and security considerations. Web 2.0 can be seen in Figure 2.3 (Antoniou et al., 2005).

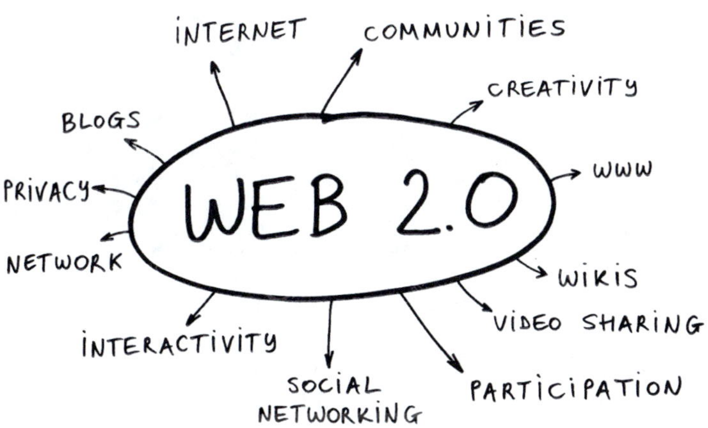

Figure 2.3. Illustration of components of web 2.0.

Source: Digiflute media labs, creative commons license.

2.1.3. Web 3.0

It is also the 3rd and most recent edition of the web, called the executable web, launched in 2014 and enables users to interact with interactive apps (Srinivasan, 2015). In other words, it is also known as the Semantic Web and customization. Web 3.0 will result in a total reimagining of the web. Conrad Wolfram's Web 3.0 idea attempts to make computers think and have a higher intellect for searching for new data rather than humans. Web 3.0 is a new approach that is being applied in a variety of industries on the web. In other words, turn the web into a massive database. At Web 3.0, it is recommended that machines behave like humans by describing precise details at a fast speed and bringing the data to the user as the definition of a word rather than searching for the same term on the web. Google, which represents the digital capabilities of Web 3.0, is one instance (Rimale et al., 2016). Figure 2.4 depicts web 3.0.

Figure 2.4. Image of web 3.0.

Source: Think ML, creative commons license.

The ability to generate 3D models and manage animation using 3D graphics software or programs is now accessible to users, while many websites still lack this functionality, such as Secondlife.com. There are levels in web 3.0, although only some have been utilized up to this point. Web 3.0 has a lot of capabilities, but it also has a lot of flaws. For example, it is harder to construct an intelligent web because it requires more website design expertise from the supplier, and it is tough to determine a user's ID on the internet (Casanovas et al., 2016).

2.2. THE WEB TECHNOLOGY STACK

A protocol stack comprises four levels employed to describe, discover, execute, and engage Web services. Web utilizes numerous standards that specify various parts of a single connection or are used in conjunction. Using a Uniform Resource Identifier (URI), a web page, word, photo, video, or sound file can be located by finding data resources on the web. Hyper Text Transport Protocol (HTTP) is a protocol accountable for web communications between server and client; it is a set of guidelines regulating the transmission of text, graphic pictures, audio, video, and other data types. Also, there's a protocol called File Transport Protocol, mainly used to transmit text, image, and audio files, among others. IP Security is an additional protocol utilized by the web to decompose and encrypt data shared between the client and the server using similar cryptographic keys (Sadeeq et al., 2018).

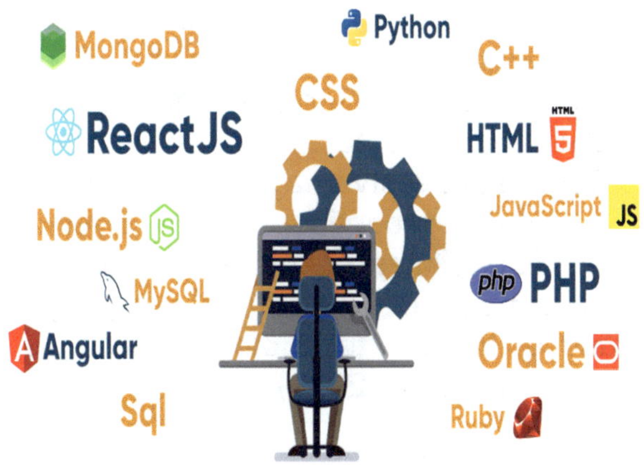

Figure 2.5. Illustration of the web technology stack.

Source: Tapan Patel, creative commons license.

2.2.1. Portals and Search Engines

An Online portal is a website that allows users to browse other websites by giving a link to them. It is designed for a specific purpose, such as dispersed apps that exchange information amongst users (Zebari et al., 2018). In other words, it can be depicted as a massive database of parts that multiple users can access simultaneously. The online portal assists users with search navigation, system integration, and various additional functions such as business analytics and distribution activities. Web portals include Netvibes, iGoogle, MSN, and NAVER (Jacksi et al., 2016). A search engine, often known as a search site, is a tool that allows users to retrieve data from any web host on a server, like the WWW. In other words, a web process utilizes specific requirements to discover data and bring up all web pages that include this term or words. Numerous sites serve as instances of search engines, such as Google, Yahoo, and so on (Jacksi et al., 2018).

2.2.2. The Semantic Web

The web is getting bigger every day, making it difficult to find data about any term or phrase since many websites contain it and many provide inaccurate information. The Semantic Web is the new phrase that Tim Berners-Lee suggested. The current web edition enables the user to use computers rather than people to find the accurate data desired. Semantic search uses a strategy that bases results on user intent and the meaning of words (Zeebaree et al., 2019). The addition of semantic material in Web pages enables the utilization of search parameters like the specified location and previous searches. To put it another way, The Semantic Web uses a technology that enables computers to comprehend human speech and respond to user queries following their meaning. The layers of the semantic web have yet to be reached as of this writing. Google is an excellent example of the semantic web. The semantic web is not so much a technique as it is an architecture that allows the generation of meaning through the utilization of protocols, markup languages, and other associated data analysis. Each successive layer in the semantic modern web stack is responsible for providing services to the layer above it while simultaneously drawing on the capabilities of the layers that came before it. In the following paragraphs, a concise description of every layer is provided. The semantic web makes use of various technologies such as URLs, XML, and RDF, among others (AL-Zebari et al., 2019)

2.2.2.1. Semantic Web Technology

Semantic web technology applies traditional semantics to the information surrounding us to provide its whole meaning. The WWW inventor envisions this capability with Connected Data technology (Jacksi & Abass, 2019). As per Sir Tim Berners-Lee, there are relationships between all forms and data sources. Some development language is used to describe and connect the web's data to make it simple for computers to interpret and interpret them. This technology enables computers to store, manage, and retrieve data based on its meaning and relevance (Berners-Lee et al., 1994).

2.2.2.2. Semantic Web Stack

It is a component of the semantic web layers, often referred to as the semantic web cake, and it depicts the semantic web's structure. The semantic web is a depiction of the languages; the stack shows the techniques used in the semantic web; these established techniques for the semantic web are arranged to make the semantic web feasible. In other words, the web information stack demonstrates that the semantic web is an abstraction of the conventional hypertext web rather than a new technology (Morville & Rosenfeld, 2006). Figure 2.5 depicts the semantic web stack.

2.2.2.3. Ontology

Though they don't have a precise understanding, ontologies are essential for the semantic web and can be considered collections of URIs. The core concept of philosophy, ontology, is the investigation of entities and their connections. In other words, it refers to all types of things currently in existence and the relationships between them. The ideas and associations on the semantic web characterize a range of topics and are also used to define the languages used in specific applications (Albert et al., 1999). This vocabulary could be straightforward or complicated.

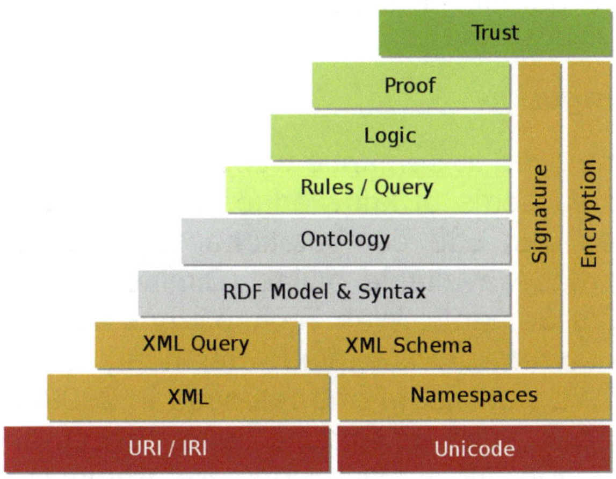

Figure 2.6. Schematic of levels of the semantic web stack.

Source: Steve Bratt, creative commons license.

2.2.2.4. Resource Description Framework

It is the paradigm commonly used to define internet resources, such as web pages and website content (Ng et al., 1998; Malviya et al., 2021). The resource's creators are included in the RDF specification, data production, and update processes. The information retrieved by a search query is tied to engine data groups or subject divisions. The RDF approach allows users to easily share websites and characteristics with additional intelligence agents. In contrast hand, RDF is an interface for another technology, such as XML, created by the World Wide Web Consortium (W3C). This model is employed to share data on the website, correct? There are RDF capabilities that enable the integration of data even when the models are fundamentally different. Apache Jena, Mobi, FRED, and Outdated-XML adobes are the most recent additions to the collection of RDF-related technologies. Relative to OWL, the network of subclasses and properties in RDF is minimal (De, 2015; Pretorius et al., 2017).

2.2.2.5. Resource Description Framework Schema

This is a collection of classes with varied features that employ RDF extensible information to define a data model, the fundamental elements offered for ontology descriptions, also known as RDF languages. These vocabularies attempt to categorize RDF resources stored in triple stores for use with the query language SPARQL (Khanzode & Sarode, 2016). The RDFS has several classes comparable to OOP classes in that they specify the resources of the class and subclass. Figure 2.6 shows an instance of RDFS. The RDFS language is frequently employed to define the main class and kinds of terms defined in RDF, and it is also used to specify features for other resources. Such as property range and domain (Knight & Burn, 2005).

2.2.2.6. Ontology Web Language

The OWL is a language employed in semantic webs to represent relationships between various sophisticated items of knowledge or sets of objects. One of the easy-to-learn languages that use computational logic is the OWL. The OWL materials were once made available online (Cimino et al., 1995). OWL is a component of the W3C's Semantic Web Technology stack, including RDF, SPARQL, and RDFS. The current OWL variant, commonly known as OWL2, was created by the W3C OWL work team and released in 2009. And the 2014 release of the 2nd edition. Tools such as Apache Jane, FRED, and Graph DB are among those included in the OWL. OWL's primary grammar depended on XML, RDFS, and RDF (Starr, 1997).

As the evolution of the web progressed through its phases, it became abundantly evident that web 0.1 served as the foundation of the web. Because it only contains a few features, it does not make it possible for users to perform any actions; instead, users can only read content on the internet. In particular, Web 0.1 only handles some design languages currently in use. Web

0.2 is an improvement in certain respects since it enables users to publish for more extended periods on the web, supports a wide variety of languages and standards, and provides enhanced levels of safety (Won et al., 2009). Although version 0.3 of the site is the most recent, it differs from editions 0.2 and 0.1 in several ways.

It contains many new capabilities that enable users to perform various tasks. On the other side, it enhances the user's capacity to upload updates and make site changes. It is also safer because it employs different strategies, like a tunnel. In addition, web 0.3 offers a 3D graph with enhanced traffic throughput. The semantic web is an additional category of the web. Web 0.3's primary characteristic is intellect, which implies that when a user searches for something, the research techniques depend on the terms and the person's mental state (Algosaibi et al., 2015).

2.3. DEVELOPMENT OF WEB PAGE, WEBSITE, AND BROWSER

2.3.1. Web Page

A web page is a type of an electronic book published in HTML. A web page might include text, images, sound, video, and multimedia experiences (Margolis et al., 1997; Rind et al., 1997). Users of web documents can go from one subject to another.

Dear students, when you go through a book, you read one page following the other in a straight line. With hypertext, you can navigate through documents in whatever works best for you and your goals. You can jump from one subject to another using hypertext.

The following are a few web page design guidelines that will assist you in creating an excellent webpage (Van et al., 2000).

1. Design the website to make an impression on the user during the first few moments of their visit.
2. Continue regularly upgrading websites with the most recent and freshest data.
3. Keep the focus on web pages. Don't display everything on one webpage; utilize different pages for different themes.
4. Ensure that the website's functionalities are available in all browsers.
5. Please verify that the website's icons and links function as they should.
6. Use reduced pictures to speed up website loading.

2.3.2. Web Site

Compiling one or even more web pages that correspond to a particular system is defined as that firm's website. A website can also be used to relate to a collection of materials that are connected in some way. The initial page that loads when a user visits a website is called the home page. There are two types of websites: those that are static and those that are dynamic. The materials of a static website are intended to stay the same, but the materials of a dynamic website are constantly being updated (Russo, 2000).

TIPS

Hypertext documents allow users to navigate from one topic to another easily.

2.3.2.1. Hyperlinks

These are the components of a hypertext file that provide navigation from one site to the other. A link might connect to a separate area of the exact text or a completely different file to play a multimedia file, download a file, or use other online tools on the WWW. Hyperlinks typically show as highlighted, colored text; they might even display as images or clickable buttons (Pollach, 2003). For instance, it will launch a website in a new tab, which you may dismiss to return to this page. A link might go to a different web page, a file, a movie, or a file type. If one is still determining whether something is a link, hover over it. The cursor must become a hand icon.

2.3.2.2. URL

Uniform Resource Locator (URL) is a sequence of characters that specifies a webpage on the WWW (Mawdsley, 2006).

2.3.2.3. IP addresses

Every machine on the web is referred to as a host computer or host. Every host computer on the network has a particular id termed an IP address, typically expressed in the format xxx.xxx.xxx.xxx, where xxx is a three-digit number ranging from 0 to 255—for instance, 192.170.0.145 (Bentley et al., 1997).

2.3.2.4. File Transfer Protocol

It is a client-server TCP/IP app that uses the internet to transmit data between 2 remote PCs. Before transferring files, a TCP link is made and remains active. Before cutting off the link, more than a single file may be sent (Cockburn & Wilson, 1996).

2.3.3. Web Browser

A web browser is a software tool that allows a person to see and connect with the text, photos, videos, songs, and other material commonly found on a Web page on the WWW or LAN. Web browsers generally use HTTP to retrieve Web pages from Web servers. The URL, viewed as an address and begins with HTTP: for HTTP connectivity, is used to identify carriers. Surfing is employing a browser to access information on the web. Internet Explorer is currently the most widely used web browser. Also available are Firefox, Chrome, Safari, and Opera. Each has its distinct style and experience, but they all have the same purpose: appropriately displaying online pages. For most web pages, any popular browser will suffice (Berners-Lee, 1992) (Figure 2.7).

Did you Know?

Hyperlink usually appears in an underlined text in a different color and may appear as an image or as a button to click.

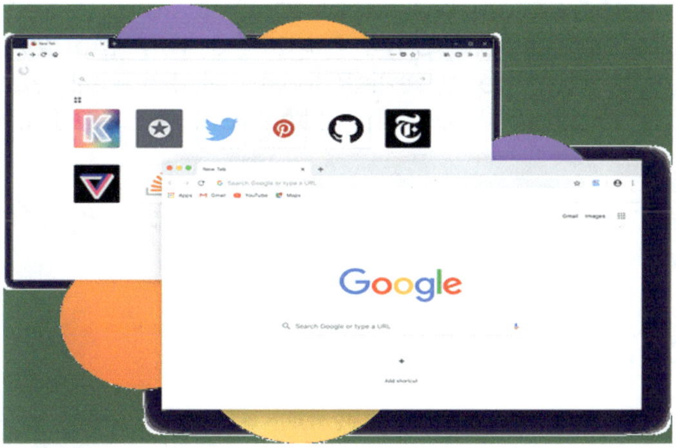

Figure 2.7. Image of Firefox vs. Google Chrome.

Source: Mozilla Foundation, creative commons license.

2.3.4. Web Server

A Web page is saved on a Remote server, which makes it accessible to other computers on the network. HTTP queries are accepted, processed, and responded to by a Web server. Web browsers, which the client machine employs to interact, send, and acquire information over the web, send these queries. A client/server connection is the relationship that exists between a Web client and the Server (Ainscough, 1996).

The function of the Web Server is to (Albert et al., 1999):

I. Access control;
II. Server-side page computation;

III. Maintenance of log; and

IV. CGI script and custom API program implementation.

2.3.5. Downloading and Upload Files

Downloading is getting information from a distant website. It is now known, dear students, that a browser can display various documents, multimedia, and other things. One might want to view a file outside the browser (Weare & Lin, 2000). This is made possible by obtaining the file and placing it conveniently on the system. Consider the scenario where one wanted to print and finish an online form. To alter it, save it on the computer and open it in the proper application.

When the link of a document is clicked, it might download without any intervention, but occasionally it will just appear in the browser. One can choose Save Target As from the context menu when you right-click the hyperlink to stop it from appearing in the browser. The location where the document is saved will be your choice.

The term "upload" refers to transmitting a document or information to a remote location (Choudhury, 2014).

ACTIVITY 2.1:

Explain the development of web pages and websites using internet technologies. Also, describe the historical evolution of the World Wide Web.

2.3.6. Bookmarks

One can quickly create a shortcut that will take them to any of the preferred websites. One can add a page to the favorites to revisit later. Bookmarks make it much simpler to locate a particular page the last time. One does not need to commit the complete address of the website to memory because it can be navigated through the bookmarked pages. Create a favorite in Internet Explorer by going to the Favorites menu and selecting the Add to Favorites option. Other browsers are like Google Chrome, but their language might differ slightly.

SUMMARY

Throughout the evolution of web development, it has been apparent that the web has evolved from a primitive web with few capabilities and control to a vast intelligence storehouse of data. Also, it has gotten simpler for all classes of consumers, as they no longer need to be knowledgeable about communication technology to use the internet. This makes it very convenient to look for any data that comes to mind, obtaining a million websites in milliseconds. The latest web iteration will be able to search for data like a human. It has become very service-oriented for the user but complicated for developers. Some layers of the semantic web still need to be defined, but it is regularly developing. In the future, the net will resemble humans, as when we look for data, it will first consider what is in our minds and comprehend the user instead of searching by keywords. In the future, the internet will be more intelligent than humans.

REVIEW QUESTIONS

1. Differentiate between web 1.0, web 2.0, and web 3.0.
2. Define web technology stack.
3. Discuss the role of the internet in the globalization of business.
4. Describe the development of the web page, website, and browser.

MULTIPLE CHOICE QUESTIONS

1. What is the difference between a Web Page and a Web Site?

a. A Web Page is a single page of information, while a Web Site is a collection of Web Pages.

b. A Web Page is a single page of information, while a Web Site is a collection of documents.

c. A Web Page is a collection of documents, while a Web Site is a single page of information.

d. A Web Page is a data collection, while a Web Site is a single page of information.

2. What is a Web Browser?

a. A program used to view information on the WWW.

b. A web-based application used to view information on the WWW.

c. An application used to store information on the WWW.

d. A program used to store information on the WWW.

3. What is Web 1.0?

a. A web-based platform for developing interactive websites.

b. A platform for developing static websites.

c. A web-based platform for developing static websites.
d. A platform for developing interactive websites.

4. What is Web 2.0?

a. A platform for developing interactive websites.
b. A platform for developing static websites.
c. A web-based platform for developing interactive websites.
d. A web-based platform for developing static websites.

5. What is Web 3.0?

a. A platform for developing interactive websites.
b. A platform for developing static websites.
c. A web-based platform for developing interactive websites.
d. A web-based platform for developing static websites.

6. What is a Portal?

a. A website that provides access to information and services on the WWW.
b. A website that provides access to information and services on the internet.
c. A web-based application that provides access to information and services on the WWW.
d. A web-based application that provides access to information and services on the internet.

7. What is a Search Engine?

a. A web-based application used to search for information on the WWW.
b. A web-based application used to search for information on the internet.
c. A website used to search for information on the WWW.
d. A website used to search for information on the internet.

Answers to Multiple Choice Questions

1. (b); 2. (a); 3. (c); 4. (c); 5. (a); 6. (a); 7. (a)

REFERENCES

1. Aghaei, S., Nematbakhsh, M. A., & Farsani, H. K., (2012). Evolution of the world wide web: From web 1.0 to web 4.0. International Journal of Web & Semantic Technology, 3(1), 1–10.
2. Ainscough, T. L., (1996). The internet for the rest of us: Marketing on the world wide web. Journal of Consumer Marketing, 13(2), 36–47.
3. Albert, R., Jeong, H., & Barabási, A. L., (1999). Diameter of the world wide web.

Nature, 401(6749), 130–131.

4. Algosaibi, A. A., Albahli, S., & Melton, A., (2015). World wide web: A survey of its development and possible future trends. In: 16th International Conference on Internet Computing and Big Data-ICOMP (Vol. 15, pp. 79–84).
5. AL-Zebari, A., Zeebaree, S. R., Jacksi, K., & Selamat, A., (2019). ELMS–DPU ontology visualization with protégé VOWL and web VOWL. Journal of Advanced Research in Dynamic and Control Systems, 11, 478–85.
6. Antoniou, G., Franconi, E., & Harmelen, F. V., (2005). Introduction to semantic web ontology languages. In: Reasoning Web (Vol. 1, pp. 1–21). Springer, Berlin, Heidelberg.
7. Bentley, R., Appelt, W., Busbach, U., Hinrichs, E., Kerr, D., Sikkel, K., & Woetzel, G., (1997). Primary support for cooperative work on the world wide web. International Journal of Human-Computer Studies, 46(6), 827–846.
8. Berners-Lee, T. J., (1992). The worldwide web. Computer Networks and ISDN Systems, 25(4, 5), 454–459.
9. Berners-Lee, T., Cailliau, R., Luotonen, A., Nielsen, H. F., & Secret, A., (1994). The worldwide web. Communications of the ACM, 37(8), 76–82.
10. Casanovas, P., Palmirani, M., Peroni, S., Van, E. T., & Vitali, F., (2016). Semantic web for the legal domain: The next step. Semantic Web, 7(3), 213–227.
11. Choudhury, N., (2014). World wide web and its journey from web 1.0 to web 4.0. International Journal of Computer Science and Information Technologies, 5(6), 8096–8100.
12. Cimino, J. J., Socratous, S. A., & Clayton, P. D., (1995). Internet as a clinical information system: Application development using the world wide web. Journal of the American Medical Informatics Association, 2(5), 273–284.
13. Cockburn, C., & Wilson, T. D., (1996). Business use of the world wide web. International Journal of Information Management, 16(2), 83–102.
14. De Leeuw, J. R., (2015). jsPsych: A JavaScript library for creating behavioral experiments in a web browser. Behavior Research Methods, 47(1), 1–12.
15. Du, X., (2009). Semantic Service Description Framework for Efficient Service Discovery and Composition (Vol. 1, pp. 3–9). Doctoral dissertation, Durham University.
16. Jacksi, K., & Abbas, S. M., (2019). Development history of the world wide web. Int. J. Sci. Technol. Re.s, 8(9), 75–79.
17. Jacksi, K., Dimililer, N., & Zeebaree, S. R., (2016). State of the art exploration systems for linked data: A review. Int. J. Adv. Comput. Sci. Appl. IJACSA, 7(11), 155–164.
18. Jacksi, K., Zeebaree, S. R., & Dimililer, N., (2018). LOD explorer: Presenting the web of data. International Journal of Advanced Computer Science and Applications, 9(1), 2–9.
19. Khanzode, C. A., & Sarode, R. D., (2016). Evolution of the world wide web: From web 1.0 to 6.0. International Journal of Digital Library Services, 6(2), 1–11.

20. King, J. D., (2008). Search Engine Content Analysis (Vol. 1, pp. 4–9). Doctoral dissertation, Queensland University of Technology.
21. Knight, S. A., & Burn, J., (2005). Developing a framework for assessing information quality on the world wide web. Informing Science, 8, 4–8.
22. Malviya, V. K., Rai, S., & Gupta, A., (2021). Development of web browser prototype with embedded classification capability for mitigating cross-site scripting attacks. Applied Soft Computing, 102(1), 106873.
23. Margolis, M., Resnick, D., & Tu, C. C., (1997). Campaigning on the INTERNET: Parties and candidates on the world wide web in the 1996 primary season. Harvard International Journal of Press/Politics, 2(1), 59–78.
24. Mawdsley, E., (2006). Using the World Wide Web for Development Research (Vol. 1, pp. 1–5). Doing Development Research, London: Sage.
25. Morville, P., & Rosenfeld, L., (2006). Information Architecture for the World Wide Web: Designing Large-Scale Websites (Vol. 1, pp. 3–6). "O'Reilly Media, Inc."
26. Nath, K., Dhar, S., & Basishtha, S., (2014). Web 1.0 to web 3.0-evolution of the web and its various challenges. In: 2014 International Conference on Reliability Optimization and Information Technology (ICROIT) (Vol. 1, pp. 86–89). IEEE.
27. Ng, H. I., Pan, Y. J., & Wilson, T. D., (1998). Business use of the world wide web: A report on further investigations. International Journal of Information Management, 18(5), 291–314.
28. Pollach, I., (2003). Communicating corporate ethics on the world wide web: A discourse analysis of selected company web sites. Business & Society, 42(2), 277–287.
29. Pretorius, S., Ikuesan, A. R., & Venter, H. S., (2017). Attributing users based on web browser history. In: 2017 IEEE Conference on Application, Information and Network Security (AINS) (Vol. 1, pp. 69–74). IEEE.
30. Rimale, Z., Benlahmar, E. H., & Tragha, A., (2016). A Semantic Learning Object (SLO) Web-Editor Based on Web Ontology Language (OWL) Using a New OWL2XSLO Approach, 7, 315–320.
31. Rind, D. M., Kohane, I. S., Szolovits, P., Safran, C., Chueh, H. C., & Barnett, G. O., (1997). Maintaining the confidentiality of medical records shared over the internet and the world wide web. Annals of Internal Medicine, 127(2), 138–141.
32. Russo, N. L., (2000). Developing applications for the web: Exploring differences between traditional and world wide web application development. Managing Web-Enabled Technologies in Organizations: A Global Perspective (Vol. 1, pp. 23–35). IGI Global.
33. Sadeeq, M. A., Zeebaree, S. R., Qashi, R., Ahmed, S. H., & Jacksi, K., (2018). Internet of things security: A survey. In: 2018 International Conference on Advanced Science and Engineering (ICOASE) (Vol. 1, pp. 162–166). IEEE.
34. Srinivasan, J., (2015). Semantic cloud architecture integration of the cloud and semantic web. IMS Manthan. The Journal of Innovations, 8(2), 1–10.

35. Starr, R. M., (1997). Delivering instruction on the world wide web: Overview and basic design principles. Educational Technology, 37(3), 7–15.
36. Van, D. D. C., Fechner, D. L., & Green-Adelsberger, K., (2000). Promotional strategies on the world wide web. Journal of Marketing Communications, 6(1), 21–35.
37. Weare, C., & Lin, W. Y., (2000). Content analysis of the world wide web: Opportunities and challenges. Social Science Computer Review, 18(3), 272–292.
38. Won, S. S., Jin, J., & Hong, J. I., (2009). Contextual web history: Using visual and contextual cues to improve web browser history. In: Proceedings of the SIGCHI Conference on Human Factors in Computing Systems (Vol. 1, pp. 1457–1466).
39. Zebari, R. R., Zeebaree, S. R., & Jacksi, K., (2018). Impact analysis of HTTP and SYN flood DDoS attacks on Apache 2 and IIS 10.0 web servers. In: 2018 International Conference on Advanced Science and Engineering (ICOASE) (Vol. 1, pp. 156–161). IEEE.
40. Zeebaree, A. Z. S. R., Adel, A. Z., Jacksi, K., & Selamat, A., (2019). Designing an ontology of E-learning system for Duhok polytechnic university using protégé OWL tool. J. Adv. Res. Dyn. Control Syst., 11, 24–37.

CHAPTER 3

HTML AND CSS: BUILDING BLOCKS OF THE WEB

UNIT INTRODUCTION

The foundation of the web is CSS and HTML, which are crucial for web development. A web page's content and structure are provided by HTML, and its visual presentation and design are provided by CSS. On the website, content is organized and formatted using Hypertext Markup Language (HTML). The structure and content of a web page, including paragraphs, images, headings, links, and more, are defined by a collection of tags and components. Thanks to HTML's standardized format, web pages can be seen on any device using a web browser (Lemme et al., 2016).

Using Cascading Style Sheets (CSS), a web page's visual look can be specified. It offers a method for styling and organizing various web page components, such as fonts, colors, backgrounds, borders, etc. CSS enables web designers to make web pages that are responsive and aesthetically pleasing, and that can be read on any device that has a web browser. Together, HTML and CSS can build a web page. While CSS handles the page's visual display and styling, HTML handles the page's organization and content. HTML and CSS make it simpler to manage and update a website by separating the presentation and content of a page. The foundation of the web is HTML and CSS, which are crucial for web development. HTML is responsible for providing a web page's content and structure, whereas CSS is responsible for the web page's visual display and styling. To design responsive and visually appealing web pages that can be read on any device with a web browser, web developers must have a solid understanding of CSS and HTML

(Park et al., 2013).

Learning Objectives

By the end of this chapter, you will be able to:

- Understand the basic concepts of the World Wide Web (WWW), including hypertext, browsers, and web servers.
- Describe the anatomy of a URL and how it is used to locate web resources.
- Identify the key components of HTML and XHTML, including syntax, rules, markup color-coding, elements, attributes, and entities.
- Create well-organized web pages using HTML text, document heads, headings, paragraphs, lists, tables, and Cascading Style Sheet (CSS) markup.

Key Terms

- Attributes
- Browsers
- Cascading Style Sheets (CSS)
- Elements
- Entities
- Extensible Hypertext Markup Language (XHTML)
- Hypertext
- Hypertext Markup Language (HTML)
- Markup C-coding
- Syntax
- Uniform Resource Locator (URL)
- Web Servers

3.1. WEB PAGES IN THEIR NATURAL HABITAT

Many other types of material can be included on web pages, including audio, pictures, text, forms, interactive games, and even video files.

Glancing the Web reveals a wealth of data and content in various formats. Although each website is unique, they use HTML, sometimes called hypertext markup language (HTML). Cascading Style Sheets (CSS) and Extensible Hypertext Markup Language (XHTML) are two more terms they will frequently encounter (Wimelius, 2004).

Every Web page uses HTML (or a decent imitation), regardless of the content. Content, graphics, and other pieces of info are elements; HTML is the mortar holding web pages together; CSS specifies how web pages should appear when displayed.

As with XHTML, CSS files, and HTML that create Web pages are merely typoscript documents. The Web functions in addition to it because of this use of text content (Lubin et al., 1993). Any TypoScript file they produce on a Windows machine will function just as well on a Mac OS or any other operating system, including any HTML, CSS, or XHTML files.

However, Website pages are more than just text documents. HTML, XHTML, or CSS is a unique type of attention-depriving, sugar-loaded TypoScript used to create web pages. To indicate how a page should appear and function, each uses a unique set of instructions that they provide inside text files (Samu et al., 1996).

3.1.1. Hypertext

Lines of text can point to another object in cyberspace, thanks to special HTML instructions. Hyperlinks are a type of pointer. The Web is held together by connections, which act as glue. Links often display in blue and are underlined in their web browser. A hyperlink will take them somewhere else when they click on it. A Web page can be created and edited in any program that can produce plain text, including Notepad and TextEdit, whether the page has hypertext. While some software tools provide fanciful options and apps to aid in creating Web pages, the text files they produce are identical to those produced by plain-text editors. But in our opinion, a straightforward text editor is better for individuals learning HTML. People only need to open TextEdit on a Mac or Notepad on a PC to get started (Barnet, 2018).

When developing HTML, avoid Word programs like WordPad or Microsoft Word. They add unnecessary code to web pages they might not want or need. The World Wide Web (WWW) lives up to its name. There are billions of hyperlinks connecting online sites that are hosted on web servers all over the world. The Internet would consist of nothing but standalone sites without these links (Tredinnick, 2007).

The Web's capacity to link to pages and other resources on a similar site or at another site accounts for a significant portion of its value.

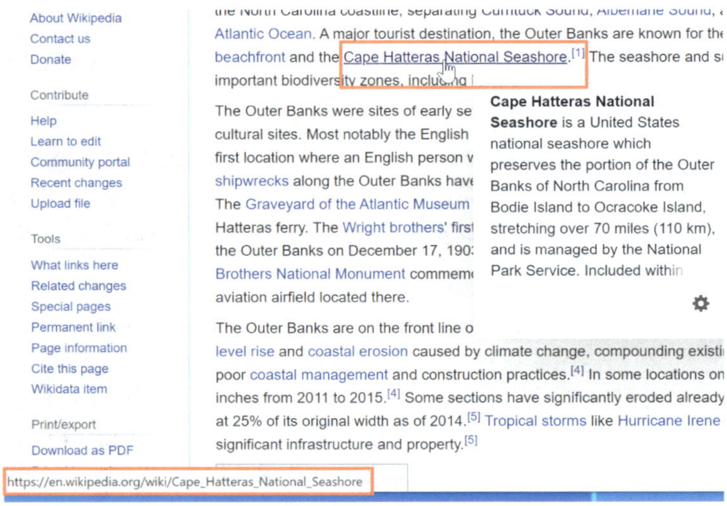

Figure 3.1. Examples of hyperlinks in a Wikipedia page.

Source: GCF global, creative commons license.

Internet Explorers were developed precisely to read markup, also known as HTML instructions, and display the outcome of the Web page.

To offer instructions to a browser, markup is stored in a text file and its content. Take a look at Figure 3.1 page as an illustration. Examining the page's underlying HTML will reveal how it is constructed and formatted (Landow & Kahn, 1993) (Figure 3.2).

Figure 3.2. This webpage utilizes a variety of components as well as various pieces of HTML and CSS syntax to produce its current aesthetic.

Source: EdTittel, creative commons license.

A picture, a title that explains the side, several sections that discuss one of their writers, and a contact element with links to a resume and a list of accomplishments are all included on this page (Koppen & Neumann, 1999).

However, the formatting of the page's various parts varies:

1. The paragraph text is smaller than the title at the apex of the page.
2. There is more white space between blocks of text than between consecutive lines of text.
3. Some text is displayed in light blue, white, and orange.

The HTML markup instructs web browsers how to present these page elements in particular ways. An HTML element (also referred to as the markup) is any text that is enclosed within angle brackets (less-than < and greater-than signs: >). A p inside of brackets (p> …/p> tags, for instance) designates content within paragraphs. The styling of the multiple HTML components used on this page is defined by CSS in the markup between the style> and /style> tags at the top of the file. In essence, that is all there is to it.

Elements are the aggregate name for tags and the text between the tags. Curly braces enclose CSS markup, while angle brackets > enclose HTML and XHTML markup (Halpin & Lavrenko, 2011).

3.1.2. Browsers

A web browser is the user's component in the web riddle. Web browsers use instructions from HTML, XHTML, and CSS to display the content of Web pages on the screen.

Always assume the content will be seen in a web browser when creating HTML. Just keep in mind that there are numerous variations of each type of browser available.

Figure 3.3. Examples of various internet browsers.

Source: Brett Howse, creative commons license.

Typically, Internet Explorers ask a Web server for and then display Web pages accessible via the Internet. Before uploading them to a Web server, they can also see HTML pages stored on their computer. They view these sites in their browser when creating their own HTML pages, often known as local pages. To get a better picture of what users will see after the website is live on the Internet, use local pages (Jackson et al., 2006).Every Web browser has a unique technique for interpreting HTML. From one browser to the next, the same HTML may not appear precisely the same. Variations will not be significant while working with basic HTML, but when they incorporate more components (such as multimedia and scripting), rendering markup becomes complex.

Some individuals utilize text-only Web browsers like Lynx because

1. They're visually impaired and can't use a graphical display.
2. They like a lean, fast Web browser that displays only text (Huynh et al., 2006).

3.1.3. Web Servers

If they can't share the HTML of their pages with the world, they are not much use to them.

That's feasible, thanks to web servers. A computer that serves as a web server:

i. Connections to the WWW
ii. Modifies software that serves websites
iii. Inquiries sent by web browsers to servers in search of web pages

Practically any machine, including the one in their home, can operate as a web server. However, Web servers are often machines devoted to the job. To publish their Web pages, they do not need to be an Internet or computer whiz, but they do need to select a Web server to host their pages on (Arlitt & Williamson, 1997):

1. Companies' IT departments might have a web server if they are creating pages for a company website. (Ask their IT expert for the details.)
2. People require a host for their Web pages when launching a new website.

Simply conducting a Google search will help them find a cheap host. GoDaddy (www.godaddy.com), which currently charges monthly costs of as little as $1.99, is one affordable host. With a little searching, they might even locate hosts for their free websites. A directory of free host companies is kept up by Free Web Hosts. Visit their website at www.free-webhosts.com (Bohrer et al., 2002).

3.2. ANATOMY OF A URL

There are billions of resources on the Web, all of which can be linked. The location of a resource is crucial for linking to it. They cannot immediately access a Web page using a Web browser's Address bar without a precise address (a Uniform Resource Locator or URL).

The common method of addressing Web resources is through URLs. Each resource—a Web page, website, or single file—has its URL. Similar to their postal address, URLs function. Figure 3.3 shows what makes up a URL (Khare, 1999).

Each element of a URL aids in indicating where to find a Web page or resource:

i. **Protocol:** defines the decorum the browser will use to appeal the file. The prefix for most URLs that begin with "http://" is the Web page protocol.
ii. **Domain:** identifies the file's location on a common Web page, such as www.sun.com. Few files (like those on a personal website) or thousands of files (like those on a sizable corporate website like www.sun.com) may be hosted by a domain.
iii. **Path:** names the order of folders they must visit to access a particular file.

For instance, they can use the /developers/evangcentral/ path to access a file in the developer's folder's evangcentral folder. **Filename:** specifies the file the browser will access from a given directory path.

The URL in shown below connects to the domain and provides a route that goes to a particular file with the name file.html even though it is not publicly available (Halle et al., 2017):

http://www.domain.com/mainfolder/subfolder/file.html

TIPS

Knowing the different components of a URL, such as the protocol, domain name, and path, is essential for navigating and accessing web resources on the Internet.

3.3. (X)HTML's COMPONENT PARTS

The mystery surrounding the X is cleared out in the next part. This part demonstrates

i. a comparison of HTML and XHTML in their various forms
ii. The structure of an HTML document, often known as its syntax

iii. The names of the essential components and components of HTML (and XHTML) markup

iv. How to make the most effective and appropriate use of the features offered by (X)HTML

v. The guidelines that specify how HTML (and XHTML) should be used

Did you Know?

The first version of HTML was released in 1993, and the latest version of HTML, HTML5, was released in 2014.

3.3.1. HTML and XHTML

Hypertext Markup Language, or HTML, is a markup language that was created to describe Web pages in the late 1980s and early 1990s. The WWW Consortium's (W3C) standard descriptions now include several references to HTML. In 1999, the final HTML specification was completed.

They receive an innovative, enhanced version of HTML grounded on the eXtensible Markup Language (XML) when they prefix HTML with an "X" to create XHTML. With regard to computers, software, and the Internet, XML is made to function and perform properly (Perlin, 2006) (Figure 3.4).

HTML vs. XHTML

Some comparisons of HTML vs. XHTML

HTML	XHTML
Tags aren't extensible	Tags are extensible
Tags are not case-sensitive	Only lowercase tags are allowed
Possible to leave off and ending tag like </body>	Tags should appear in pairs
Overlapping tags	No overlapping tags

Figure 3.4. Difference between HTML and XHTML.

Source: Any difference between, creative commons license.

The original formulation of HTML has some irregularities that can cause heartburn for software that reads HTML documents. On the other hand, XHTML uses a syntax that is far more predictable and regular, making it simpler for software to process. HTML will eventually be replaced by XHTML; however, HTML is still in use. This book discusses both types and walks them through the process of adding an X to their own HTML texts to convert them to XHTML.

i. Most HTML and XHTML markup is identical.

ii. In rare cases, HTML and XHTML markup must be used differently.

iii. In unusual instances, the markup for HTML and XHTML may appear somewhat differently.

This book demonstrates how to write code compatible with XHTML and HTML (Levering & Cutler, 2006).

3.3.2. Syntax and Rules

HTML is a simple language for recitation the contents of Web pages. Even little effort is required with XHTML. When they know how to utilize a little (X)HTML, their components are simple. There are three different sorts of components in both HTML and XHTML markup:

1. **Attributes:** Details concerning a particular occurrence of an element.
2. **Entities:** pseudo-ASCII text characters, such as accented letters (É) and copyright symbols (). or SGML, or The Standard Generic Markup Language, is where entities come from.
3. **Elements:** Utilizing tags, you may distinguish between the various components of an HTML page.

There are various combinations of elements, attributes, and entities in every piece of XHTML and/or HTML markup that describes the content of a Web page (Adida et al., 2008).

3.3.3. Markup Color-Coding

Developers color-code the XHTML, HTML, and CSS information in their code samples to make it easier to understand the different types of markup. When reading all of their code listings, bear in mind the following color key.:

1. **Purple** gives the DOCTYPE assertion in (X)HTML documents. SGML is a completely different markup language than the one being used here. SGML provides guidelines that (X)HTML pages must adhere to while creating and presenting content. Code for character entities is likewise covered by this (Whitehead & Russell, 2008).
2. **Light green** represents standard HTML and XHTML markup.
3. **Dark green** represents XML markup
4. **Orange** represents CSS, markup
5. **Blue** represents JavaScript

Because it adversely impacts readability when code appears in the body copy, they only colored markup in code guides and elements. As they will see in the descriptions of the html>, head>, and title> elements in their first paragraph discussing HTML markup here, they use a different, monospaced font.

Additionally: If developers use an HTML editor, like Dreamweaver, HTML Kit, Kompozer, or anything else, they discover that these applications also use colored text to help them distinguish between different types of markup. The problem is that none of these tools perform this task similarly, and none follow our approach.

They chose colors that would be simple to understand on a four-color printed page, while others chose their hues to look appealing on LCDs (Brooks & Brooks, 2017).

3.3.4. Elements

(X)HTML's building blocks are called elements. They serve as descriptions for all of the text on their page. Tags and the material contain makeup elements. The two primary categories of elements are:

1. Material-containing elements consisting of a tag pair and any material that appears in between the opening and closing tags of the pair
2. Components that add content to the page by employing a single tag (Kennedy & Musciano, 2002).

3.3.4.1. Tag Pairs

A tag pair indicates the beginning and end of elements that define content. This is how start and end tag pairs appear:

<tag>…</tag>

Content — such as paragraphs, headings, tables, and lists — always uses a tag pair:

i. The start tag (<tag>) indicates, "The element begins here."
ii. The end tag (</tag>) indicates, "The element ends here."

Amid a start tag and an end tag is where the actual material is located. For instance, the paragraph element (p>) is used to enclose paragraph text on the Ed Tittel page in Listing 1–1 (CSS inline markup is omitted for clarity):

<p>In 1986, Ed began contributing articles on computer-related topics to a monthly magazine with a Macintosh focus. He has written for magazines like LAN Times, Network World, Mac World, and LAN Magazine since 1989. In 1991, he began working on his first book, and by 1994, he had contributed to more than a dozen distinct works **</p>** (Sánchez-Villamil et al., 2006).

3.3.4.2. Single Tags

Empty elements (since they have no content) are those that add something to the page, and they use one tag like this:

<tag />

Line breaks and images use one tag since they do not add anything to the HTML file.

Prior to the closing greater-than sign, a forward slash should be placed after the last unfilled element in an XHTML document., a significant distinction between it and HTML. This is thus because XHTML is based on XML, and the XML standard requires that unfilled elements be closed with a slash, as shown here:

<tag/>

However, they should include a space before the concluding slash, as shown here, to make this type of HTML legible inside older browsers (Held et al., 2012):

<tag />

Because they are unfamiliar with XHTML, outdated browsers can ignore the closing slash using this space. The space is ignored by more recent browsers that comprehend XHTML, and they interpret the tag exactly, which is tag/> (following XML regulations).

Although empty elements don't require a slash in HTML, this syntax is deprecated (i.e., considered obsolete despite still appearing in some markup). This is how an empty HTML element appears:

<tag />

Listing 1–1 practices the image tag (<img />) to contain an image on the page:

<img src="images/header. gif" alt="header graphic" width="794" height="160" />

A picture is referred to via the img element. The file that the image /> element points to is replaced when the page is displayed by the browser (an attribute performs the pointing, as seen in the following section). What occurs in HTML as image> seems in XHTML as img /> (and this applies to other single tag elements) following the XHTML guideline that was previously mentioned.

Elements in HTML or XHTML cannot be invented. If they utilize elements that don't belong to this set, all browsers will ignore their use of legal (X)HTML elements. The HTML 4.01 or XHTML 1.0 specs outline the elements they can utilize (Kim et al., 2008).

3.3.4.3. Nesting

Nested elements are often combined in page structures. Consider their nested components as a set of tidy suitcases that nest inside one another.

A bulleted list, for instance, uses two different types of components:

i. The <ul> element specifies that the list is unordered (bulleted).
ii. The <li> elements mark each item in the list.

When combining elements in this way, make sure to fully shut the inside element before closing the outside element (Wang & Weiss, 2022):

<ul>…<li>Item 1</li>…<li>Item 2</li> </ul>

3.3.5. Attributes

How an element describes a material or performs allows for variation thanks to attributes. Elements can be used in many ways depending on the situation, thanks to attributes. The src attribute, for instance, is used by the img /> element to identify the site of the image they want to utilize on their page:

<img src="images/header. gif" alt="header graphic" width="794" height="160" />

Inside this particular instance of HTML, the img /> element acts as an overall signal to the viewer that they want to present an img; the src attribute, in this particular case, identifies header.gif as the image that they wish to include inside this particular instance of HTML. The alt element provides a TypoScript alternative for the photo that can be displayed in a browser that only supports text. Other characteristics offer guidance on how to present the image in a certain format (Petrovski & Bizer, 2017). After the element name but before the ending sign, they add attributes to the start tag of the element they want them with, as shown here:

<tag attribute="value" attribute="value">

They are free to include the characteristics and their associated values in any order within the first tag or only one tag; but, in accordance with the standards governing XML syntax, the values of attributes must always be enclosed in quotation marks (Vadivu et al., 2012).

Each (X)HTML element supports the usage of a number of different attributes, but users are unable to freely combine and match the various components and attributes. Certain attributes will utilize any text provided as a value since the value might be anything; for example, it could be the URL of an image or a website that the user wishes to connect to. Others, such as the choices they offer for how text should be aligned within a table column, come with a predetermined set of possible values for the property.

The standards for HTML 4.01 and XHTML 1.0 detail the precise attributes that users are allowed to use with each specific element, as well as the values (if any are explicitly defined) that each attribute may take (Shinzato & Sekine, 2013).

3.3.6. Entities

The Web is made possible by text, yet it has several restrictions. They can use entities, which are unique characters, on their website.

3.3.6.1. Non-ASCII Characters

ASCII text at its most fundamental level defines just a limited number of characters. Certain special characters, such as fractions, copyright signs, and characters with accents, are not supported by this implementation.

The result of translating a section of text from the website shown in Figure 3.2 into German is displayed in Figure 3.5. The translated text includes three instances of the letter u with an umlaut (u).

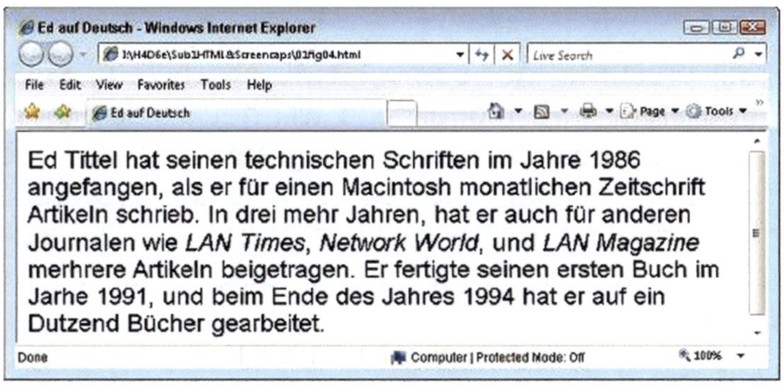

Figure 3.5. All text characters cannot be represented by ASCII text; hence HTML entities are used in their place.

Source: Ed Tittel, creative commons license.

An umlauted u is not available in ASCII text; hence HTML utilizes entities to represent it. The character it refers to takes the entity's place in the browser. Entities are marked with an ampersand

(&) at the beginning and a semicolon (;) at the end to indicate that they are derived from SGML. They color-code entities purple to reflect this. The entities in the following markup are bold (Brooker & Rohl, 1965):

<html>

<head> <style type="text/css"> body { font-family: sans-serif; font-size: large; } cite { font-family: serif; font-style: italic;

}

</style> <title>Ed auf Deutsch</title> </head> <body>

The umlauted u is represented by the entity ü.

3.3.6.2. (X)HTML Character Codes

The ISO-Latin-1 character set's encodings are provided by default, and associated entities can be called upon and used without specific modifications. But to tell the browser to interpret Unicode character codes when using one of the other encodings listed before, appropriate markup must be used. (Unicode is an international standard; in fact, it is ISO standard 10646.) It has enough character codes to support most uncommon alphabets in addition to a wide variety of additional symbols and nonalphabetic characters. Although all browsers handle UTF-8, support for UTF-16 character codes should appear within the next year or two. This will make it possible for browsers to cope with non-Roman alphabets like Arabic, katakana (Japanese), and Hangul (Korean) more successfully, which certain browsers currently find difficult to render correctly (Li & Momoi, 2001).

3.3.6.3. Tag Characters

HTML-savvy software will presume that some HTML characters, such as the greater-than and less-than signs, are hidden and will not display them on the finished Web page. These characters include the greater-than and less-than signs. They are required to make their choices clear to the browser in order for the greater-than or less-than signs to appear on their page. By making use of the following entities, they are able to display characters that are frequently a part of the concealed HTML markup:

i. greater-than sign (>): >
ii. less-than sign (<): <
iii. ampersand (&): &

While the and > marks are used in markup, they serve as directions to the browser rather than rendering anything on the page. Include the entities for these symbols in their markup if they need them on the web page, like this:

<p> The paragraph element designates a paragraph in some text:**</p>**

<p><p>This is a paragraph.**</p></p>**

The markup above uses entities to describe the and > symbols in the second line and tags to create a paragraph in the first line (Carey & Manic, 2016).

3.4. WEB PAGES COMPOSITION

In (X)HTML files, comments contain text not shown on the final page.

Each comment is recognized by two unique markup character sequences.:

i. Use the character!-- to begin each comment.
ii. Add the character --> to the end of each comment

The succeeding code includes comments that describe each markup element's purpose and place within the hierarchy of HTML markup.

An arrangement of elements forms a structure:

1. Certain elements are only able to exist inside other elements.
2. Certain components are necessary for a properly organized (X)HTML document (Heer & Chi, 2001).

<html>··<!-- Any HTML document that is well-formed should always have this tag appear close to or at the start of the content. --> <head>··<!-- The information needed to label the entire HTML document is provided by the head element. document -->

<title>Welcome to Ed Tittel.com</title> <!-- The text in the title element appears in the title bar of the browser window when the page is viewed -->

</head> <!-- closes the head element -->

<body>··<!-- The content that appears on any Web page appears or is invoked from inside the body element -->

<!-- Skip a bunch of copy here . . . -->

<!-- Subtitle text -->

<h1>Contact:</h1>

<!-- List -->

<ul>

<li><b>Email:</b> etittel at yahoo dot com</li>

```
<li><b>Address:</b> 2443 Arbor Drive, Round Rock, TX 78681–
2160</li>

<li><b>Phone:</b> 512–252–7497 (No solicitors, please)</
li> <li>List of publications available in: <a href="docs/v_et.doc"
target="_blank">MS Word</a></li>

<li>Resume available in: <a href="docs/Resu-et13.doc" target="_
blank">

MS Word</a></li>

</ul></body>··<!-- End of the body section -->

</html>·· <!-- End of the HTML document -->
```

(Oh et al., 2016).

3.4.1. Organizing HTML Text

In HTML documents, text can be structured in various ways besides the head and body sections.

3.4.2. Document Heads

In addition to a title, they can declare a variety of labels and information in the head section, mostly to characterize the content that follows. Examples of this information include the character sets used, metadata about the current document, scripts that will be called, and stylistic details. Real content is found in the body section, which also contains most (X)HTML components (Jung & Kwon, 2005).

Remember

Organizing HTML text involves structuring and formatting content using HTML tags to enhance readability and user experience on web pages.

3.4.3. Document Headings

The HTML document head is distinct from headings defined by the elements h1 through h6. While the head identifies or characterizes the entirety of the document, individual headings arrange the material that follows them. In the Ed Tittel page example, the h1 element draws attention to the Contact block at the bottom of the page (Budhiraja & Mago, 2020).

3.4.4. Paragraphs and More

When people wish to display continuous text on a web page, they can do so by utilizing the paragraph element, which is denoted by the letter p and is comprised of the tags p> and /p>. The hr /> element can establish horizontal rules (lines).

In addition, HTML provides a selection of tools for stressing or emphasizing text within paragraphs (Jaruskulchai & Kruengkrai, 2003).

3.4.5. Lists

The definition of unordered or bulleted lists is made simple by HTML. Other list types, such as numbered lists, can be created using various tools. To build as many layers of hierarchy as their list may require (say, when describing a difficult subject or simulating a table of contents with multiple heading levels they want to reflect), lists can be nested inside other lists (Cohen et al., 2002).

3.4.6. Tables

HTML offers several listing tools in addition to markup for constructing tables. (Tables were widely utilized in HTML design for various page layouts, but they are now only used for tables, as they should be.) Since markup includes structure, they can include it while defining a table.

1. Take charge of the arrangement of the rows and columns.
2. Distinguish between column heads and table data (Oogane & Asakawa, 1998).

3.4.7. Cascading Style Sheet Markup

In addition to any combination of these three formats, CSS markup can appear in separate style-sheet documents, a block of text in the document's head, and as an addition to specific HTML elements' style attributes. CSS allows for far more precise control over font selection, background, text color usage, text alignment, placement of other website elements, and much more (Keller & Nussbaumer, 2009).

ACTIVITY 3.1:

You are tasked with creating a website for a small business. Describe the HTML tags and CSS properties you would use to create a responsive navigation bar and footer that looks visually appealing and is easy to navigate on both desktop and mobile devices.

SUMMARY

Chapter Three of the book covers the fundamental building blocks of the WWW: HTML and CSS. The chapter begins by introducing readers to the basic concepts of the web, such as hypertext, browsers, and web servers. The anatomy of a URL is also discussed, explaining how URLs are used to locate web resources. Next, the chapter delves into the details of HTML and XHTML, including syntax, rules, markup color-coding, elements, attributes, and entities. Readers will learn the basic structure of HTML documents and how to use different HTML tags to create headings, paragraphs, lists, tables, and other types of content. The chapter also covers CSS, which is a style sheet language used to describe the presentation and layout of web pages, separate from their content. Readers will learn how to apply CSS markup to their HTML documents to improve the overall appearance and visual design of their web pages. Overall, this chapter provides a solid foundation for readers who want to create well-organized and visually appealing web pages using HTML and CSS.

REVIEW QUESTIONS

1. What is hypertext, and how is it used on the WWW?
2. Explain the role of web servers in delivering web content to clients.
3. What are the different parts of a URL, and what do they represent?
4. How does markup color-coding help in creating HTML and XHTML documents?
5. What are the different types of HTML elements and attributes, and how are they used in web page design?
6. What is the purpose of Cascading Style Sheets (CSS), and how does it improve the design of web pages?
7. Create an HTML document with a heading, a paragraph of text, and a bulleted list.

MULTIPLE CHOICE QUESTIONS

1. What is a browser?

a. A markup language used to create web pages
b. A computer that stores and delivers web content to clients over the Internet
c. A software application that allows users to access and view web pages on the Internet
d. A unique address that identifies the location of a web resource on the Internet

2. What is XHTML?

a. A stricter version of HTML that follows XML rules and syntax
b. A style sheet language used to describe the presentation and layout of web pages

c. A set of rules that define the structure and grammar of a programming language or markup language
d. A special character or symbol that is not available on a standard keyboard

3. **What is an attribute in HTML?**
   a. The building blocks of HTML and XHTML documents
   b. A special property that modifies the behavior or appearance of HTML or XHTML elements
   c. A software application that allows users to access and view web pages on the Internet
   d. A text that contains links to other documents or resources
4. **What is the purpose of Cascading Style Sheets (CSS)?**
   a. To describe the structure and grammar of a programming language or markup language
   b. To identify the location of a web resource on the Internet
   c. To describe the presentation and layout of web pages, separate from their content
   d. To modify the behavior or appearance of HTML or XHTML elements
5. **What is the basic structure of an HTML document?**
   a. Head and body
   b. Paragraphs and headings
   c. Tables and lists
   d. Elements and attributes
6. **What is the purpose of entities in HTML?**
   a. To describe the presentation and layout of web pages, separate from their content
   b. To modify the behavior or appearance of HTML or XHTML elements
   c. To provide special characters or symbols that are not available on a standard keyboard
   d. To create links between web resources

Answers to Multiple Choice Questions

1. (c); 2. (a); 3. (b); 4. (c); 5. (a); 6. (c)

REFERENCES

1. Adida, B., Birbeck, M., McCarron, S., & Pemberton, S., (2008). RDFa in XHTML: Syntax and processing. Recommendation, W3C, 7(41), 14.
2. Arlitt, M. F., & Williamson, C. L., (1997). Internet web servers: Workload characterization

and performance implications. IEEE/ACM Transactions on Networking, 5(5), 631–645.

3. Barnet, B., (2018). Hypertext before the web–or, what the web could have been. SAGE Handbook of Web History, 4, 215–226.
4. Bohrer, P., Elnozahy, E. N., Keller, T., Kistler, M., Lefurgy, C., McDowell, C., & Rajamony, R., (2002). The case for power management in web servers. Power Aware Computing, 4, 261–289.
5. Brooker, R. A., & Rohl, J. S. (1965). Atlas Autocode reference manual. University of Manchester. Department of Computer Science, 12(1), 56-60.
6. Brooks, D. R., & Brooks, D. R., (2017). Introducing HTML. Programming in HTML and PHP: Coding for Scientists and Engineers, 45, 1–10.
7. Budhiraja, S. S., & Mago, V., (2020). A supervised learning approach for heading detection. Expert Systems, 37(4), 12520.
8. Carey, H. J., & Manic, M., (2016). HTML web content extraction using paragraph tags. In: 2016 IEEE 25th International Symposium on Industrial Electronics (ISIE) (Vol. 2, pp. 1099–1105). IEEE.
9. Cohen, W. W., Hurst, M., & Jensen, L. S., (2002). A flexible learning system for wrapping tables and lists in HTML documents. In: Proceedings of the 11th International Conference on World Wide Web (Vol. 1, pp. 232–241).
10. Halle, M., Demeusy, V., & Kikinis, R., (2017). The open anatomy browser: A collaborative web-based viewer for interoperable anatomy atlases. Frontiers in Neuroinformatics, 2(1), 11, 22.
11. Halpin, H., & Lavrenko, V., (2011). Relevance feedback between hypertext and semantic web search: Frameworks and evaluation. Journal of Web Semantics, 9(4), 474–489.
12. Heer, J., & Chi, E. H., (2001). Identification of web user traffic composition using multi-modal clustering and information scent. In: Proc. of the Workshop on Web Mining, SIAM Conference on Data Mining (Vol. 1, pp. 51–58).
13. Held, C., Kimmerle, J., & Cress, U., (2012). Learning by foraging: The impact of individual knowledge and social tags on web navigation processes. Computers in Human Behavior, 28(1), 34–40.
14. Huynh, D. F., Miller, R. C., & Karger, D. R., (2006). Enabling web browsers to augment web sites' filtering and sorting functionalities. In: Proceedings of the 19th Annual ACM Symposium on User Interface Software and Technology (Vol. 1, pp. 125–134).
15. Jackson, C., Bortz, A., Boneh, D., & Mitchell, J. C., (2006). Protecting browser state from web privacy attacks. In: Proceedings of the 15th International Conference on World Wide Web (pp. 737–744).
16. Jaruskulchai, C., & Kruengkrai, C., (2003). A practical text summarizer by paragraph extraction for Thai. In: Proceedings of the Sixth International Workshop on Information Retrieval with Asian Languages (Vol. 1, pp. 9–16).

17. Jung, S. W., & Kwon, H. C., (2005). A scalable hybrid approach for extracting head components from web tables. IEEE Transactions on Knowledge and Data Engineering, 18(2), 174–187.
18. Keller, M., & Nussbaumer, M., (2009). Cascading style sheets: A novel approach towards productive styling with today's standards. In: Proceedings of the 18th International Conference on World Wide Web (Vol. 1, pp. 1161, 1162).
19. Kennedy, B., & Musciano, C., (2002). HTML & XHTML: The Definitive Guide (Vol. 1, p. 680). Sebastopol: O'Reilly.
20. Khare, R., (1999). Anatomy of a URL (and other internet-scale namespaces, part 1). IEEE Internet Computing, 3(5), 78.
21. Kim, H. L., Passant, A., Breslin, J. G., Scerri, S., & Decker, S., (2008). Review and alignment of tag ontologies for semantically-linked data in collaborative tagging spaces. In: 2008 IEEE International Conference on Semantic Computing (Vol. 1, pp. 315–322). IEEE.
22. Koppen, E., & Neumann, G., (1999). Active hypertext for distributed web applications. In: Proceedings. IEEE 8th International Workshops on Enabling Technologies: Infrastructure for Collaborative Enterprises (WET ICE'99) (Vol. 1, pp. 297–302). IEEE.
23. Landow, G. P., & Kahn, P., (1993). Where's the hypertext: The Dickens web as a system-independent hypertext. In: Proceedings of the ACM Conference on Hypertext (Vol. 1, pp. 149–160).
24. Lemme, S., Sutter, J., Schlinkmann, C., & Slusallek, P., (2016). The basic building blocks of declarative 3D on the web. In: Proceedings of the 21st International Conference on Web3D Technology (Vol. 1, pp. 17–25).
25. Li, S., & Momoi, K., (2001). A composite approach to language/encoding detection. In: Proc. 19th International Unicode Conference (Vol. 1, pp. 1–14).
26. Lubin, Y., Ellner, S., & Kotzman, M., (1993). Web relocation and habitat selection in desert widow spider. Ecology, 74(7), 1915–1928.
27. Oh, J., Ahn, W. H., & Kim, T., (2016). MVC architecture driven restructuring to achieve client-side web page composition. In: 2016 7th IEEE International Conference on Software Engineering and Service Science (ICSESS) (Vol. 3, pp. 45–53). IEEE.
28. Oogane, T., & Asakawa, C., (1998). An interactive method for accessing tables in HTML. In: Proceedings of the Third International ACM Conference on Assistive Technologies (Vol. 1, pp. 126–128).
29. Park, T. H., Saxena, A., Jagannath, S., Wiedenbeck, S., & Forte, A., (2013). Towards a taxonomy of errors in HTML and CSS. In: Proceedings of the Ninth Annual International ACM Conference on International Computing Education Research (Vol. 1, pp. 75–82).
30. Perlin, N., (2006). The X factor: From HTML to XHTML. In: 2006 IEEE International Professional Communication Conference (Vol. 1, pp. 190–192). IEEE.
31. Petrovski, P., & Bizer, C., (2017). Extracting attribute-value pairs from product

specifications on the web. In: Proceedings of the International Conference on Web Intelligence (Vol. 2, pp. 558–565).

32. Samu, F., Sunderland, K. D., Topping, C. J., & Fenlon, J. S., (1996). A spider population in flux: Selection and abandonment of artificial web-sites and the importance of intraspecific interactions in Lephthyphantes tenuis (Araneae: Linyphiidae) in wheat. Oecologia, 106, 228–239.
33. Sánchez-Villamil, E., Santos-Antón, S., Ortiz-Rojas, S., & Forcada, M. L., (2006). Evaluation of alignment methods for HTML parallel text. In: Advances in Natural Language Processing: 5th International Conference on NLP, FinTAL 2006 Turku, Finland, August 23–25, 2006 Proceedings (Vol. 1, pp. 280–290). Springer Berlin Heidelberg.
34. Shinzato, K., & Sekine, S., (2013). Unsupervised extraction of attributes and their values from product description. In: Proceedings of the Sixth International Joint Conference on Natural Language Processing (Vol. 1, pp. 1339–1347).
35. Tredinnick, L., (2007). Post-structuralism, hypertext, and the world wide web. In: ASLIB Proceedings (Vol. 59, No. 2, pp. 169–186). Emerald Group Publishing Limited.
36. Vadivu, P. S., Sumathy, P., & Vadivel, A., (2012). Image retrieval from WWW using attributes in HTML TAGs. Procedia Technology, 6, 509–516.
37. Wang, J., & Weiss, R. E., (2022). Local and global topics in text modeling of web pages nested in web sites. Computational Statistics & Data Analysis, 173, 107518.
38. Whitehead, P., & Russell, J. H., (2008). HTML: Your Visual Blueprint for Designing Web Pages with HTML, CSS, and XHTML (Vol. 9, pp. 14–16). John Wiley & Sons.
39. Wimelius, H., (2004). Fundamentals of user perception and interaction: Environmental psychology applied in a study of web pages. Psychology J., 2(3), 282–303.

CHAPTER 4

JAVASCRIPT: THE LANGUAGE OF THE WEB

UNIT INTRODUCTION

An interactive and dynamic website can be made using the programming language JavaScript. Brendan Eich (1996) created it in while he was employed by Netscape Communications Corporation. JavaScript runs on the browser used by the user instead of the server because it is a scripting language that works on the client side. In order to update a web page's content without needing a page refresh, JavaScript can be used. This makes it possible for a more interactive and dynamic web experience. With the help of tools like Node.js, JavaScript is additionally utilized on the side of the server, enabling programmers to create server-side applications. As a result, full-stack frameworks for JavaScript such as React and Angular, that can be used to create entire web applications, have been created. JavaScript is a flexible language with many applications outside of web development. It can be applied to the creation of desktop and mobile applications, video games, and even the programming of robots. Overall, understanding JavaScript is a requirement for any web developer, and it is a valuable skill for every programmer to possess due to its widespread use and versatility (Severance, 2012; Wrifs-Brock & Eich, 2020).

Learning Objectives

- At the end of this chapter, readers will be able to:
- Understand the definition and specifications of JavaScript

- Learn the advantages and limitations of JavaScript
- Familiarize with JavaScript development tools
- Understand JavaScript syntax and code structure
- Learn how to enable JavaScript in different browsers
- Understand the different ways of placing JavaScript in HTML documents
- Learn about JavaScript variables, data types, and scope
- Understand JavaScript operators and their types

Key Terms

- Arithmetic Operators
- Assignment Operators
- Bitwise Operators
- Chrome
- Client-side JavaScript
- Comments in JavaScript
- Comparison Operators
- Conditional Operator
- Data Types
- Development Tools
- External File
- Firefox
- Internet Explorer
- JavaScript
- JavaScript Enabling
- JavaScript Operators
- JavaScript Placement
- JavaScript Syntax
- JavaScript Variables
- Logical Operators
- Non-JavaScript Browsers
- Opera
- Reserved Words
- Type of Operator
- Variable Scope

4.1. DEFINITIONS AND SPECIFICATIONS

JavaScript is a flexible programming language for computers. Its implementations enable scripts running on the client side to interact with users and create dynamic pages, and it is most frequently used as a component of web pages.

It is an object-oriented programming (OOP) language that can be interpreted.

LiveScript was the original name of JavaScript, yet Netscape changed it to JavaScript, perhaps in response to the buzz that Java was causing.

LiveScript, the predecessor to JavaScript, made its debut in Netscape 2.0 in 1995. Netscape, Internet Explorer, and other popular web browsers all contain the general-purpose language's core.

The basic JavaScript language was standardized by the ECMA-262 Specification.

1. JavaScript is a simple, interpreted programming language.
2. Constructed for the development of network-centric applications.
3. Integrates with and complements Java.
4. Integrated and complementary to HTML.
5. Cross-platform and open (Bodin et al., 2014; Chaudhuri et al., 2017).

> **Did you Know?**
>
> Visual Studio Code, a free and open-source code editor developed by Microsoft, is one of the most popular JavaScript development tools used by developers worldwide.

4.1.1. Client-Side JavaScript

Client-side JavaScript is the most popular variation of the language. For the script's code to be recognized by a browser, it must be incorporated into or referenced from an HTML document.

It implies that a website need not be static HTML, but rather may contain programs that communicate with users, manage browsers, and produce HTML content on the fly.

Over conventional CGI server-side scripts, the JavaScript client-side mechanism offers a number of benefits. JavaScript, for instance, can be used to determine whether a user has entered an email address that is correct in a form field (Figure 4.1).

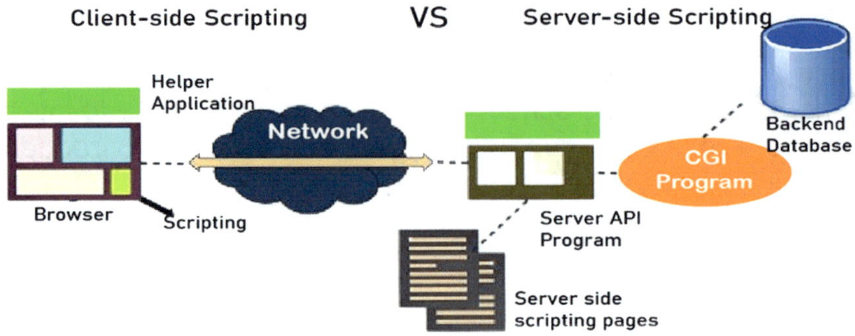

Figure 4.1. Difference between server-side scripting and client-side scripting.

Source: Tech Differences, Creative Commons License

When a user submits a form, JavaScript is run, and just if all of the entries are correct are they sent to a web server. User-initiated events, including button clicking, link navigation, and various other explicit or implicit user actions, can be caught using JavaScript (Ocariza et al., 2016).

4.1.2. Advantages of JavaScript

The qualities of using JavaScript are:

1. **Less Server Interaction**: User input can be verified before the page is sent to the server. Because of the reduced server traffic, your server will be under less stress.
2. **Providing Visitors with Immediate Feedback:** They are not required to wait for the page to reload to find out if they forgot to enter something.
3. **Enhanced Interactivity:** You can design interfaces that respond when a user mouses over them or presses a key on the keyboard to activate them.
4. **Richer Interfaces:** To give your website visitors a Rich Interface, you may employ JavaScript to include things like drag-and-drop components and sliders (Ahmed, 2014; Lerner et al., 2013).

4.1.3. Limitations of JavaScript

JavaScript can't be used as a legitimate programming language. It does not have the following crucial components:

1. It is not possible to read or write files using Client-side JavaScript. This is still here for security purposes.

2. Since no such support is available, JavaScript may not be employed in networking applications.
3. JavaScript lacks multithreading and multiprocessor support.
4. Once more, JavaScript is a simple, interpreted programming language that allows you to add interactivity to HTML pages that would otherwise be static (Andreasen et al., 2017).

4.1.4. JavaScript Development Tools

The lack of expensive development tools is one of JavaScript's key advantages. You can begin by using a basic text editor like Notepad. You are not even required to purchase a compiler because it is a language that is interpreted and used in a web browser.

Several vendors have developed excellent JavaScript editing tools to simplify our lives. These are a few of them:

1. **Microsoft FrontPage:** FrontPage is a well-known HTML editor created by Microsoft. Web designers can create interactive websites with the help of the JavaScript tools that FrontPage also offers.
2. **Macromedia Dreamweaver MX:** Among professionals who work in web development, Macromedia Dreamweaver MX is an extremely well-liked HTML and JavaScript editor. It offers a number of useful prebuilt JavaScript components, works well with databases, and complies with new standards like XHTML and XML.
3. **Macromedia HomeSite 5:** Macromedia's HomeSite 5 is a popular JavaScript editor and HTML that can be used to efficiently manage personal websites (Bienfait & Ertl, 2013).

4.1.5. JavaScript Today

The most recent revision to the ECMAScript standard in more than four years will be ECMAScript Edition 5. The only very slight difference between JavaScript 2.0 and Edition 5 in the ECMAScript standard is that JavaScript 2.0 matches to Edition 5.

On the internet, you can find the JavaScript 2.0 specification.

Today, the ECMAScript standard is followed by both Netscape JavaScript and Microsoft JScript, though both languages continue to support features that are not included in the standard (Chaqfeh et al., 2022).

4.2. JAVASCRIPT SYNTAX

JavaScript declarations that are inserted between the <**script**>... </**script**> HTML tags on a web page can be used to implement JavaScript (Figure 4.2).

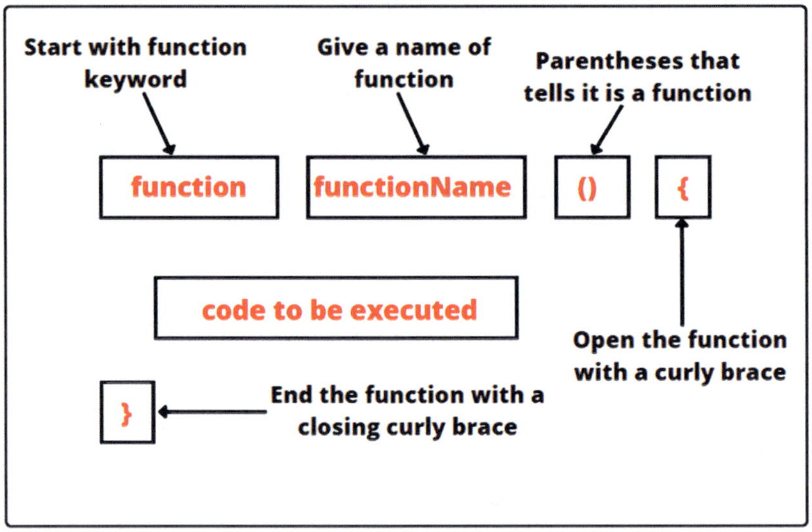

Figure 4.2. JavaScript function syntax declaration.

Source: Scientech easy, creative commons license.

The**<script>** tags, which contain your JavaScript, can be placed anywhere on your website, but it is typically advised that you keep it inside the**<head>** tags.

The browser program is informed to begin interpreting all of the text within these tags as scripts by the <script> tag. Your JavaScript will have the following basic syntax.

```
<script ...>

JavaScript code

</script>
```

Two crucial attributes are required by the script tag:

1. **Language:** The language that you are using for your scripts is indicated by this attribute. Usually, JavaScript will be its value. Although the use of this attribute has been phased out in the latest versions of HTML (and XHTML, its successor).
2. **Type:** It is now advised to set this attribute's value to "text/ javascript" to denote the scripting language being used.

The following is the syntax for your JavaScript.

```
<script language="javascript" type="text/javascript">

JavaScript code

</script> (Kim et al., 2022)
```

4.2.1. JavaScript Code

Let's print out a sample of "Hello World" first. We surrounded our JavaScript code with an optional HTML comment. To protect the code we wrote to a browser that doesn't support JavaScript, do this. The comment is concluded by a "//-->." In this case, "//" in JavaScript denotes a comment, so we added it to stop browsers from interpreting the final portion of the HTML responses as JavaScript code. We then make a function document call which inserts an address into our HTML file (Figure 4.3).

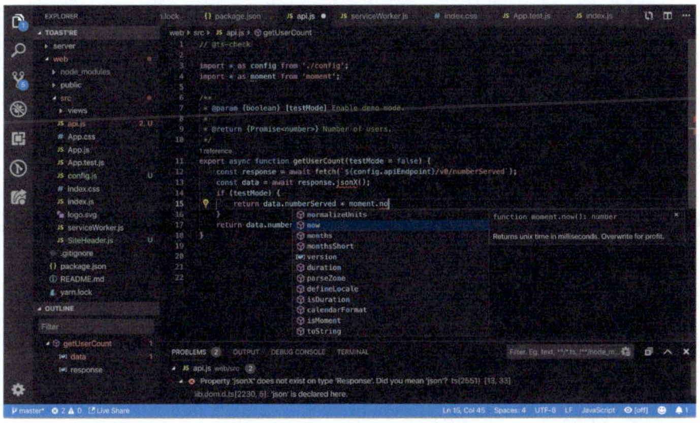

Figure 4.3. An example of JavaScript in visual studio code.

Source: Visual studio code, creative commons license.

The text, HTML, or both can be written using this function. Consider a look at the code below.

```
<html>

<body>

<script language="javascript" type="text/javascript">

<!--

document.write ("Hello World!")

//-->
```

```
</script>
</body></html>
```

The output of this code is as follows:

Hello World! (Guarnieri & Livshits, 2009)

4.2.1.1. Whitespace and Line Breaks

Programs written in JavaScript ignore newlines, tabs, and spaces. You are free to arrange and indent your programs in a way that is orderly and consistent, making the code simple to read and comprehend.

This includes using tabs, spaces, and newlines easily throughout your program (Ferguson et al., 2013).

4.2.1.2. Semicolons are Optional

As in C, C++, and Java, simple statements are usually followed by a semicolon character in JavaScript. However, JavaScript permits you to leave out this semicolon if you separate every one of your statements onto their own line. The following code, for instance, might have been written without semicolons.

```
<script language="javascript" type="text/javascript">
<!--...var1 = 10...var2 = 20 //-->
</script>
```

However, you must employ semicolons when organized in just one line as shown below:

```
<script language="javascript" type="text/javascript">
<!--
var1 = 10; var2 = 20;
//-->
</script>
```

Note: Semicolons are a good programming technique (Reid et al., 2013).

4.2.1.3. Case Sensitivity

A case-sensitive language is JavaScript. This necessitates consistent letter capitalization when typing the language's key phrases, variables, function names, and additional identifiers. As a result, in JavaScript, identifiers such as Time and TIME have different meanings.

NOTE: When writing JavaScript variable and function names, caution should be exercised (Zaidi & Zaidi, 2017).

4.2.2. Comments in JavaScript

JavaScript accepts comments written in C and C++ formats. Thus:

1. JavaScript treats any text among a // as well as the end of the line as a comment and ignores it.
2. A comment is considered to be anything that's within the symbols /* and */. This might take up several lines.
3. JavaScript also understands the opening HTML comment sequence, <“!--. Like the // comment, JavaScript addresses it as a single-line comment.
4. 4. JavaScript does not recognize the HTML comment ending sequence -->, so it must be written as //--> (Nascimento et al., 2021; Chandra et al., 2016).

4.3. JAVASCRIPT ENABLING

JavaScript support is already built into every modern browser. You may frequently need to manually turn on or off this support. The process for turning on and off JavaScript support in Chrome, Firefox, Internet Explorer, and Opera is described in this chapter (Romano et al., 1998; Brown et al., 2020).

4.3.1. JavaScript in Internet Explorer

The steps to enable or disable JavaScript in the Internet Explorer browser are as follows:

1. From the menu, select Tools -> Internet Options.
2. From the dialogue box, choose the Security tab.
3. Select Custom Level from the menu.
4. From the menu, select Custom Level.
5. Under Active scripting, select the radio button for Enable.
6. At last, select OK and exit.

You must choose the Turn off radio button in Active scripting in order to stop Internet Explorer from supporting JavaScript (Stothard, 2000) (Figure 4.4).

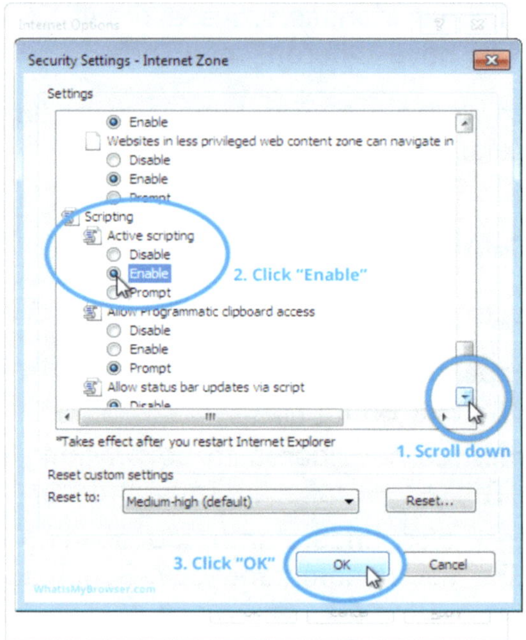

Figure 4.4. JavaScript enabling in internet explorer.

Source: What is my browser, creative commons license.

4.3.2. JavaScript in Firefox

The steps to enable or disable JavaScript in Firefox are as follows:

1. Click to open a new tab ->, then type about: config into the address field.
2. The warning dialogue can be found after that. I'll exercise caution, I swear!
3. A list of configure choices can then be found in the browser.
4. Type the word JavaScript. enabled into the search box.
5. By selecting the toggle option from the context menu when you right-click on the value of that option, you can either enable or disable JavaScript there.

If JavaScript.enabled is true, clicking the toggle changes it to false. If JavaScript is turned off, clicking the toggle turns it on (Hackett & Guo, 2012; Ugawa et al., 2019).

4.3.3. JavaScript in Chrome

The steps to enable or disable JavaScript in Chrome are as follows (Figure 4.5):

1. In your browser, select the Chrome menu in the top right corner.
2. Choose Settings.
3. At the bottom of the page, click Show advanced settings.
4. Select the button of Content settings in the Privacy section.
5. Choose "Do not permit any site to execute JavaScript" or "Permit all sites to operate JavaScript (recommended)" under the "Javascript" section (Seo & Kim, 2014; He et al., 2021).

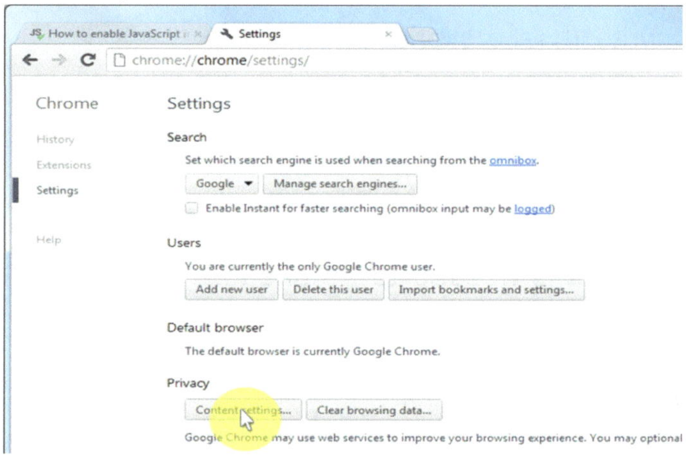

Source: Josh Brolin, creative commons license.

Figure 4.5. Enabling JavaScript in chrome.

Remember

Enabling JavaScript in Firefox allows users to experience dynamic and interactive web content, such as online games, animations, and other rich media, that would otherwise be unavailable or limited without JavaScript functionality.

4.3.4. JavaScript in Opera

The steps to enable or disable JavaScript in Opera are as follows:

1. Select Preferences under Tools-> in the menu.
2. From the dialogue box, choose the Advanced option.
3. From the items listed, pick Content.
4. Choose Enable JavaScript checkbox.
5. At last, select OK and exit.

You shouldn't check the **Enable JavaScript checkbox** if you want to turn off JavaScript support in Opera (Mehrnazhad et al., 2016).

4.3.5. Warning for Non-JavaScript Browsers

The user can see a warning message if JavaScript is required to perform an important task by using the **<noscript>** tag.

Following the script block, you may add a **noscript** block as follows:

```
<html>
<body>
<script language="javascript" type="text/javascript">
<!—
```

```
document. write ("Hello World!")
//-->
</script>
<noscript>
Sorry...JavaScript is needed to go ahead.
</noscript>
</body></html>
```

Now, the message from </noscript> will appear on the screen if the user's browser cannot handle JavaScript or if JavaScript is not enabled (Reips, 2007).

4.4. JAVASCRIPT PLACEMENT

JavaScript code can be inserted anywhere within an HTML document with relative ease. However, the following are the methods that people prefer to use for including JavaScript within an HTML file:

1. Write in <head>...</head> section.
2. Write in <body>...</body> section.
3. Write in <body>...</body> and <head>...</head> sections.
4. Include the script in a separate file and in the head>.../head> section (Afsari, 2017).

4.4.1. JavaScript in <head>...</head> Section

You should put the script in its head as shown if you want it to run when a certain event occurs, like when a user presses somewhere (Leeuw, 2015).

```
<html>
<head>
<script type="text/javascript">
<!--
function sayHello() { alert("Hello World")
}
//-->
</script>
</head>
<body>
Click here for the result
<input type="button" onclick="sayHello()" value="Say Hello" />
</body>
</html>
```

This code will create these results:

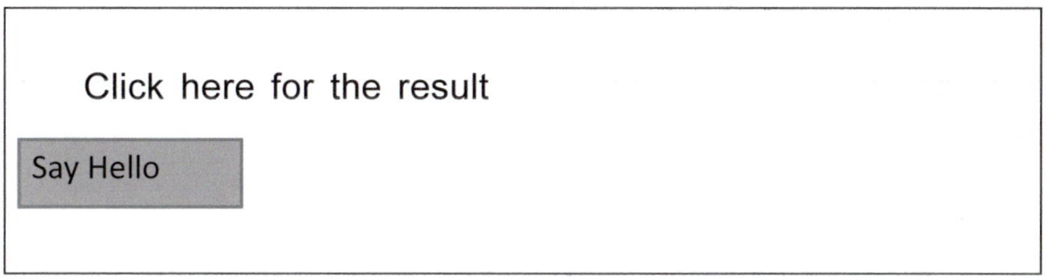

4.4.2. JavaScript in <body>...</body> Section

The script passes in the <body> section of the document if you need it to execute as the page loads and create content for the page. In this scenario, you wouldn't have any JavaScript-defined functions. Consider the code below (Harder & Harder, 2018).

```
<html><head>
</head>
<body>
<script type="text/javascript">
<!--
document.write("Hello World")
//-->
</script>
<p>This is web page body </p>
</body>
</html>
```

This code will create the results as follows:

Hello World

This is web page body

4.4.3. JavaScript in <body> and <head> Sections

As shown below, you can combine the code for JavaScript in the <head> and <body> sections (Bhangal et al. 2003).

```
<html>
<head>
<script type="text/javascript">
<!--
function sayHello() { alert("Hello World")
}
//-->
</script>
```

```
</head>
<body>
<script type="text/javascript">
<!--
document.write("Hello World")
//-->
</script>
<input type="button" onclick="sayHello()" value="Say Hello" />
</body>
</html>
```

This code will create the results as follows.

HelloWorld

Say Hello

4.4.4. JAVASCRIPT IN EXTERNAL FILE

As you use JavaScript more frequently, you might discover instances where you reuse the same JavaScript code across different pages of a website.

You are not required to maintain the same code in different HTML files. You may save JavaScript in a separate file and then consist of it in your HTML files using the script tag, which offers a mechanism for doing so.

Here is an illustration of how to use the **script** tag's **src** attribute to include a separate JavaScript file in your code for HTML.

```
<html>
<head>
<script type="text/javascript" src="filename.js" ></script>
</head><body>
. </body></html>
```

Writing all of the JavaScript source code in a plain text file with an extension of ".js" and including that file as demonstrated above are the requirements for using JavaScript from a separate source. For instance, you could include the filename.js file and leave the subsequent content in the **filename.js** file, then use the **sayHello** function within your HTML file (Tilkov & Vinoski, 2010).

```
function sayHello() { alert("Hello World")
}
```

4.5. JAVASCRIPT VARIABLES

4.5.1. JavaScript Datatypes

The range of data types that a programming language can support is one of its most fundamental features. These are the kinds of values that a programming language can represent and work with.

TIPS

Understanding JavaScript datatypes, such as numbers, strings, and Booleans, is essential for writing efficient and effective JavaScript code.

You can work with three basic data types in JavaScript:

1. Numbers, such as 123, 120.50 etc.
2. Strings of text, such as "This text string" etc.
3. Boolean, such as true or false.

The trivial data types null and undefined, which each define a single value, are also defined by JavaScript. JavaScript also supports a combined data type called an object in addition to the aforementioned primitive data types. Objects will be covered in depth in a different chapter.

Note: Java does not distinguish between floating-point values and integer values. In JavaScript, floating-point values are used to represent all numbers. JavaScript uses the IEEE 754-defined 64-bit floating-point format to represent numbers (Ugwa et al., 2019).

4.5.2. JavaScript Variables

Variables are a feature of many programming languages, including JavaScript. You can think of variables as named containers. These containers can be used to store data, and you can then identify the data by just naming the container.

In a JavaScript program, a variable must first be declared before it can be used. The **var** keyword is used to declare variables as follows.

```
<script type="text/javascript">
<!-- var
money;
var name;
```

```
//-->
</script>
```

You can also declare multiple variables with the same **var** keyword as follows:

```
<script type="text/javascript">
<!-- var money, name;
//-->
</script>
```

Variable initialization is the act of keeping the value in a variable. Initializing variables can be done either when they are first created or afterward when you require them. For instance, you could make a variable called money and later give it the value of 2000.50. You can initialize another variable by giving it the following value.

```
<script type="text/javascript">
<!--
var name =
"Ali"; var
money; money = 2000.50;
//-->
</script>
```

Note: Only declare or initialize variables with the **var** keyword once throughout the lifespan of the document.

The same variable should not be declared twice. The language JavaScript is **untyped**. As a result, any data type can be stored in a JavaScript variable. In contrast to many other languages,

JavaScript does not require you to specify the type of information the variable will store when you declare it. A variable's value type may change while a program is running, and JavaScript handles this automatically (Vouillon & Balat, 2014).

4.5.3. JavaScript Variable Scope

The area of your program where a variable is defined is its scope. Variables in JavaScript only have two scopes.

1. **Global Variables:** A variable that is global can be defined in any part of your JavaScript code because it has a global scope.
2. **Local Variables:** Once a local variable has been defined, it can only be used within the defined function. The parameters of a function are always specific to that function.

A local variable with an identical name has preference over any variable that is global outside of the main body of a function.

You can effectively hide a global variable by declaring a local variable or function parameter with an identical name. Take a look at the example below.

```
<script type="text/javascript">

<!--

var myVar = "global"; // Declare a global variable function checkscope() {

var myVar = "local"; // Declare a local variable document.write(myVar);

}

//-->

</script>
```

It will create the result as follow:

Local

JavaScript Variable Names

Keep the following guidelines in mind when giving name to your variables in JavaScript.

1. None of the JavaScript-reserved keywords should be used as variable names. The next section includes a list of these keywords. Break and Boolean variable names, for instance, are invalid.
2. Variable names in JavaScript shouldn't begin with a number (0–9). They have to start with a letter or an underscore. For instance, 123test is not a valid variable name, whereas _123test is.
3. Case matters when naming variables in JavaScript. As an illustration, Name, as well as name, is two distinct variables (Theisen, 2019).

4.5.4. JavaScript Reserved Words

The Table 4.1 provides an outline of all words that are reserved in JavaScript. They cannot be used as object names, loop labels, JavaScript variables, functions, or techniques (Severance, 2012).

Table 4.1. List of JavaScript Reserved Words

abstract boolean break	else	Instance of	switch synchronized
byte	enum	int	this
case	export	interface	throw
catch	extends	long	throws transient
char	false	native	true
class	final	new	try
const continue debugger default delete	finally	null	typeof
do	float	package	var
double	for	private protected public	void
	function	return	volatile
	goto	short	while
	if	static	with
	implements import	super	
	in		

Source: Tutorials point, creative commons license.

4.6. JAVASCRIPT OPERATORS

4.6.1. Operator

Consider a straightforward expression. The sum of 4 and 5 is 9. The operands in this instance are 4 and 5, and the operator is '+.' These operators are supported by JavaScript (Figure 4.6).

1. Arithmetic Operators
2. Comparison Operators
3. Logical (or Relational) Operators
4. Assignment Operators
5. Conditional (or ternary) Operators

Let's examine each operator individually (Mirshokraie, 2014).

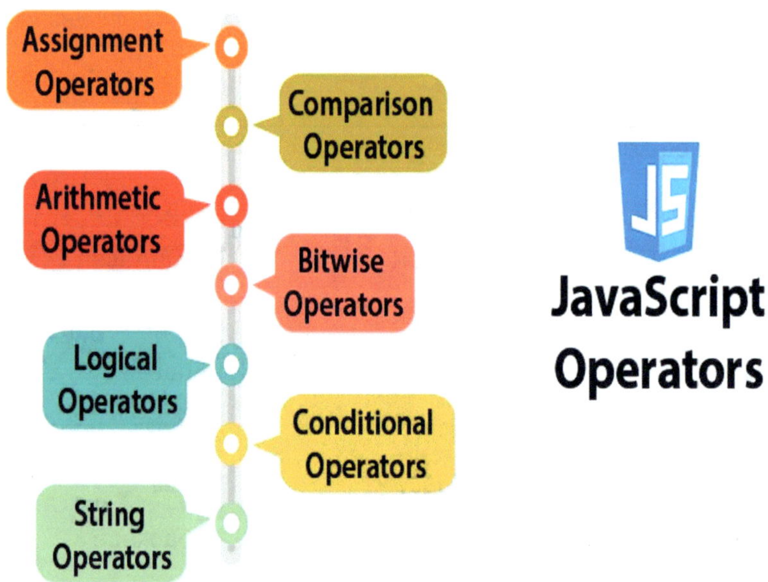

Figure 4.6. Schematic of the JavaScript operators.

Source: Beth K, creative commons license.

4.6.2. Arithmetic Operators

These arithmetic operators are supported by JavaScript:

If variable A has a value of 10 as well as variable B has a value of 20, then (Cowell & Cowell, 2003) (Table 4.2):

Table 4.2. Arithmetic Operators in JavaScript

Sl. No.	Operator and Description
1	+ (Addition) Adds two operands Ex: A + B will give 30
2	- (Subtraction) Subtracts the second operand from the first Ex: A – B will give -10
3	> (Greater than) Checks if the value of the left operand is greater than the value of the right operand, if yes, then the condition becomes true. Ex: (A > B) is not true.
4	< (Less than) Checks if the value of the left operand is less than the value of the right operand, if yes, then the condition becomes true. Ex: (A < B) is true.
5	>= (Greater than or Equal to) Checks if the value of the left operand is greater than or equal to the value of the right operand, if yes, then the condition becomes true. Ex: (A >= B) is not true.
6	<= (Less than or Equal to) Checks if the value of the left operand is less than or equal to the value of the right operand, if yes, then the condition becomes true. Ex: (A <= B) is true.

Source: Tutorials point, creative commons license.

4.6.3. Comparison Operators

In JavaScript, the subsequent comparison operators are supported (Arslan & Arslan, 2018) (Figure 4.7):

Comparison Operators

>	Greater Than
>=	Greater Than or Equal To
<	Less Than
<=	Less Than or Equal To
==	Equal To
===	Strict Equal To
!=	Not Equal To
!==	Strict Not Equal To

Figure 4.7. Comparison operators in JavaScript.

Source: Tree house, creative commons license.

4.6.4. Logical Operators

In JavaScript, a number of logical operators are supported (Borghetti et al., 2010) (Figure 4.8):

Logical Operators

Operator	Meaning	Example	Result
&&	Logical and	(5<2)&&(5>3)	False
||	Logical or	(5<2)||(5>3)	True
!	Logical not	!(5<2)	True

Figure 4.8. Logical operators in JavaScript.

Source: Sushant kumar, creative commons license.

4.6.5. Bitwise Operators

In JavaScript, a number of bitwise operators are supported:

If variable A has a value of 2 as well as variable B has a value of 3, then (Kim et al., 2017) (Table 4.3):

Table 4.3. Bitwise Operators in JavaScript

Sl. No	Operator and Description
1	& (Bitwise AND) It performs a Boolean AND operation on each bit of its integer arguments. Ex: (A & B) is 2.

<table>
<tr><td>2</td><td>| (BitWise OR)

It performs a Boolean OR operation on each bit of its integer arguments.

Ex: (A | B) is 3.</td></tr>
<tr><td>3</td><td>^ (Bitwise XOR)</td></tr>
<tr><td></td><td>It performs a Boolean exclusive OR operation on each bit of its integer arguments. Exclusive OR means that either operand one is true or operand two is true, but not both.

Ex: (A ^ B) is 1.</td></tr>
<tr><td>4</td><td>~ (Bitwise Not)

It is a unary operator and operates by reversing all the bits in the operand.

Ex: (~B) is -4.</td></tr>
<tr><td>5</td><td><< (Left Shift)

It moves all the bits in its first operand to the left by the number of places specified in the second operand. New bits are filled with zeros. Shifting a value left by one position is equivalent to multiplying it by 2, shifting two positions is equivalent to multiplying by 4, and so on.

Ex: (A << 1) is 4.</td></tr>
<tr><td>6</td><td>>> (Right Shift)

Binary Right Shift Operator. The left operand's value is moved right by the number of bits specified by the right operand.

Ex: (A >> 1) is 1.</td></tr>
<tr><td>7</td><td>>>> (Right shift with Zero)

This operator is just like the >> operator, except that the bits shifted in on the left are always zero.

Ex: (A >>> 1) is 1.</td></tr>
</table>

Source: Tutorials point, creative commons license.

4.6.6. Assignment Operators

In JavaScript, the following kinds of assignment operators are supported (Figure 4.9):

Operator	Example	Equivalent Expression (m=15)	Result
=	y = a+b	y = 10 + 20	30
+=	m +=10	m = m+10	25
-=	m -=10	m = m-10	5
*=	m *=10	m = m*10	150
/=	m /=10	m = m/10	1.5
%=	m %=10	m = m%10	5
**=	m**=2	m = m**2 or $m = m^2$	225
//=	m//=10	m = m//10	1

Figure 4.9. Assignment operators in JavaScript.

Source: Rajesh kumar, creative commons license.

Note: Bitwise operators follow the same reasoning, so they will <<=, >>=, >>=, &=, |= and ^= (Brooks, 2007).

4.7. MISCELLANEOUS OPERATORS

The conditional operator (?:) and the type of operator are two JavaScript operators that will be covered in this article (Myalapalli, 2015).

4.7.1. Conditional Operator (?:)

The conditional operator initially tests the expression for a true as well as false value, and then, based on the outcome of the test, operates any of the two given statements (Table 4.4).

Table 4.4. Conditional Operators in JavaScript

Sl. No	Operator and Description
1	?: (Conditional) If Condition is true? Then value X: Otherwise value Y

Source: Mirshokraie et al., Creative Commons License.

4.7.2. Type of Operator

Prior to its single operator, which can be of any type, the kind of operator is a single operator. The value it holds is a string that specifies the operand's data type. If the operand is a string, number, or Boolean value, the type of operator assesses to "number," "string," or "boolean" and returns true or false depending on the evaluation. The type of Operator's return values are listed in Table 4.5 (Logozzo & Veter, 2010).

Table 4.5. Type of operators in JavaScript

Type	String Returned by typeof
Number	"number"
String	"string"
Boolean	"boolean"
Object	"object"
Function	"function"
Undefined	"undefined"
Null	"object"

Source: Guha et al., creative commons license.

ACTIVITY 4.1:

You are working on a web application that allows users to filter and sort data based on different criteria. Describe how you would use JavaScript functions and objects to implement this functionality, and provide an example of how you would test your code.

SUMMARY

Chapter Four introduces the reader to JavaScript, the language of the web. The chapter begins with an overview of JavaScript, including its definitions and specifications, advantages, limitations, and development tools. Next, the chapter covers JavaScript syntax, including code and comments. The chapter then moves on to discussing JavaScript enabling in popular web browsers such as Internet Explorer, Firefox, Chrome, and Opera, as well as warning for non-JavaScript browsers. The placement of JavaScript in web pages is also discussed, including in the head and body sections, as well as external files. The chapter concludes by covering JavaScript variables, datatypes, variable scope, reserved words, and operators such as arithmetic, comparison, logical, bitwise, assignment, conditional, and typeof.

REVIEW QUESTIONS

1. What is JavaScript and what is it used for?
2. What are the advantages and limitations of using JavaScript?
3. Where can JavaScript be placed in an HTML document?
4. What are JavaScript variables and what is their purpose?
5. What are JavaScript operators and what are their different types?
6. How can JavaScript be enabled in different web browsers?
7. What is the purpose of the conditional operator and what is its syntax?

MULTIPLE CHOICE QUESTIONS

1. What is the purpose of JavaScript?

a. To create web pages
b. To style web pages
c. To add interactivity to web pages
d. To connect to databases

2. What are the advantages of using JavaScript?

a. It is easy to learn
b. It can add interactivity to web pages
c. It can create web pages
d. It is a server-side programming language

3. Where can JavaScript be placed in an HTML document?

a. Only in the <head> section
b. Only in the <body> section
c. Both in the <head> and <body> sections

d. Only in an external file

4. What is the purpose of JavaScript variables?

a. To store data

b. To create functions

c. To style web pages

d. To connect to databases

5. What is the purpose of comparison operators in JavaScript?

a. To perform arithmetic calculations

b. To compare values

c. To perform logical operations

d. To assign values

6. What is the purpose of the conditional operator in JavaScript?

a. To compare values

b. To assign values

c. To perform arithmetic calculations

d. To make decisions

Answers to Multiple Choice Questions

1. (b); 2. (a); 3. (b); 4. (c); 5. (d); 6. (a)

REFERENCES

1. Afsari, K., Eastman, C. M., & Castro-Lacouture, D., (2017). JavaScript object notation (JSON) data serialization for IFC schema in web-based BIM data exchange. Automation in Construction, 77(1), 24–51.
2. Ahmed, M. Z., (2014). Which one is better-JavaScript or jQuery. International Journal of Computer Science and Mobile Computing, 3(6), 193–207.
3. Andreasen, E., Gong, L., Møller, A., Pradel, M., Selakovic, M., Sen, K., & Staicu, C. A., (2017). A survey of dynamic analysis and test generation for JavaScript. ACM Computing Surveys (CSUR), 50(5), 1–36.
4. Arslan, E., & Arslan, E., (2018). Conditional statements and comparison operators. Learn JavaScript with p5. JS: Coding for Visual Learners, 89(1), 61–76.
5. Bhangal, S., Jankowski, T., Bhangal, S., & Jankowski, T., (2003). Further JavaScript. Foundation Web Design, 35(1) 203–233.
6. Bienfait, B., & Ertl, P., (2013). JSME: A free molecule editor in JavaScript. Journal of Cheminformatics, 5(1), 1–6.

7. Bodin, M., Charguéraud, A., Filaretti, D., Gardner, P., Maffeis, S., Naudziuniene, D., & Smith, G., (2014). A trusted mechanized JavaScript specification. ACM SIGPLAN Notices, 49(1), 87–100.
8. Borghetti, J., Snider, G. S., Kuekes, P. J., Yang, J. J., Stewart, D. R., & Williams, R. S., (2010). 'Memristive' switches enable 'stateful' logic operations via material implication. Nature, 464(7290), 873–876.
9. Brooks, D. R., (2007). Fundamentals of the JavaScript language. An Introduction to HTML and JavaScript: For Scientists and Engineers, 67–106.
10. Brown, F., Renner, J., Nötzli, A., Lerner, S., Shacham, H., & Stefan, D., (2020). Towards a verified range analysis for JavaScript JITs. In: Proceedings of the 41st ACM SIGPLAN Conference on Programming Language Design and Implementation (pp. 135–150).
11. Chandra, S., Gordon, C. S., Jeannin, J. B., Schlesinger, C., Sridharan, M., Tip, F., & Choi, Y., (2016). Type inference for static compilation of JavaScript. ACM SIGPLAN Notices, 51(10), 410–429.
12. Chaqfeh, M., Coke, R., Hu, J., Hashmi, W., Subramanian, L., Rahwan, T., & Zaki, Y., (2022). JSAnalyzer: A web developer tool for simplifying mobile web pages through non-critical JavaScript elimination. ACM Transactions on the Web, 16(4), 1–31.
13. Chaudhuri, A., Vekris, P., Goldman, S., Roch, M., & Levi, G., (2017). Fast and precise type checking for JavaScript. Proceedings of the ACM on Programming Languages, 1(OOPSLA), 1–30.
14. Cowell, J., & Cowell, J., (2003). JavaScript and XHTML. Essential XHTML™ Fast: Creating Dynamic Web Sites with XHTML and JavaScript, 15(1), 157–176.
15. De Leeuw, J. R., (2015). jsPsych: A JavaScript library for creating behavioral experiments in a web browser. Behavior Research Methods, 47(1), 1–12.
16. Eich, B., & McKinney, C. R. (1996). JavaScript Language Specification. Techn. Ber. Netscape Communications, Nov, 96-002.
17. Ferguson, R., Heilmann, C., Ferguson, R., & Heilmann, C., (2013). HTML and JavaScript. Beginning JavaScript with DOM Scripting and Ajax, 12(1), 69–100.
18. Guarnieri, S., & Livshits, V. B., (2009). GATEKEEPER: Mostly static enforcement of security and reliability policies for JavaScript code. In: USENIX Security Symposium (Vol. 10, pp. 78–85).
19. Guha, A., Saftoiu, C., & Krishnamurthi, S., (2010). The essence of JavaScript. In: ECOOP 2010–Object-Oriented Programming: 24th European Conference, Maribor, Slovenia, June 21–25, 2010. Proceedings 24 (pp. 126–150). Springer Berlin Heidelberg.
20. Hackett, B., & Guo, S. Y., (2012). Fast and precise hybrid type inference for JavaScript. ACM SIGPLAN Notices, 47(6), 239–250.
21. Harder, J., & Harder, J., (2018). What is JavaScript? Graphics and Multimedia for the Web with Adobe Creative Cloud: Navigating the Adobe Software Landscape, 50(1), 881–898.

22. Kim, H. Y., Kim, J. H., Oh, H. K., Lee, B. J., Mun, S. W., Shin, J. H., & Kim, K., (2022). DAPP: Automatic detection and analysis of prototype pollution vulnerability in node.js modules. International Journal of Information Security, 21(1), 1–23.
23. Kim, M., Jeong, H. J., & Moon, S. M., (2017). Small footprint JavaScript engine. Components and Services for IoT Platforms: Paving the Way for IoT Standards, 103–116.
24. Lerner, B. S., Politz, J. G., Guha, A., & Krishnamurthi, S., (2013). TeJaS: Retrofitting type systems for JavaScript. ACM SIGPLAN Notices, 49(2), 1–16.
25. Logozzo, F., & Venter, H., (2010). Rata: Rapid atomic type analysis by abstract interpretation–application to JavaScript optimization. In: Compiler Construction: 19th International Conference, CC 2010, Held as Part of the Joint European Conferences on Theory and Practice of Software, ETAPS 2010, Paphos, Cyprus, March 20–28, 2010. Proceedings 19 (pp. 66–83). Springer Berlin Heidelberg.
26. Mehrnezhad, M., Toreini, E., Shahandashti, S. F., & Hao, F., (2016). Touch signatures: Identification of user touch actions and PINs based on mobile sensor data via JavaScript. Journal of Information Security and Applications, 26(1), 23–38.
27. Mirshokraie, S., Mesbah, A., & Pattabiraman, K., (2014). Guided mutation testing for JavaScript web applications. IEEE Transactions on Software Engineering, 41(5), 429–444.
28. Myalapalli, V. K., & Karri, S., (2015). Optimizing front end applications and JavaScript. Innovative Research in Science, Engineering and Technology. 4(6), 6–10.
29. Nascimento, R., Figueiredo, E., & Hora, A., (2021). JavaScript API deprecation landscape: A survey and mining study. IEEE Software, 39(3), 96–105.
30. Ocariza, F. S., Bajaj, K., Pattabiraman, K., & Mesbah, A., (2016). A study of causes and consequences of client-side JavaScript bugs. IEEE Transactions on Software Engineering, 43(2), 128–144.
31. Reid, J., Valentine, T., Reid, J., & Valentine, T., (2013). JavaScript nuts and bolts. JavaScript Programmer's Reference, 22(1), 25–56.
32. Reips, U. D., (2007). The methodology of internet-based experiments. The Oxford Handbook of Internet Psychology, 45(1), 373–390.
33. Romano, Jr. N. C., Nunamaker, Jr. J. F., Briggs, R. O., & Vogel, D. R., (1998). Architecture, design, and development of an HTML/JavaScript web-based group support system. Journal of the American Society for Information Science, 49(7), 649–667.
34. Seo, H., & Kim, H., (2014). Low-power encryption algorithm block cipher in JavaScript. Journal of Information and Communication Convergence Engineering, 12(4), 252–256.
35. Severance, C., (2012). Javascript: Designing a language in 10 days. Computer, 45(2), 7, 8.
36. Stothard, P., (2000). The sequence manipulation suite: JavaScript programs for analyzing and formatting protein and DNA sequences. Biotechniques, 28(6), 1102–1104.

37. Theisen, K. J., (2019). Programming languages in chemistry: A review of HTML5/ JavaScript. Journal of Cheminformatics, 11(1), 11.
38. Tilkov, S., & Vinoski, S., (2010). Node.js: Using JavaScript to build high-performance network programs. IEEE Internet Computing, 14(6), 80–83.
39. Ugawa, T., Iwasaki, H., & Kataoka, T., (2019). eJSTK: Building JavaScript virtual machines with customized datatypes for embedded systems. Journal of Computer Languages, 51(1), 261–279.
40. Vouillon, J., & Balat, V., (2014). From bytecode to JavaScript: The Js_of_ocaml compiler. Software: Practice and Experience, 44(8), 951–972.
41. Wirfs-Brock, A., & Eich, B., (2020). JavaScript: The first 20 years. Proceedings of the ACM on Programming Languages, 4(HOPL), 1–189.
42. Zaidi, R., & Zaidi, R., (2017). Introduction to JavaScript. JavaScript Essentials for SAP ABAP Developers: A Guide to Mobile and Desktop Application Development, 12(1), 1–13.

CHAPTER 5

OBJECT-ORIENTED PROGRAMMING

UNIT INTRODUCTION

To address a problem, we typically start by thinking about it in a broad sense, on a higher level of abstraction. We try to calculate the available resources, such as money; in other words, we dissect the issue. If resources are limited, humans have been known to resort to sleight of hand. For example, if we cannot find sufficient wallpaper, we might be unable to conceal some secret locations; however, things like furniture, photographs, and so on can help. It indicates that we try to organize the solution using the resources at our disposal following a plan. Together, abstraction, decomposition, and organization make up what we call a paradigm (Sanders & Dorn, 2003). These three steps are necessary for solving every problem. The functional paradigm was the foundation of the previous programmers' experiences (Xinogalos et al., 2006).

Assume that we will travel to Trieste by automobile, and at this point, we have begun to plan how we will do so. In accordance with the tenets of an outdated programming paradigm, we ought to have conceived of the problem as a matter of function operating on data:

1. Please think of the issue despite a process that really can solve it, such as how to collect essential things, how to run a car, and so on. This is the first step in the abstraction level (Briot et al., 1998).

2. At the deconstruction level, you should think about how to segment all processing in smaller, more manageable processing components or functions, like the procedures involved in actually transferring an automobile from one location to another. We are aware that driving in cities differs greatly from driving on highways. We pay some thought to simple tasks like turning off and starting the car. So, we will create some functions;
3. In terms of the organization, make sure that our functions are set up to communicate with one another following the regulations. We create iterations of function calls, sending various parameters to the functions, etc. (Wiener & Pinson, 1988).

This is the Hint: Conventional programming practices tend to isolate data, and the processes that manipulate it, or at least do not actively advocate examining them together. This is an unusual strategy; we must create a number of information forms, then create a number of processes that work with these structures (Kanaki & Kalogiannakis, 2018).

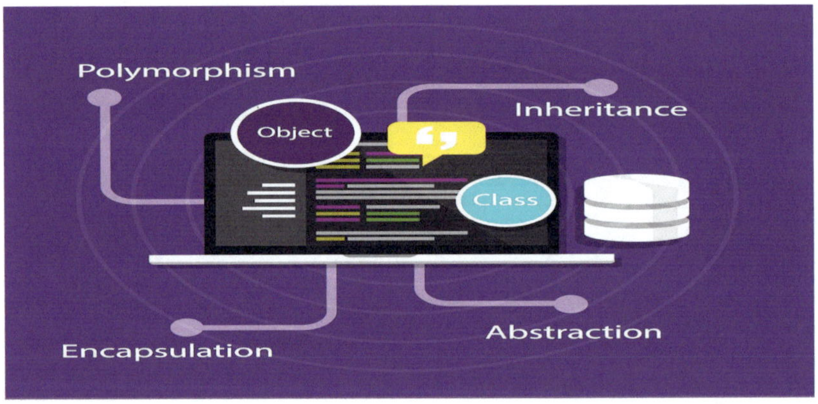

Figure 5.1. Object oriented programming with a real-world scenario.

Source: Hashim Lokasher, creative commons license.

In a real-world scenario, we first consider the general road before beginning to consider how to navigate the traffic of the many towns & cities pass through. After that, we might think about where would be the greatest area to stop for a meal, to rest, etc. Finally, we may consider the specifics of the trip, including how to plan the scheduler for this kind of adventure so that we arrive at a given restaurant at such a specific time (Figure 5.1). An example of an object-oriented way of thinking is the following: We look at things in terms of their connections to one another:

1. On a higher level of abstraction, we think of several autonomous agents (objects) cooperating, such as the automobile, ourselves, goods to take, etc. (Cox, 1986).
2. At the level of decomposition, we determine the categories of items on which to partition the overall project;
3. At the organizational level, we produce the correct quantity of items of each type (Wu, 2006).

Learning Objectives

The information that the readers would be able to acquire after finishing this chapter is as follows:

- A world that is based on objects
- The defining features of an item programming language
- The idea of encapsulation comes in third.
- the idea of passing on a family business
- An introduction to polymorphism's fundamentals
- An introduction to the foundations of handling exceptions
- The use of distributed objects with RMI and CORBA
- An overview of object-oriented programming and design

Key Terms

- Abstraction
- Class
- Distributed Objects
- Encapsulation
- Inheritance
- Messages
- Object-Oriented
- Programming
- Sample
- Variables

5.1. AN OBJECT-ORIENTED WORLD

An object-oriented language need to provide these three extremely crucial explicit qualities in order to adhere to the OOP paradigm (Uzakov et al., 2019). This is viewed from the perspective of a programmer. When we are seeking to find solutions to real-world problems using our object-oriented programming (OOP), we make considerable use of these notions as models for those difficulties. These three ideas are as follows:

1. Encapsulation,
2. inheritance,
3. polymorphism (Mylopoulos et al., 1999).

Abstraction can be thought of as an implicit quality. We utilize it in specifying ADT for short or new abstract data types.

5.1.1. Encapsulation Example

In the event that we decide to drive to Trieste, let's use the steering system of such a vehicle as an illustration of encapsulation. If we decided to take a car, this is what would happen.

When the initial models hit the roads, the function of a car's steering mechanism hasn't altered all that much. Users can start using it right away because of its uniform user interface.

For instance, turning the steering wheel in a clockwise direction will cause the car to turn right, and doing it in a anticlockwise direction will cause it to turn left.

Remember

Object-oriented programming (OOP) is a programming paradigm based on objects, which can contain data and code to manipulate that data.

So, in the framework of the object-oriented paradigm, this mechanism is viewed as an object. We don't know the implementation specifics, thus we can use them without any technical knowledge. A select few of us have access to further information; they know that each automaker has a somewhat different way of implementing this strategy (Atkinson et al., 1990).

The interface is conventional, but when the mechanism is altered by something like a rent trailer, we run into problems (Figure 5.2).

In exchange, the component that controls the vehicle's direction consists of many advanced subsystems, each with its own state, behaviors, interface, and implementation. The steering mechanism components that utilize these interfaces are the only ones with access to them, not the driver (Bergin et al., 2005).

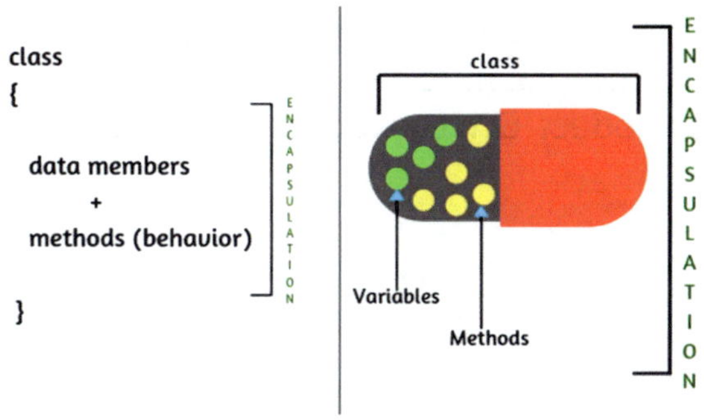

Figure 5.2. Illustration of the encapsulation.

Source: Scientech easy, creative commons license.

Encapsulation is a technique that is frequently used in OOP, and it is intended to conceal the implementation while exposing the interface (Yan, 2009).

5.1.2. Inheritance Example

Inheritance is another pointer in the direction of OOP (Smith & Robson, 1990). Consider the situation of a person who recently purchased an older home as an analogy. After purchasing the property, the individual does not typically tear down the old house and start from begin while constructing a new one; rather, he will typically make changes to the existing one. In OOP, this means that the individual derives from the home that already exists, or, to put it another way, that he extends it; hence, he is responsible for building subclasses of house that is already in existence. The characteristics of the old house have been carried over into the new one.

It is a highly typical technique to create new, enhanced things by employing new definitions that augment previously established definitions (Hirshfield & Ege, 1996). It is one of the sayings of OOP, which promotes the reuse of components already present in programs.

Don't make the same mistake twice! Reuse the code, and don't start from scratch!

5.1.3. Polymorphism Example

Polymorphism, from the Greek (polys), means "one name, many shapes," which makes it arguably the most elusive idea to pin down, especially in terms of everyday speech. The Greek root for the polymorphism is morphe, meaning "name" (Sridharan et al., 2013). In keeping with our automobile theme, I'd like to compare polymorphism to the automatic transmission on your car. Imagine there are three modes: Drive, Neutral, and Reverse (Figure 5.3).

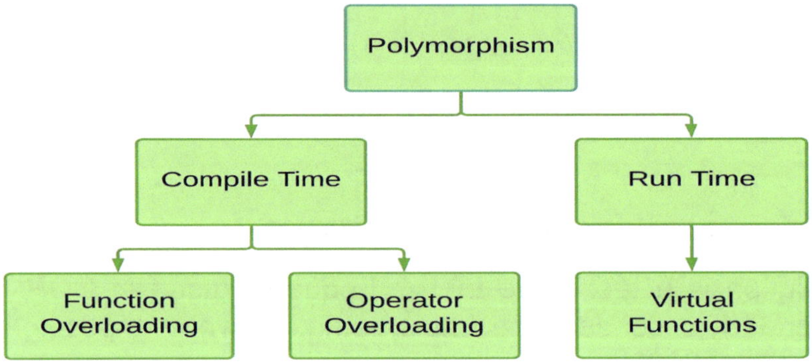

Figure 5.3. Polymorphism and its components.

Source: Geeks for Geeks, creative commons license.

We know that just one approach may be called the Reverse technique. When we put the gear selector into Neutral, the car's engine is severed from connecting to the transmission system.

We put the car in Drive to go forward while driving it. The mechanism of the automatic transmission system determines at runtime, based on various sets of conditions, which version of the Drive function to apply to every specific circumstance. The circumstances at hand will determine the particular implementation of the function that will be utilized. This is comparable to something that's known as runtime polymorphism (Srinath, 2017).

As a result, the automobile displays polymorphic behavior when moving in the direction of forward motion, but it displays non-polymorphic behavior when driving in the direction of backward movement.

Polymorphism is a technique that allows the behavior of an example of type to be altered depending on the present circumstances.

We can summarize our instances (Rentsch, 1982):

This is an object-oriented world that we live in. An item programming paradigm is an approach to computer programming that strives to write programs in a way that models how humans comprehend the world.

The following recommendation can serve as a foundation for constructing an initial description of OOP (Xu, 2013):

The solution to problem must be similar to the problem, and anyone observing the answer must be able to identify the problem even if they were not aware of it beforehand.

The use of OOP to construct a stacking class out of which stack items can be instantiated is an excellent illustration of this principle from the realm of computers (Stroustrup, 1995). Programmers familiar with queues, stacks, and other data structures analogous to stacks will be able to recognize them as a stack with no additional prior knowledge if a stack is applied as instantiated, as an object, a class and described as suitable.

5.1.4. A Word of OOP Vocabulary

Languages before OOP and those after having different programming paradigms and vocabularies (Lange & Nakamura, 1997). Class methods have replaced procedures; you are a prime example of this shift.

Let's take OOP as an extra example. We can declare an abstract data type by encapsulating the data type's implementation type and the interface to a data type inside a class.

After that, the instantiation procedure can produce one or more instances of the class.

An object is a term used to refer to an example of a class.

Everything possesses a state and acts in a particular manner (Booch, 1994).

The current values which are recorded in the local variables are what determines the state of the system.

How the object behaves is established by the example methods of the classes from which it was instantiated.

The classes or subclasses that makeup inherited types of abstract data are derived from either the base classes or the superclasses (Joines & Roberts, 1999). While developing subclasses, we start by extending their parent classes. The programmer creates instances of objects within the program and communicates with those objects by calling the methods associated with the class (or member functions). To "construct an instance of a class" is what is meant by "instantiate" an object.

OOP involves the definition of abstract data types, the encapsulation of those types of abstract data into classes, the creation of instantiations of objects, and the transmission of messages to objects (Andrianoff & Levine, 2002). Nearly every action or object referenced in OOP terminology has evolved to be expressed by a multitude of distinct phrases, which further confuses the meaning of these words. These terms are usually ambiguous and frequently depend on the author or authors who first published the particular book you're currently enjoying reading. We can change the state of an object in a variety of ways, such as by sending it a message, using one of its ways, or using any of its member functions.

5.2. IMPORTANCE OF OOP

Object-Oriented Programming, sometimes known as OOP, is a paradigm of programming that is utilized in the process of developing software applications (Sridharan et al., 2013). It is predicated on the idea of objects, which are packages that include information and function. The primary objective of OOP is to ease the process of developing software by partitioning complex issues into smaller, relatively manageable parts.

Modularity is a significant advantage that comes with using OOP. The ability to write and test code in separate modules is what we mean when discussing modularity (Hadjerrouit, 1999). This capacity makes it much simpler to manage huge software projects. The OOP modular method enables programmers to break down complex problems into smaller, relatively manageable components, making designing and maintaining code simpler.

Reusability is another significant advantage that comes with using OOP. The capacity to reuse code in various settings is what we mean when we talk about reusability (Gottlob et al., 1996). This can help programmers save both time and effort. OOP makes it possible to reuse code by introducing the idea of inheritance, which permits the construction of new classes that are derived from existing courses and inherit the attributes and operations of the base class from which they are derived. Another essential advantage of OOP is its flexibility (Kölling, 1999). The capacity of an item to behave in a manner dependent on the circumstances in which it is utilized is called flexibility. This enables the object to assume a variety of different shapes. The OOP makes this flexibility possible by introducing the idea of polymorphism, which permits things to take on various distinct forms (Salvaneschi et al., 2014).

Scalability is also another significant advantage that comes with OOP. The capacity to remove or add objects without disrupting the rest of the code is what we mean when we talk about scalability. OOP is a scalable programming method, meaning that objects may be added to or removed from a program without introducing unexpected side effects (Zimmermann et al., 1992).

Encapsulation is the key to OOP's provision of a safe programming method, which brings us to the conclusion of this chapter (Kölling, 1999). The internal data of an object can only be accessed once it has been encapsulated, which makes it harder for unauthorized code to change the object's properties or gain access to its data. In general, OOP is a significant programming paradigm that gives a method for creating software that is scalable, modular, reusable, flexible, and safe. As a result, it is a crucial tool for developing reliable and effective software applications.

5.3. THE CHARACTERISTICS OF AN OOP

After going through the fundamentals of what makes an object-oriented program tick, let's dive into the specifics of the inquiry at hand.

5.3.1. An Object

Let's take a look at these three overarching inquiries.

1. What exactly are objects when talking about OOP?
2. What kinds of things should serve as the program's objects while designed to be object-oriented?
3. What is OOP that distinguishes it from conventional procedural programming and suggests that it might be superior to the latter?

Put, and adopting a highly liberal point of view:

An example of data type is referred to as an object.

The two objects are declared in the JAVA code piece that follows.

The very first thing is an example of a straightforward integer variable that goes by the name tired. Some people in the field of computer science do not believe this to be a real object. They believe that an object ought not to be an essential part of the language itself. This may be true in general, but remember that we are interpreting things quite broadly (Figure 5.4).

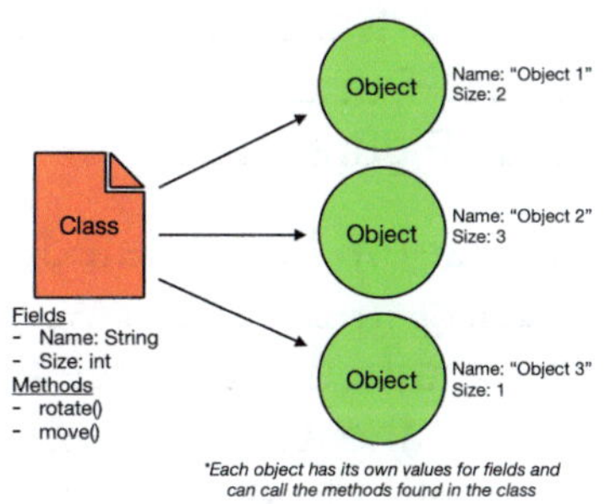

Figure 5.4. Illustration of an object.

Source: Jordan Burroughs, creative commons license.

The other object is an example of an abstract data type called a Person. The thing in question is called man, and the data type is Person (Pokkunuri, 1989).

```
...
int tired; // an example of an int type
Person man; // an instance of abstract data type
// recognized as a Person
...}
```

The integer data type derives from so-called primitive types, that are built into the language. You might already be conscious of this or be able to infer it.

It is expected that you established and declared an abstract type person Named in your code. From a linguistic perspective, this is a novel type of data (Rahnev et al., 2014).

5.3.2. Abstraction

The declaration of an abstract type of data containing a specification of t behavior and data representation of the class is referred to as abstraction. It demonstrates the different types of data that may be stored with new kinds of data and the various ways it can be manipulated JAVA programmers define the data representation and the behaviour of a new type (present the specification to the compiler) using the keyword class. (Kölling, 1999).

It means that a new type's specifications are converted into a form that the programmer can know and operate with by using the keyword class. This allows the compiler to produce more accurate results.

After the new type has been specified, one or more examples of that type of object can be transitioned from the abstract to the concrete state of existence. Put another way, an instance of such an object can be created (Figure 5.5).

After the object has been instantiated, it is referred to as having a state and behaving in a certain way. The behavior of an item is governed by the methods it possesses, while the status of an object is identified by the values that are now stored in its data variables (instance methods or member functions) (instance variables) (Nygaard, 1986).

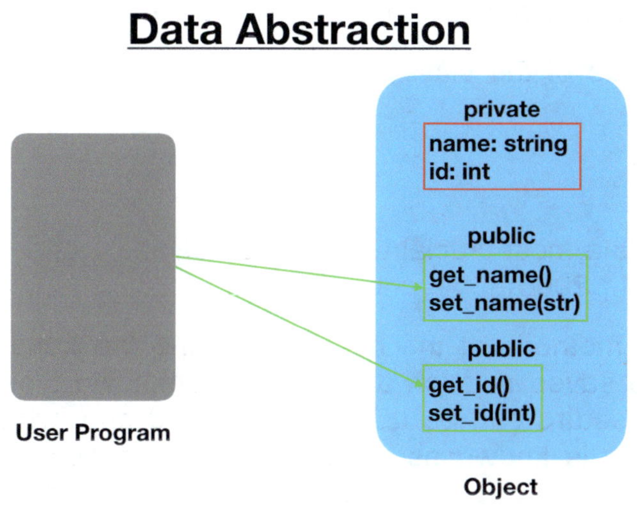

Figure 5.5. Schematic of the abstraction.

Source: Pankaj, creative commons license.

As a graphical user interface (GUI) component, the button is the most common example. If a button is considered an object, its behavior and state can be readily envisioned by us (Xinogalos et al., 2006). It can exist in various shapes, including sizes, positions, captions, etc. At any particular point, the information held in the local variables of the button object determines which of these states the button will be in. A property of an object is a collection of one or even more local variables that describe the object's current state.

Similarly, an action predefined for the button will typically be triggered whenever it is clicked using a mouse.

On the one hand, each independent button object possesses instance variables, values that define the condition of the button anywhere at a given time. On the other hand, each button object contains a particular fundamental behavior to react to a click or other event, which can then be used in conjunction with an action (Agarwal et al., 1996).

5.3.3. Sample Class Definition

Let's create a working example now by trying to construct the code to model a human being. Many will say it's like their daily routine when they alternate between working and resting. Every member of the group must report their current state, whether they are awake & able to work, sleepy, or overjoyed. There will be three instance variables in this class: an integer for weariness, a string for name, and a second string for origin (Embley et al., 1991).

This is what the line that corresponds to it looks like:

class Human { // code of the class

...

}

The word "class" is the most crucial term in the definition, and its full name is Human (Concas et al., 2006).

The three instance methods of the new type define the behaviors of the new type. Data can be saved in such an object of unknown type, given the name setPerson. This feature can be used. The second one, which retrieves data from an object and is known as getHumanInfo, can access previously saved information (Wiedenbeck et al., 1996). The final one is known as Work, and it is responsible for putting into action changes to an object called weary, which belongs to the class Human. The code also isn't displayed now; we will look at it later.

These are the lines that correspond to each other (Lange & Nakamura, 1997):

// data storage instance method with a void setPerson parameter (int state, String na, String orig) { ...

}

// display information about a person String using an instance method getHumanInfo() { ...

}

// Work on the instance method String Work() { ...

}

This new type can be expanded by including other behaviors through the setting up of different methods, and this is something that we can do.

After the new type has been specified, we can construct examples of this type, also known as objects. We may interact with those objects as we interact with the other variables produced from primitive data types.

5.4. ENCAPSULATION

Encapsulation the first of three key ideas that influence the creation of object-oriented software (Santos, 2014). On a conceptual level, we consider the cooperation of distinct agents. Lastly, we put a representation of data and behavior into a class, allowing us to describe both the implementation and interface of the course.

An enclosed design is one that, by standard procedures for OOP, typically conceals its execution from the class user and reveals just its interface (Gatziu & Dittrich, 1992). After going through these steps, a clementine seed was produced. Realization of all of its behavior is obscured from us; all we know is how to cultivate it, and we are familiar with its user interface.

Because of the experiences of human beings, we are aware of the seeds' interface, and we have class documentation that describes the interface. But, God did not offer detailed documentation on how sources are implemented. An average user typically does not need to understand how well the steering system of an automobile is developed, and most people are unaware of the specifics of the mechanism's implementation. To produce and perhaps alter the user-level documentation, a class designer needs to have documentation on the commission.

In passing, I should mention that JAVA has a specialized method for producing documentation, which will be discussed in the following courses.

Java employs the terms public, protected, & private to restrict access to a class's constituent components. The meanings of the initial two phrases can be determined with little effort (Hogg, 1991). The final period, protected, confers exclusive access privileges to the members of derived classes from the base classes to the members of the inherited classes.

Typically, users who use an attractive class are unable to modify the values of its local variables without using the class's interface (Banciihon, 1988).

Can you recall the code fragments that we provided? Now, let's examine the source in its entirety.

```
class Human {


int tired; // instance variables

String name;     // of the class

String origin; //


// instance method for storing and retrieving data

void setPerson (int state, String na, String orig) {

tired = state; 10 name = na;
```

```
origin = orig;
} // end method setPerson

// instance method to display info of a human
String getHumanInfo() {
String info;
info = ("My name is" +
name + " and I am" +
origin + " ");
if (tired > 1)
info = info +
("I am very tired.");
else
info = info +
("and I am ready to work.");
return info;
} // end method showHumanInfo

void drinking(){
System.out.println(
"I like drink with friends");
}//end drinking()

// instance method Work
String Work() {
if (tired < 2) {
tired ++;
```

```
return
("Ouff . working again…");
}
else
return
("Sorry can't work, being too exhausted.");
} // end method Work

String rest() {
if (tired < 1)
return
 ("Not very tired, so going to a party.");
else {
tired --;
return
("Sleeping, hhhharrarrrdrrhhhh…");
}
}
} // end class Human definition

// Driver program

class ex1 { // defining the controlling class
public static void main(String[] args) { // define main

Human obj = new Human ();
obj.setPerson(0, "Olexiy," "Ukrainian"); //store data
```

```
// Get info about Olexiy

System.out.println (obj.getHumanInfo());

} //end main

} //end ex1 class
```

In general, the class should consist of public methods for them to be accessible to a user. All of the classes and techniques in our software are, by default, accessible to the public. Invoking those methods allows the class to save, read, and modify values (Korson & McGregor, 1990). The setPerson method was used in the software that was just shown to insert data about me, and then the getHumanInfo function was used to retrieve information about me.

The program that we are looking at does not have any secret implementation. This isn't a well-designed program from an OOP perspective, but at the same time, it is too simplistic! (Civello, 1993).

Please note that we utilized the setPerson and getHumanInfo methods in our program. There is a remark of special significance regarding the names of procedures that begin with set and get (Chidamber & Kemerer, 1991):

In Java, the keywords "set" and "get" at the beginning of the names of methods have a specific significance. Specifically, the JAVA Beans Application Programming Interface (API) introspection feature considers such names to indicate design patterns to alter the object's properties.

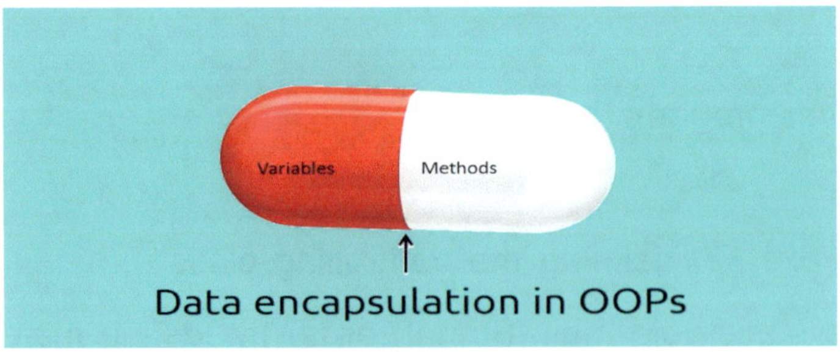

Figure 5.6. Illustration of the encapsulation, class, methods and variables.

Source: Geek Bot, creative commons license.

Object-oriented styles are not considered to be good design by default. There has been widespread agreement upon basic design standards for classes in an effort to improve the quality of designs created. Typically, the data members are held in confidence (Canfora et al., 1999). Typically, the interface comprises solely of methods and has relatively few member functions, if any. This is a mechanism for hiding the in question implementation (Figure 5.6).

On the other hand, the data members intended for use as symbolic constants are publicly disclosed and defined in a way that prevents their values from being modified. This is the only exception to the general rule.

The methods provided by the interface should either be used to control access to the private local variables or offer a means to reach them. The interface ought to be as general as is humanly possible, meaning that it shouldn't be tied down to a specific implementation in any way (Schultz & Axelsen, 2016). It indicates that from a functional standpoint, the method's arguments should have the same significance. If, for whatever reason, it becomes necessary to change the implementation, the change should be carried out in such a way as to prevent the interface from being altered.

In our software, the only variables and methods we use are example variables and example methods. The class methods and class variables are the following topics for discussion.

Did you Know?

Instance and class variables are types of variables used in OOP to store data and state information for objects and classes, respectively.

5.4.1. Instance and Class Variables

Our program exclusively employs exemplary variables and procedures. A discussion of class procedures and class variables is required. Just what are you trying to say? What purpose do they serve for us?

Each example of such a type or object stores its data in a collection of variables known as "instance variables" that are defined in a certain manner. These variables are handled as distinct entities and are stored in distinct memory regions (Sarcar, 2022). A single period specifies the required connecting operator for object instance access. With our software, you may access the name of the object obj by putting obj.name into the field.

It is feasible to speculate about it (Sanders et al., 20008):

All objects that belong to a class share the same set of variables. They are pretty comparable to the concept of global variables. There is only one instance of such a class variable stored in Memory, and all of the objects that belong to that class have access to it.

Class variables have a beneficial property in that they can be accessible even if no item of the type has been instantiated. This is a very significant aspect of class variables. You may get to them by using the dot operator, which is used to link the variable name with the class name.

5.4.2. Instance and Class Methods

1. Two distinct types of methods can be assigned to a class:
2. Procedures specific to instances; and
3. Methods specific to categories (Alrashidi et al., 2014).

Suppose you are familiar with the circumstances surrounding instance variables & class variables. In that case, you can readily speculate that methods that are designated as static belong to the class, whereas ways that are not static belong to the instance. Instance methods are "tied" to the objects to which they are applied since they require a thing of the class to be invoked (Guidec et al., 1996). Using the illustrative method on a particular object will have accessibility to the object's instance variables. It's crucial to remember that forms of a class have direct access to member variables that Class methods cannot access members outside of the class. They have no access to the instance's data or methods (Ågerfalk, 1999). The incredible quality of class methods is that you can call them by just referring to the class name rather than needing first to create an instance of the class. Using the right joining operator on the name of lass and the name of the method, one may retrieve class methods in the same way as class variables can be accessed.

5.4.3. Sample Program

A significant portion of what we've been talking about is probably going to be easier to comprehend when it is viewed in the context of an actual application (Freeman-Benson & Borning, 1992). The following Output will be generated by the software and shown on a standard output device:

```
---------------

This cat has child(ren): 100

This cat has legs: 4

---------------

This cat has a child(ren): 1220. This cat has legs: 4
```

Let's look at some of the fascinating snippets of code that make up the program before we move on to the listing of it.

The declaration of 2 member variables of class is displayed in the first intriguing piece of code that we will look at. The first is an example variable with the name legs, while the second is a class variable with the name child.

int child; // declare an example variable 'child' static int legs; // declare a class variable 'legs'

The declaration of variables in Java typically looks something like this, with the name of the type coming first, then the Variable's name is declared (Clark, 2006). The point of interest in the discussion setting is that we use the fixed keyword in the statement of the class variable.

The following code demonstrates the definitions of two distinct approaches (with the bodies of methods deleted for brevity). The class method is referred to by its shorthand name, classMethod, whereas the instance method is referred to by its shorthand name, instanceMethod (Kosbar & Schneider, 1992).

```
void { instance method() { // define an instance method

// body of method deleted for brevity

} //end instance method()

   static void class method() {        //define} a class method

//body of method deleted for brevity

} //end class method()
```

Most procedure or member function declarations in Java look like this: first comes the name of the return type (void indicates that nothing is returned), next comes the name method, and then comes the formal parameter list. The method's body is subsequently wrapped in a corresponding set of curly braces and returned to its original state { } (Jacobson, 1993).

You may probably anticipate correctly at this point: utilizing static keywords inside the specification of the class method is the crucial point to consider.

The following snippet of code is a single sentence extracted from the main structure of one of the procedures. This statement will cause the Output to be shown on the device designated as the standard Output. This single phrase exhibits some of the syntax complexity present in an object-oriented program using overloaded operators, classes, class variables and instance methods (Voigt et al., 2010).

```
System.out.println("This cat has legs: "

+ legs);
```

This assertion is comprised of three parts that are connected with periods.

The first component is the word System, the name of one of the classes included in the standard JAVA class library. To provide context, the System class is immediately loaded into Memory whenever a new Java program is started.

A period serves as the connection between the term out and the name of the System class. The System class contains a member variable whose name is "out," and "out" is the name of that Variable (Kniesel & Theisen, 2001).

The public class variable is being used for the member variable named out. Because of this, it is now feasible to access this Variable by combining the name of the class with the name of the Variable and then separating the two words with a period.

It is important to note that the joining operator used is a period, and the class uses two types out is attached to the phrase println (Sutcliffe, 1991). In addition to being a class variable, the Variable out is also a references Variable, and it stores a reference to an instance of PrintStream class.

An instance method with the name println can be found in the PrintStream class (). There are ten different overloaded variants of the println() procedure contained within the PrintStream class. The version being used in this instance has a behavior that causes its strings argument to be shown on the device designated as the standard Output.

Now think about the String that is passed to println method like it is given below (Xianzhong & Zhenyu, 1991):

("This cat has child(ren): "

+ child)

The literal strings in Java are enclosed in quotation marks, much like in C. Java loads the plus sign in this way because it has the ability to concatenate texts as well as the addition operator in arithmetic (Boyapati et al., 2002). Also, despite the fact that their right operand has never been and isn't already a string, the overloaded plus operations have the ability to push it into the string representation. If the correct operand is not already a string, then this is the case. In this case, the right operand is the example variable, also known as an instance variable, rather than a string. The sample variable's value is first converted to a reticulation by overload plus operators, and then it is concatenated with the left operand. The stages are carried out in the sequence they are given above.

Now, let's take a second look at the two identical techniques as before, but this time, let's keep the bodies of methods intact for additional research.

// instance method void instanceMethod ( ) {

```
System.out.println("This cat has child(ren): "

+ child);

} // end instanceMethod static void classMethod ( ) {

System.out.println("This cat has legs: "

+ legs);

} // end classMethod
```

The code that allows access to the class member may be seen in the bodies of the methods, as shown above. It is essential to remember that one member is an example variable denoted by the name child. In contrast, the other membership variable is a class object represented by the name legs (Howard, 1988).

The class method known as the class Method is only permitted to display and access the class variable. In contrast, the instance method known as a child can access and display both the provided to make and the class variable. Class methods can't access instance variables.

```
class ex2 { // defining the controlling class public static void main(String[] args) { // define main......... // code

} //end main

} //end ex2 class
```

Now have a look at the breakdown of the primary approach that is provided down below. The governing method of a JAVA application must be referred to as the "main method" or "function." This requirement does not apply to applets (Skoglund, 2003). In the straightforward application that we are developing, the process of instantiating an object and accessing its instance and class method will be handled by code located in the ex2 function.

Remember that to use an instance method, you need to contact it via an object of a class. This is required to gain access to an instance method. The following snippet of code is found in the main procedure, and it creates an instance of an object with the name "mour" that belongs to the class "cat.."

```
cat mour = new cat();
```

This is a standard statement used in Java for creating an instance of an object.

The new operator requests the operating system to provide memory "from the heap" to store one instance of an object with the typical cat (Lau & Taweel, 2007).

Suppose the necessary amount of Memory is properly allotted. In that case, the address of the memory block in question will be put into a reference variable that goes by the name of mour. If the operation cannot be completed, the JAVA run time engine will throw an error. There is a subtype of exception known as this one, and it can be either ignored or captured by the application so that it can be processed. If it is disregarded, the runtime environment will terminate the program. Later on, we will talk about handling exceptions.

As soon as we have direct access to an item of a class (access to an object instance that refers to an object of a class), we seem to be capable of making use of this instance variable to obtain the ability to access the public member's factors of course and also to invoke a general procedure that is associated with a class. This is possible because that instance variable refers to an item of a class. An instance of this principle can be seen in the code snippet below.

This Bit of code contains two statements and may be found here. These statements utilize a reference variable known as mour in conjunction with the period to gain access to the instance variable and instance method of an object (Bansiya & Davis, 2002). The period is also required. It's indeed important to remember that the object of a class is the only way to access the instance methods and variables.

// access instance variable via objects: mour.child=100;

//access instance method via the object mour.instanceMethod();

It is crucial to note that it is unnecessary to utilize an instance of the class to access either the class variable or the class method. This accessibility is of equal significance (Menzies & Haynes, 1996). The following code contains two statements, both of which use the class name to gain access to the class variable or the class method associated with the class.

// access class variable via the class mour.legs = 4;

// access class method via the class mour.classMethod();

Access to class variables & class methods could be gained in one of two ways: through an object of the class or simply by referring to the class by its name (Singh & Kahlon, 2011). Please note that we do not assign a new value to the class variable "leg" because this value is used by both of the objects in the class. Cat: mour and meow.

At long last, we finished putting everything together using the JAVA program.

/* Copyright 2001, O.Ye. Tykhomyrov

The second example, ex2.java

Illustrates instance and class variables along with 4 instance and class methods.

*/

```
class cat {
int child; // instance variables 'child'
static int legs; // class variable 'legs'
1
// instance method
void instanceMethod () {
System.out.println("This cat has child(ren): "
+ child);
} // end instanceMethod
static void classMethod () {
System.out.println("This cat has legs: "
+ legs);
} // end classMethod
}
// Driver program

class ex2 { // defining the controlling class
public static void main(String[] args) { // define main

// instantiate an object of the class cat
cat mour = new cat();
cat meow = new cat();
// access instance variable via objects:
mour.child=100;
```

```
meow.child=1220;
// access class variable via the class
mour.legs = 4;

System.out.println("---------------");
// access instance method via the object
mour.instanceMethod();
// access class method via the class
mour.classMethod();
System.out.println("---------------");
meow.instanceMethod();
4meow.classMethod();
} //end main
} //end ex2 class
```

5.4.4. Messages

Messages are also referred to as member functions at times.

A method or membership function can be invoked at any time and thus constitutes a message (Atkinson et al., 1990). A message is sent from the computer program to an object, instructing the object to use the method, and the program may also pass parameters to the method for use.

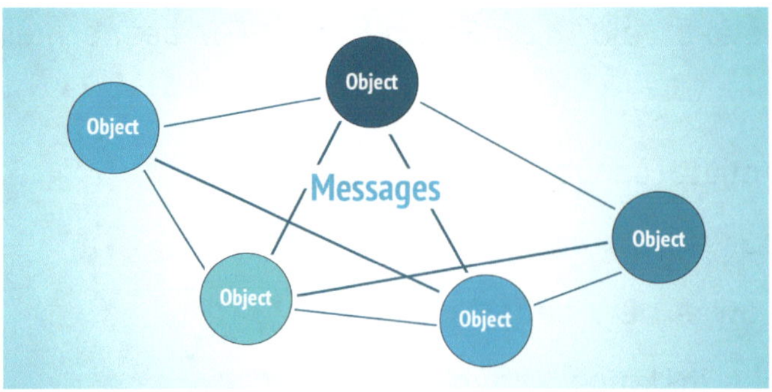

Figure 5.7. Schematic of the messages in OOP.

Source: Branko Babić, creative commons license.

Someone wrote lately that an object-oriented program is nothing more than a collection of objects scattered around and communicating via messages (Schäfer & Rauch, 2004). This is perhaps a bit of an exaggeration, but it's not far off from the actual situation (Figure 5.7).

5.4.5. Constructors, Destructors, and Garbage Collection

The majority of object-oriented systems, as well as some non-object-oriented programs, place a significant emphasis on using dynamic Memory, allocation, and reclamation from the heap (Bugliesi & Jamil, 1994). Any specific language or language system, such as the Java virtual machine, ought to carry out at least one operation in Memory:

1. to ensure that Memory is made available to the program only when it is required
2. to ensure that Memory is made available to the program only when it is required
3. reusing it as necessary (Kifer et al., 1995).

Failing to address this crucial problem leads to a problem known as "memory leakage."

Constructors are employed to create and perhaps initialize objects (Voigt, 2009):

```
// instantiate an object of the class cat

cat mour = new cat();
```

In Java, constructors, like other methods, can be overloaded with additional functionality. The issue of overload will be tackled after this (Bracha & Ungar, 2004). In a nutshell, method overloading refers to multiple methods with the same name. The listing of actual parameters is what the compiler uses to decide which version to operate (Figure 5.8).

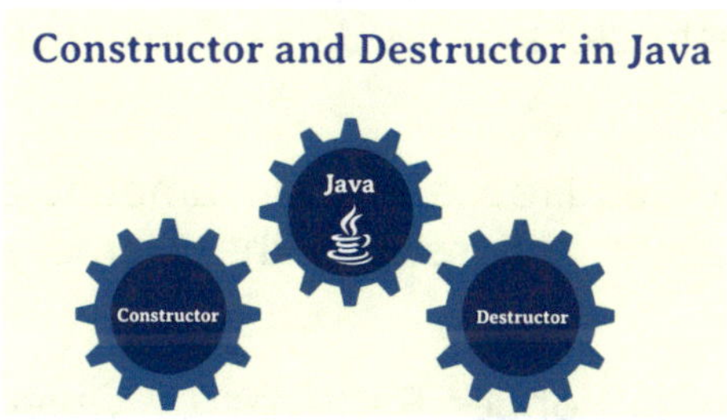

Source: Educba, creative commons license.

Figure 5.8. Example of constructor and destructor in Java.

In this particular line, the new operator serves two purposes: first, it allows dynamic Memory from the heap; second, it acts as a function Object() { [native code] } to build the object in the memory space that was allotted for it. The memory location address where the thing is stored is the value returned and given to the reference variable that goes by the name mour (Narayanan et al., 1998). An error will be generated if the Memory can not be allocated.

When you create a new class in Java, you do not have the option to provide a function Object() { [native code] }; instead, Java defines a default function Object() { [native code] } for you that does not require any parameters.

Another option is to define your function Object() { [native code] }, which does not require any arguments (Lu & Potter, 2006). The process of defining a function Object() { [native code] } is very similar to the operation of defining a method; however, constructors must share the same name as the class, they cannot include return statements, and they cannot have a return type.

The following snippet of code illustrates the essential components of a Java program, which is analogous to the one that was just discussed but has been updated to make use of a parameterized function Object() { [native code] } (Wiedenbeck et al., 1999).

```
...

String name;

// Parameterised constructor cat (String n) { name=n;}

...

System.out.println("This cat named " +

name +

" has child(ren): "

+ child); ... cat mour = new cat("Pirat"); ...
```

Destructors: When the program no longer requires an object, the software will often call on a specialized method called a destructor to execute cleanup on the object. C++ supports destructors, while JAVA doesn't support destructors (Clarke & Drossopoulou, 2002).

When an object no longer requires a certain amount of Memory, JAVA supports an additional mechanism that returns the Memory to an operating system.

Reclaiming Memory That's No Longer Required by Objects Utilized in the Program (Boyapati et al., 2003). The sanitation worker is a component of the runtime running in a low-priority thread. It is responsible for reclaiming Memory that's no longer required by objects utilized in the program. If no longer reference variables refer to the object, an object in Java is said to be in a state where it is eligible for garbage collection.

5.5. INHERITANCE

Encapsulation is the first important trait distinguishing an object-oriented program from other types. The other one is passing down family traditions. Let's take a look now, shall we?

After purchasing an older home in which to reside, a person can consider tearing it down and rebuilding it to combine it with another, more contemporary home that is also cozier, all without destroying the original folder structure. So, following the completion of the renovation, the house would be classified as a subclass of the house that previously existed. The characteristics of the old house have been carried over into the new one (Figure 5.9).

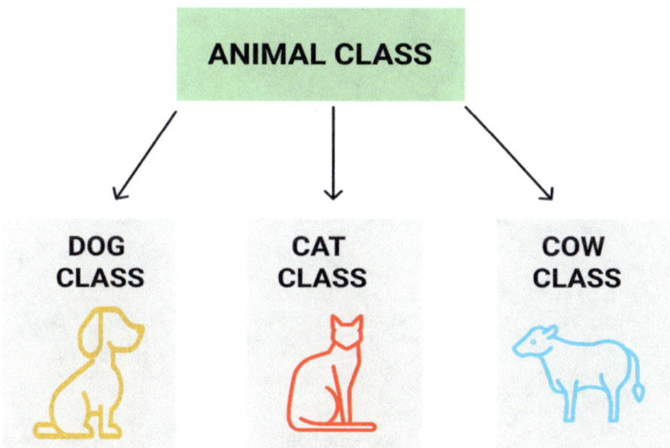

Figure 5.9. Example of inheritance in OOP.

Source: Patrick, creative commons license.

The same is true for the OO program: in most cases, a class can inherit the properties and capabilities of another class (Singh, 1995). Yet, one can circumvent this system by employing a variety of strategies.

Many people refer to the original class as the "base class" or the "superclass," whereas the newly created class is sometimes referred to as the "derived class" or the "subclass." Expanding base class or the superclass is another name commonly used to refer to inheritance.

There is a clear order to inheritance (Oren et al., 2007). To put it another way, a class has the potential to be both a subclass and a superclass of other courses.

The derived class takes on behavior and the data representation of the base class, except for situations in which the derived class overrides some of the base class's methods to alter the behavior. Additionally, the derived class can introduce additional data representations and behaviors specific to the needs of the derived class.

Generally speaking, a program can instantiate instances of a base class in addition to objects of a class derived from the base class. By designating the base class as abstract, it is also feasible to prevent instances of the class name from being instantiated in certain circumstances. Suppose the base class is indeed an abstract base class, which is a class that does not exist independently of its ability to be derived from other classes. In that case, the program cannot instantiate objects of the base class itself but implement objects of classes derived from a base class (Figure 5.10).

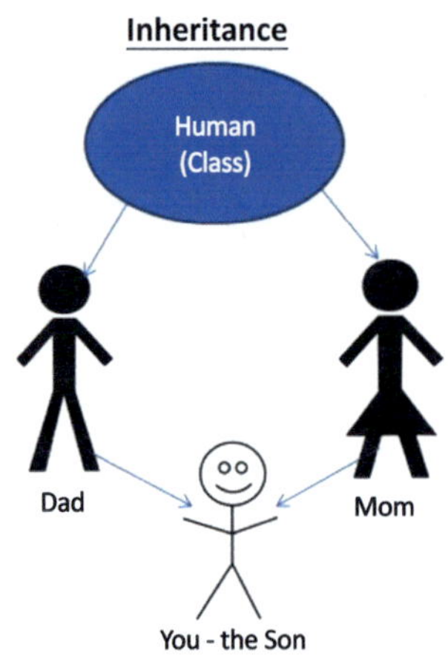

Figure 5.10. Example of inheritance.

Source: Mukesh Chaudhary, creative commons license.

The inheritance mechanism in Java makes constructing an organized hierarchy of classes possible (Rahnev et al., 2014).

When numerous abstract types of data share characteristics, you can build their similarities into a single location class and divide their unique qualities into distinct derived categories. This allows you to design your abstract types of data more efficiently. One of the functions of inheritance is to do this.

Remember that we have established a class Human, yet not everyone is the same. We have different races, sexes, cultures, religions, and other things that distinguish us from one another. Yet, we all share quite a few characteristics, such as having two legs, upper limbs, and one head. We all can study, sleep, etc. The developed class Human is equipped with methods to signify a human state regarding the possibility of working. Because of this, the Human class we have developed uses this as its shared parameter.

We can derive a Gentleman or Woman class from this introductory class. They indeed enjoy their relaxation in quite different ways: the Lady enjoys chatting with her neighbors over a cup of tea, while the Gentleman spends much of his time enjoying a pint of beer in his local watering hole.

After this, objects of classes will be able to work with all of the Human parameters and the new ones (Halbert & O'Brien, 2000).

With this hierarchical class system, you may have noticed that inheritance develops the structure from one of the most general to the least general. This is because inheritance works in Reverse. This is standard practice.

You serve as an illustration here. In the next section of code, there is a single line that must not be skipped; it is the line that defines the Lady & Gentleman subclasses (Joines & Roberts, 1999):

class Lady extends Human { … } class Gentleman extends Human { …

}

The Lady & Gentleman classes are demonstrated to be subclasses of the Human class by the usage of the keyword extends.

Let's look at the subsequent portion of the changed code if you don't mind.

. . . .

// a new method public void drinking(){ System. out.println

("Drinking tea with my neighbors"); }

We announced the addition of a new method of drinking. Naturally, the Gentleman uses the same precise strategy, but this time pertaining to beer!

Another potentially sensitive section of the code demonstrates manipulation with a method declared in a base class, Human (Ducournau & Habib, 1987). To access that technique, you must first type the term super, then the period, sometimes known as the dot operator.

// changing mathod getHumanInfo public String getHumanInfo() {String info; info=super.getHumanInfo(); info=info+"and I am a lady."; return info;

}

The final portion of the code illustrates how to use newly created classes. This is nothing new.

...

Gentleman me = new Gentleman(); Lady anne = new Lady();

me.setPerson (0, "Olexiy," "Ukrainian"); //store data you. setPerson(0, "Anne," "Russian"); //store data

System.out.println(me.getHumanInfo()); System.out.println(you. getHumanInfo()); ...

5.5.1. Single and Multiple Inheritance

Multiple inheritances is a feature supported by OOP languages like C++ (Lieberman, 1986). This indicates that a new class could be derived from far more than one class name to achieve the desired results (Halbert & O'Brien, 1987). In certain circumstances, this is an advantage, yet, in other cases, it can lead to issues. Although JAVA does not provide multiple inheritances, the same result can be achieved using a specialized mechanism known as an interface. This is only offered to let you know that OOP languages may or may not have the tools to accomplish the same goals and that this is a possibility.

5.5.2. The ISA Relationship

You could overhear folks talking about their ISA connections every once in a while. The origin of this language goes back further to more fundamental concepts than you might initially expect (Singh, 1994).

Figure 5.11. Difference between IS-A and HAS-A.

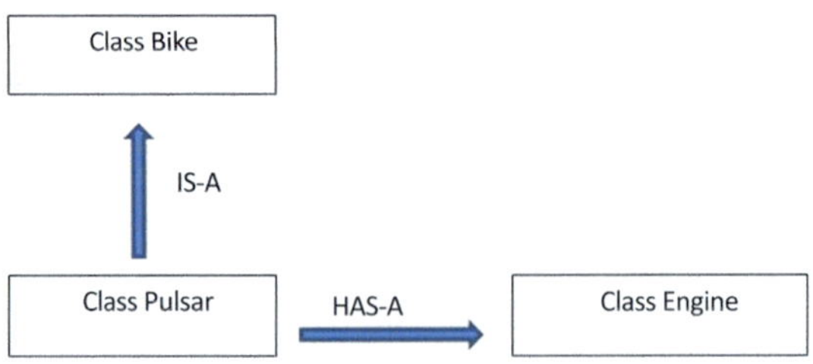

Source: Satendra Singh Bhati, creative commons license.

Object-oriented designers frequently work hard to perfect inheritance as a modeling technique for situations where a derived class "kind of" corresponds to the base class (Baclawski & Indurkhya, 1994). For instance, a lady "sort of" qualifies as a human. A wife "sort of" fits the bill for a lady, etc. (Figure 5.11).

The acronym ISA is often used to refer to this kind of connection.

5.6. POLYMORPHISM

Polymorphism is the final property that must be present in an object-oriented language (Alkazemi & Grami, 2012).

The word "polymorphism" comes from the Greek language. It signifies "one thing, many shapes" or something along those lines. In OOP, polymorphism refers to "one interface, numerous methods" and indicates that the compiler does not intuitively recognize some functions or operators (Muntean et al., 2018). The JAVA programming language does not support operators' overloading, yet it facilitates the overriding and overloading of methods.

5.6.1. Overloading Methods as a Form of Polymorphism

The ability to replace any one of the three C functions is perhaps the most well-known example of polymorphism,

1. abs()
2. labs()
3. fabs()

by a solitary JAVA function referred as ABS().

C calls for using three distinct functions, the specifics of which are determined by the data types (Ducournau, 2002). In Java, you need to remember one name for the function, regardless of the data type, whether int, long, or float. When referring to this scenario, the term "overloaded function or method" is typically used. A compiler can recognize this scenario, and the polymorphism that occurs during compile time is given the name compile time polymorphism Several authors also mention static binding or early binding when discussing this particular scenario. Most of the time, they do not regard function overload as a "real" form of polymorphism.

5.6.2. Overloading of Operators

Polymorphism of this sort is possible in so many non-OOP languages (Bruce et al., 1995). For example, the "+" operator adds any form of data when working in the C programming language. This polymorphic activity has always been an inherent part of the language, and the programmer cannot change it or exercise any control over it (Figure 5.12).

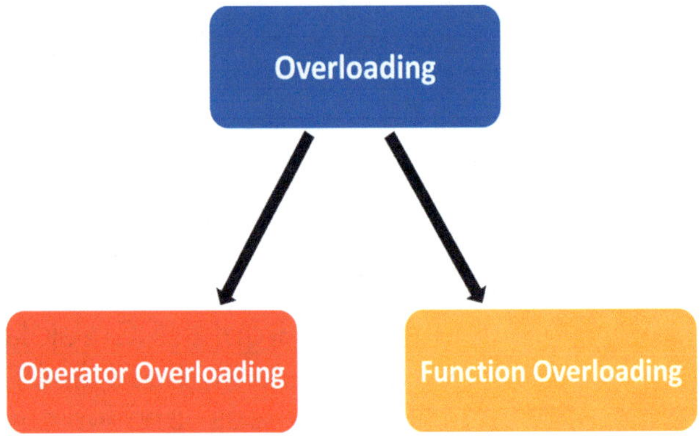

Figure 5.12. Overloading and its types.

Source: Java point, creative commons license.

C++ gives the programmer the option and, including one or two exceptions, the obligation of defining the behavior of practically any operator that can be applied to an item of a new category. This can be done only if the class is written in C++ (Wong et al., 2017).

JAVA does not provide operator overloading, but in many circumstances, overloaded operators will give a much clearer and more intuitive syntax (Åkerblom & Wrigstad, 2015).

5.6.3. Overriding Methods as a Form of Polymorphism

The words override & overload is not interchangeable, including how they are written or spoken or the meanings they convey. The concept of overloading a method is unrelated to the practice of overriding a method (Sandhu & Singh, 2008).

There is more to the story than just the methods of overloading and the operators who engage in it. Runtime polymorphism is the term used to describe the situation in which a derived class modifies the behavior of procedures specified in a base class, typically to meet the unique requirements of the derived class (Wilde & Huitt, 1992).

The concept of overriding a procedure in a base class in Java is supported, which allows objects of a derived class to force the base class method to act differently relative to those objects (Binder,

2000). In other words, the behavior of a process called drinking() described in the base class but overwritten within the derived class would change based on whether it was invoked by an item of a base class or by an item of the derived class. The drinking() method is defined in the base class but overruled in the derived class.

Reference variables of such a base-class type in Java can reference an item of any class obtained from the same base class as the base class.

Suppose an overruled method is called utilizing that evidence consistently. In that case, the system can determine, at the running time, which edition of the method is based on the object's true form rather than the local type variable used to call the process. This determination will be based on the fact that the system can decide which version the method can use based on the true object type. The following piece of Java code illustrates this fact.

In the first step, an overridden method with the same name is called drinking() while referring to an object of the base class. In the second step, an overridden method with the same name is called drinking() while referring to a thing of the derived class.

In the first scenario, the drinking() method from the base class is the one that is called. In the second scenario, the drinking() method from the derived class is the one that is called. This is of no importance (Wilde et al., 1993).

Finally, as the third step, an overridden method with the name drinking() is called upon a base-class reference that points to an obtained object. When something like this is carried out, the implementation of the invoked method is defined within the derived class rather than the one defined within the base class. This is the crux of what runtime polymorphism is all about (Nordlander, 2002).

```
// This program illustrates the runtime polymorphism.

//  Output of the program should be as followed:

// My name is null and I am null and I am ready to work.

// I like drink with friends

// My name is Olexiy and I am Ukrainian and I am ready to work.

//  and I am a Gentleman.

// I like drinking beer in my favorite pub

// My name is Olexiy and I am Ukrainian and I am ready to work.

//  and I am a Gentleman.
```

```
// I like drinking beer in my favorite pub


class ex4 {

public static void main(String args[]) {

// Human class ref to Human class object

Human   obj = new Human();

// Gentleman class ref to Gentleman class object 17 Gentleman me =new Gentleman(); 18 // set information about me:

me.setPerson (0, "Olexiy," "Ukrainian");

// Display informatio about obj: 22 System.out.println(obj.getHumanInfo()); 23 // invoke method named drinking:

obj.drinking();


// Display information about me: 27 System.out.println (me.getHumanInfo()); 28 // invoke method named drinking:

me.drinking();


// Human class ref to Gentleman class object

obj = me;


// Display information about obj:

System.out.println (obj.getHumanInfo());

// invoke method named drinking:

obj.drinking();

3}

3}
```

In practically all JAVA programming, the concepts of inheritance & method overriding are utilized. Even the well-known "Hello World" Java applet needs to have the Applet class expanded, and it also needs to override the paint() method.

5.7. EXCEPTION HANDLING

Exception management is essential to the operation of JAVA, even though OOP does not consider it to be a core notion (Weimer & Necula, 2004). As a result, it would be beneficial to talk about it for a bit in a more generic way (Figure 5.13).

We shall make an effort to take a cursory glance at the following subjects:

i. What does it mean to make an exception?
ii. How do we raise exceptions and catch them when they occur?
iii. Once we have identified an exception, what steps should we take next?
iv. How can we take advantage of an exception class hierarchy the development environment makes available to us?
v. Would the management of exceptions provide any benefits for us?

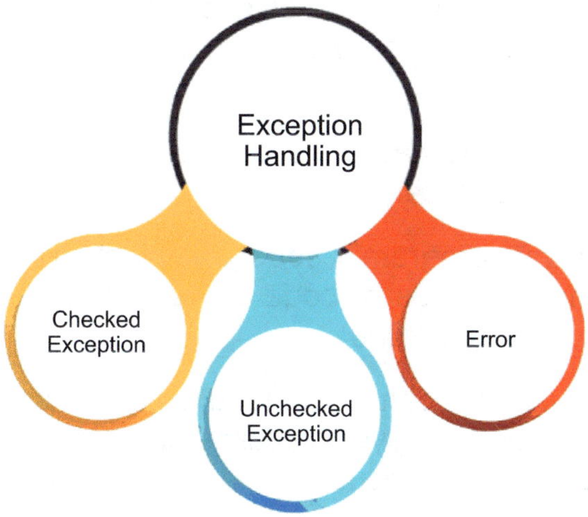

Figure 5.13. Illustration of the exception handing.

Source: Java point, creative commons license.

5.7.1. Exception Hierarchy

One possible definition of exception is presented in the following sentence:

An occurrence during a program that deviates from the typical order in which instructions are carried out is an exception.

Monitoring exceptional conditions inside a program and automatically switching control to specialized exception-handling code created by a programmer are made feasible by exception-handling capability (Romanovsky et al., 2003).

Then, we attempt to run the statements in a block of code enclosed in braces.

Following that, a programmer's code or even the runtime system directly raises this exception item of a certain kind of uncommon condition found within that block. The Java exception is an object directly or indirectly descended from the class Throwable (Poo et al., 2007).

There are two subclasses of the Java Throwable class (Xu, 2013):

1. An error signifies a non-catchable error that should not have happened. The JAVA interpreter typically exits after displaying a message in response to errors (O'Grady & Seshadri, 1991).
2. An exception denotes a strange circumstance that needs to be handled carefully to avoid program termination.

There is a subset of the possible exceptions which Java can automatically throw for which capturing and processing are optional. The compiler permits you to disregard the exceptions in this subset (Holmes & Joyce, 2001). If it happens, the runtime system will catch an ignored exception and end the program.

To compile your program, the application's code must automatically recognize the remaining exceptions that Java can throw.

Recognized implies that the program's code will catch the exception and handle the object to use another piece of code or pass it to the next level of the method-invocation tree (Kienzle, 2000).

After that, the JAVA application can execute a block of code denoted by finally. This code block is typically employed to carry out some required cleanup regardless of the probability of an exception.

It is required that the throws keyword be included in the declaration of a method's signature if the method can pass an exception on to the subsequent level of the invocation hierarchy (Bloom & Zdonik, 1987). If your program detects and handles an exception, the code used can be as complex or straightforward as you choose to make it. The reality is that you can satiate the requirements of the compiler by simply ignoring it once you've found it. Depending on the kind of exception, this might be a good idea, or it could be that it's not a good idea at all.

A Throwable JAVA class provides the methods inherited by all exception objects.

5.7.2. Advantages of Using Exception Handling

In comparison to "conventional" methods of error management, exception handling offers several benefits, including the following:

Separating Error Handling Code derived from the "regular" one provides a mechanism to isolate the specifics of what to do if something unusual happens from a normal logical way of the computer code; in other words, it is a way to handle exceptions (Campéas et a., 2005).

Spreading Errors Up The Call Stack makes it possible to take corrective action at a higher level in the program (Miller & Lennox, 1991). This makes it possible for the corrective measures to be still executed in the procedure that calls that one whenever there is an error;

The ability to establish a comparable hierarchical system for exception handling is enabled by grouping Types Of errors & Error Differentiation, which then groups them logically (Cabral & Marques, 2007).

5.8. DISTRIBUTED OBJECTS WITH CORBA AND RMI

It is possible to create software that functions over the internet by utilizing software that is written in a variety of languages and runs on various platforms, just as it is feasible to build a house by purchasing the necessary components from a variety of sellers. This is made easier for us via CORBA.

TIPS

Distributed objects can be created using technologies such as CORBA and RMI to enable communication between objects running on different machines.

Common Object Request Brokers Architecture is what is meant to be abbreviated as CORBA (Chaumette, 1998).

CORBA is an open standard for just architecture and architecture used by computer applications to collaborate across networks. It is not dependent on any particular manufacturer. It makes it possible for a CORBA-based program from one vendor to interact with a CORBA-based program from another vendor running on nearly any other machine, network, operating system, and programming language (Raptis et al., 2001). This can happen regardless of which company created the first CORBA-based application (Figure 5.14).

CORBA can be helpful in a variety of contexts. CORBA is the option that most prominent businesses and even some that aren't that big choose because it helps integrate machines from various manufacturers with varying levels of computational capacity.

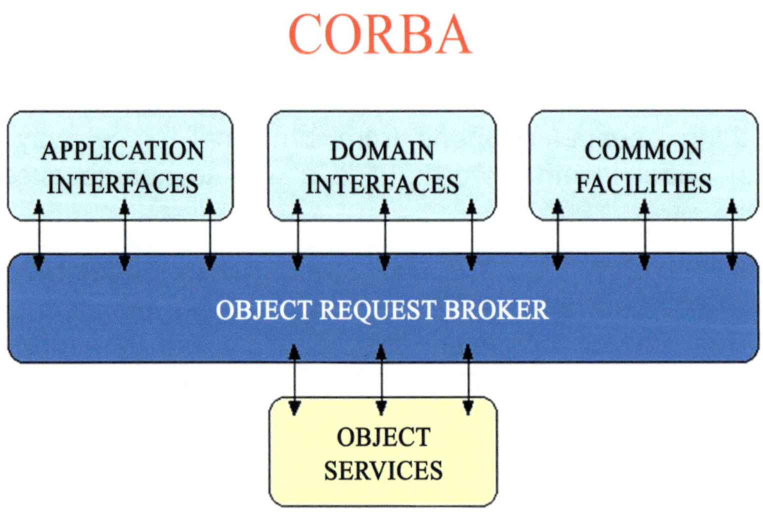

Figure 5.14. Schematic of the COBRA.

Source: Steve Vinoski, creative commons license.

The capability to manage a large number of clients, which ultimately leads to widespread deployment on web servers, is one of its most notable and significant qualities. CORBA is used by many of the most popular websites on the internet. Real-time and embedded systems are compatible with specialized variants of the CORBA programming language.

CORBA makes this avenue available in general. CORBA is comparable to a feature in JAVA called RMI, which performs most of the same functions (Stal, 1999).

RMI imparts the capacity for your objects to communicate with one another and share information via a network (Hibbard et al., 2002). As a result, establishing a client-server architecture for a large distributed system is a relatively straightforward process. Remote Method Invocation is what RMI stands for in its full name.

Communication between RMI and CORBA is probably not very quick, which means it is irrelevant for time-sensitive operations. However, it would be a decent solution for remote monitoring, in which the system response is not as crucial as other tasks.

Objects are the building blocks of CORBA applications (Saleh et al., 1999). Objects are autonomous units of software that run in the background, combine data and functionality, and frequently reflect something that exists in the physical world. Hence, the key concept behind both CORBA and RMI is the maintenance of logical consistency alongside the maintenance of the characterized as the ability of an object's implementation and interface.

5.8.1. CORBA Versus RMI

Even though RMI and CORBA both provide the same function, the two are incompatible! When using RMI, Java must be used to implement both the user application and the remote object. The definition of the interface is nothing more than a standard JAVA interface (Sventek, 1998).

1. RMI offers a lightweight and JAVA-specific mechanism enabling objects to interact with one another across networks, as well as the tools necessary to make this mechanism function properly. The JAVA virtual machine is packaged with the necessary tools, classes, and other components.
2. CORBA is both a standard and an infrastructure for integrating objects connected to a network (Hyde & Fleisch, 1998). Various suppliers must adhere to the CORBA definition when developing tools, libraries, and the like for various programming languages and operating systems.
3. The CORBA specification assures that several systems can work together.
4. Sun Microsystems offers a CORBA implementation for the Java programming language.
5. RMI and CORBA are inconsistent with one another (Plášil & Stal, 1998).

5.9. INTRO TO OBJECT-ORIENTED DESIGN

OOP is a technology in its own right; however, it is better to think of OOP as the execution of the object-oriented design procedure. Object-oriented design is a technique in its own right; however, it is often considered distinctive from OOP (Wirfs-Brock & Johnson, 1990).

Many books have been produced that describe various strategies for achieving OOD, and although we are going to talk about and cover some of those issues here, we aren't going to cover all of them. From my perspective as a physicist, programming is not a theory in and of itself but rather a method that can assist us in solving specific problems. But, the standard technique to demonstrate how to produce an OO program is to teach how to make the first pass to find classes, data members, & methods to construct the OO program. This is the first step in creating an OO program.

Provide a textual description of the solution to the problem, followed by utilizing nouns and verbs to define the classes, data members, and methods required in the design (Wirfs-Brock & Wilkerson, 1989). This is a typical approach, and it may be pretty helpful.

Consider the following tale as an explanation of the answer to a challenge involving object-oriented design. This description will serve as the basis for creating a straightforward object-oriented program. The nouns will provide us with clues regarding the classes and the data elements that will be required, while the verbs will provide us with a notion of the required methods.

Conceive a digital Counter that consists of two bits and possesses the following capabilities:

1. Setting the values of the Counter to 00 is what it means to initialize it;
2. raising the value of Count by one from its previous state
3. To "display" anything means to make its contents visible, which is what the Counter does (Shalloway & Trott, 2005).

It is expected that the following skills will be offered for each Bit:

1. to alter the value of Bit so that it has a zero;
2. to get a value that was saved in the Bit;
3. To add a 1 to a value that is now being stored within Bit and to return the carry by the truth table that is presented below (Basili et al., 1996):

0 + 0 = 0, c = 0 0 + 1 = 1, c = 0 1 + 0 = 1, c = 0 1 + 1 = 0, c = 1

A test program has to create an instance of the Counter object, then put it through its paces by incrementing it four times and showing the final value.

The following should appear in the Output of the test program (Coleman et al., 1992):

```
00

01

10

11
```

The program may look like this:

```
/* Counter designing */


class Bit{
```

```
int value;
void set(){//method to set the value of the Bit to 0
value = 0;
}//end set()

int get(){//method to get the value stored in the Bit
1return value;
}//end get()

//method to implement binary addition 14  // we provide the table here:
int add(int inValue){
1int carry = 0;
1if((value == 0) && (inValue == 0)){//0+0=0,c=0
carry = 0;
}else if((value == 0) && (inValue == 1)){//0+1=1,c=0
value = 1;
carry = 0;
}else if((value == 1) && (inValue == 0)){//1+0=1,c=0
carry = 0;
}else if((value == 1) && (inValue == 1)){//1+1=0,c=1
value = 0;
carry = 1;
}//end if statement

   return carry;
   }//end add()
   }//end class Bit
```

```
class Counter{
Bit fstbit = new Bit();//instantiate two bit objects.y
Bit scndbit= new Bit();

//method to initialize the bit objects to 0
void initialize(){
fstbit.set();
scndbit.set();
}//end initialize()

//method to add 1 to lsb and have it ripple up
// through all three bits of the Counter
void increment(){
scndbit.add(fstbit.add(1));
}//end increment()

//method to display the value of each Bit in the Counter
void show(){
System.out.println("" + scndbit.get() + fstbit.get());
}//end show()

}//end class Counter

//controlling class required by Java application
class ex5 {
public static void main(String[] args){
```

```
//instantiate a Counter object
Counter myCounter = new Counter();
myCounter.initialize();//initialize the counter object
myCounter.show(); //display contents of counter object
//increment and display counter object
for(int cnt = 0; cnt < 3; cnt++){
myCounter.increment();//increment it
myCounter.show();//display it
}//end for loop
}//end main()

}
```

The software consists of a class called Bit with a data member called value and methods that can set and add a 1 to value of instance variable, a instance variable and get the instance variable while returning the carry from binary addition (Gamma et al., 1993). In addition, the program includes a class that is called value. You can find these objects in the description as nouns or verbs.

As you observe for yourself, the design culminated in creating a class called Counter. Three embedded Bit entities inside this class served as derived classes or data members. This class includes an initialize method for setting the two counters to the value 00 in its default state.

There is another method in this class called increment, and it adds one to the Bit with the lowest value, a carry from the smallest Bit to a middle section, and adds a carry from the middle Bit to the most significant Bit. This is an example of the ripple pattern produced by a binary counter.This class also contains a show method that displays the values included in every one of the two Input objects so that they correspond to their significance level, starting with the most significant and working its way down to the least important (Bansiya & Davis, 2002).

In addition, this program includes a class known as ex5, which is not referred to by any particular noun in the description above. This is because Java programs are required to have a control subclass, and in this specific instance, the control class is called ex5.

5.10. FINAL REMARKS OF OOP

OOP needs a different approach to the design of computer programs (Filman et al., 2000). Multiple class hierarchies must have their shared behaviors and features recognized and explained. Most of the work is finished once class hierarchies have been outlined. Some objects have new instances generated for them, and their methods are called. The benefits of OOP are as follows:

1. The ability to reuse code while maintaining its individuality through inheritance and encapsulation.
2. Maintainability: modifications made to a superclass are propagated to all of the classes that inherit from it (Meyer, 1997).
3. The ability to maintain code's independence through encapsulation. The implementation details are hidden from view, and the only part of the object that the outside world may see is its interface.
4. An extremely high level of code organization and modularity is especially crucial for projects of a substantial scale; 8. prompts you to think before you code. The following are the drawbacks:
5. So because the inheritance mechanism should be implemented at runtime, compiled programs are typically larger than their uncompiled counterparts.
6. Compilated programs are typically slower than their uncompiled counterparts since subclasses need to look up inherited code before calling it (Enrich et al., 1994).

ACTIVITY 5.1:

Write a simple program using an object-oriented programming language such as Java or Python to demonstrate the basic principles of OOP, including classes, objects, and inheritance.

SUMMARY

Introduction to OOP is a chapter that provides an overview of the world of OOP. The chapter begins by defining OOP and its primary objective, making programming more object-oriented. It then discusses the characteristics of an OOP language, which include data abstraction, encapsulation, inheritance, and polymorphism. The concept of encapsulation is then explained in detail, along with its primary advantage of improved code maintainability. The purpose of heritage in OOP is also discussed, which is to reuse code and reduce redundancy. The basics of polymorphism are then introduced, which involves the ability of an object to take on many forms. The chapter also covers the fundamentals of exception handling: catching and responding to errors. Furthermore, the chapter provides an overview of distributed objects and how they can be enabled using CORBA and RMI. Finally, the chapter introduces the concept of object-oriented design and its importance in programming. Overall, the chapter provides a comprehensive understanding of the world of OOP and its essential concepts, making it a necessary read for anyone interested in programming.

REVIEW QUESTIONS

1. What exactly is meant by the term "object-oriented programming," and what are its fundamental goals?
2. What distinguishes an entity programming language from other types of languages?
3. Please define encapsulation and explain the key benefit it offers.
4. What is inheritance, and how does it function in object-oriented programming?
5. Please provide an overview of polymorphism and discuss the significance of this concept in object-oriented programming.
6. What does the term "exception handling" mean, and how does it contribute to the programming process?
7. What exactly are distributed items, and how can one utilize CORBA and RMI to use them?
8. Please walk me through the steps of object-oriented design and explain why they are necessary for programming.

MULTIPLE CHOICE QUESTIONS

1. What is the primary objective of Object-Oriented Programming?

a. To reduce the size of the program

b. To simplify the code

c. To make programming more object-oriented

d. To make programming language easier to learn

2. **Which of the following is a characteristic of an Object-Oriented Programming Language?**
   a. Functional programming
   b. Imperative programming
   c. Object-oriented programming
   d. Both a and b
3. **Which of the following is the primary advantage of encapsulation?**
   a. Improved program performance
   b. Improved code readability
   c. Improved code reusability
   d. Improved code maintainability
4. **What is the purpose of inheritance in Object-Oriented Programming?**
   a. To reduce the size of the program
   b. To simplify the code
   c. To make programming more object-oriented
   d. To reuse code and minimize redundancy
5. **Which of the following best describes polymorphism?**
   a. The ability to create objects from classes
   b. The power of an object to take on many forms
   c. The ability to define types with multiple methods
   d. The ability to define various classes with the same name
6. **What is exception handling in Object-Oriented Programming?**
   a. The process of creating custom exceptions
   b. The method of catching and responding to errors
   c. The process of debugging the code
   d. The method of optimizing the program
7. **What is the purpose of CORBA and RMI?**
   a. To improve program performance
   b. To improve code readability
   c. To enable distributed objects
   d. To improve code reusability
8. **What is object-oriented design?**
   a. The process of defining classes and objects
   b. The method of creating a user interface

c. The process of optimizing the program
d. The process of debugging the code

Answers to Multiple Choice Questions

1. (c) 2. (c) 3. (d) 4. (d)
5. (b) 6. (b); 7. (c) 8. (a)

REFERENCES

1. Agarwal, R., Sinha, A. P., & Tanniru, M., (1996). The role of prior experience and task characteristics in object-oriented modeling: An empirical study. International Journal of Human-Computer Studies, 45(6), 639–667.
2. Ågerfalk, P. J., (1999). Encapsulation or availability. In: Seminar in Scandinavia (IRIS 22):" Enterprise Architectures for Virtual Organizations (Vol. 1, pp. 37).
3. Åkerblom, B., & Wrigstad, T., (2015). Measuring polymorphism in python programs. In: Proceedings of the 11th Symposium on Dynamic Languages (Vol. 1, pp. 114–128).
4. Alkazemi, B. Y., & Grami, G. M., (2012). Utilizing BlueJ to teach polymorphism in an advanced object-oriented programming course. Journal of Information Technology Education. Innovations in Practice, 11(1), 271.
5. Alrashidi, M., Callaghan, V., & Gardner, M., (2014). An object-oriented pedagogical model for mixed reality teaching and learning. In: 2014 International Conference on Intelligent Environments (Vol. 1, pp. 202–206). IEEE.
6. Andrianoff, S. K., & Levine, D. B., (2002). Role playing in an object-oriented world. In: Proceedings of the 33rd SIGCSE Technical Symposium on Computer Science Education (Vol. 1, pp. 121–125).
7. Atkinson, M., Dewitt, D., Maier, D., Bancilhon, F., Dittrich, K., & Zdonik, S., (1990). The object-oriented database system manifesto. In: Deductive and Object-Oriented Databases (Vol. 1, pp. 223–240). North-Holland.
8. Baclawski, K., & Indurkhya, B., (1994). The notion of inheritance in object-oriented programming. Communications of the ACM, 37(9), 118–119.
9. Banciihon, F., (1988). Object-oriented database systems. In: Proceedings of the Seventh ACM SIGACT-SIGMOD-SIGART Symposium on Principles of Database Systems (Vol. 1, pp. 152–162).
10. Bansiya, J., & Davis, C. G., (2002). A hierarchical model for object-oriented design quality assessment. IEEE Transactions on Software Engineering, 28(1), 4–17.
11. Basili, V. R., Briand, L. C., & Melo, W. L., (1996). A validation of object-oriented design metrics as quality indicators. IEEE Transactions on Software Engineering, 22(10), 751–761.

12. Bergin, J., Stehlik, M., Roberts, J., & Pattis, R., (2005). Karel J. Robot: A Gentle Introduction to the Art of Object-Oriented Programming in Java (2nd edn., pp. 1–10). Redwood City: Dream Songs.
13. Binder, R., (2000). Testing Object-Oriented Systems: Models, Patterns, and Tools (3rd edn., pp. 2–6). Addison-Wesley Professional.
14. Bloom, T., & Zdonik, S. B., (1987). Issues in the design of object-oriented database programming languages. In: Conference Proceedings on Object-Oriented Programming Systems, Languages and Applications (Vol. 1, pp. 441–451).
15. Booch, G., (1994). Coming of age in an object-oriented world. IEEE Software, 11(6), 33–41.
16. Boyapati, C., Lee, R., & Rinard, M., (2002). Ownership types for safe programming: Preventing data races and deadlocks. In: Proceedings of the 17th ACM SIGPLAN Conference on Object-Oriented Programming, Systems, Languages, and Applications (Vol. 1, pp. 211–230).
17. Boyapati, C., Liskov, B., & Shrira, L., (2003). Ownership types for object encapsulation. ACM SIGPLAN Notices, 38(1), 213–223.
18. Bracha, G., & Ungar, D., (2004). Mirrors: Design principles for meta-level facilities of object-oriented programming languages. ACM SIGPLAN Notices, 39(10), 331–344.
19. Briot, J. P., Guerraoui, R., & Lohr, K. P., (1998). Concurrency and distribution in object-oriented programming. ACM Computing Surveys (CSUR), 30(3), 291–329.
20. Bruce, K. B., Schuett, A., & Van, G. R., (1995). PolyTOIL: A type-safe polymorphic object-oriented language. In: ECOOP'95—Object-Oriented Programming, 9th European Conference, Åarhus, Denmark, August 7–11, 1995 9 (Vol. 1, pp. 27–51). Springer Berlin Heidelberg.
21. Bugliesi, M., & Jamil, H. M., (1994). A logic for encapsulation in object oriented languages. In: Programming Language Implementation and Logic Programming: 6th International Symposium, PLILP'94 Madrid, Spain, September 14–16, 1994 Proceedings 6 (Vol. 1, pp. 215–229). Springer Berlin Heidelberg.
22. Cabral, B., & Marques, P., (2007). Exception handling: A field study in java and. net. In: ECOOP 2007–Object-Oriented Programming: 21st European Conference, Berlin, Germany, July 30-August 3, 2007; Proceedings 21 (Vol. 1, pp. 151–175). Springer Berlin Heidelberg.
23. Campéas, A., Dony, C., Urtado, C., & Vauttier, S., (2005). Distributed exception handling: Ideas, lessons and issues with recent exception handling systems. In: Rapid Integration of Software Engineering Techniques: First International Workshop, RISE 2004, Luxembourg-Kirchberg, Luxembourg, November 26, 2004: Revised Selected Papers 1 (Vol. 1, pp. 82–92). Springer Berlin Heidelberg.
24. Canfora, G., De Lucia, A., & Di Lucca, G. A., (1999). An incremental object-oriented migration strategy for RPG legacy systems. International Journal of Software Engineering and Knowledge Engineering, 9(1), 5–25.

25. Chaumette, S., (1998). JEM-DOOS: The Java/RMI based distributed objects operating system of the JEM project. In: Computing in Object-Oriented Parallel Environments: Second International Symposium, ISCOPE 98 Santa Fe, NM, USA, December 8–11, 1998 Proceedings 2 (Vol. 1, pp. 135–142). Springer Berlin Heidelberg.
26. Chidamber, S. R., & Kemerer, C. F., (1991). Towards a metrics suite for object oriented design. In: Conference Proceedings on Object-Oriented Programming Systems, Languages, and Applications (Vol. 1, pp. 197–211).
27. Civello, F., (1993). Roles for composite objects in object-oriented analysis and design. In: Proceedings of the Eighth Annual Conference on Object-Oriented Programming Systems, Languages, and Applications (Vol. 1, pp. 376–393).
28. Clark, D. R., (2006). Overview of object-oriented programming. Beginning Object-Oriented Programming with VB 2005: From Novice to Professional (2nd edn., pp. 3–9).
29. Clarke, D., & Drossopoulou, S., (2002). Ownership, encapsulation and the disjointness of type and effect. In: Proceedings of the 17th ACM SIGPLAN Conference on Object-Oriented Programming, Systems, Languages, and Applications (Vol. 1, pp. 292–310).
30. Coleman, D., Hayes, F., & Bear, S., (1992). Introducing objectcharts or how to use statecharts in object-oriented design. IEEE Transactions on Software Engineering, 18(1), 8, 9.
31. Concas, G., Marchesi, M., Pinna, S., & Serra, N., (2006). On the suitability of yule process to stochastically model some properties of object-oriented systems. Physica A: Statistical Mechanics and its Applications, 370(2), 817–831.
32. Cox, B. J., (1986). Object Oriented Programming: An Evolutionary Approach (Vol. 1, pp. 2–8). Addison-Wesley Longman Publishing Co., Inc.
33. Ducournau, R., & Habib, M., (1987). On some algorithms for multiple inheritance in object oriented programming. In: ECOOP'87 European Conference on Object-Oriented Programming: Paris, France, June 15–17, 1987 Proceedings 1 (Vol. 1, pp. 243–252). Springer Berlin Heidelberg.
34. Ducournau, R., (2002). "Real world" as an argument for covariant specialization in programming and modeling. In: Advances in Object-Oriented Information Systems: OOIS 2002 Workshops Montpellier, France, September 2, 2002 Proceedings 8 (Vol. 1, pp. 3–13). Springer Berlin Heidelberg.
35. Embley, D. W., Kurtz, B. D., & Woodfield, S. N., (1991). Object-Oriented Systems Analysis: A Model-Driven Approach (2nd edn., pp. 2–4). Yourdon Press.
36. Enrich, H. D., Engels, G., Paredaens, J., & Wegner, P., (1994). Fundamentals of Object-Oriented Languages, Systems and Methods (Vol. 95, pp. 5–10). In Dagstuhl Seminar Report.
37. Filman, R. E., Friedman, D. P., & Norvig, P., (2000). Aspect-Oriented Programming is Quantification and Obliviousness (Vol. 1, pp. 3–9).
38. Freeman-Benson, B. N., & Borning, A., (1992). Integrating constraints with an object-oriented language. In: ECOOP'92 European Conference on Object-Oriented

Programming: Utrecht, The Netherlands, June 29–July 3, 1992 Proceedings 6 (Vol. 1, pp. 268–286). Springer Berlin Heidelberg.

39. Gamma, E., Helm, R., Johnson, R., & Vlissides, J., (1993). Design patterns: Abstraction and reuse of object-oriented design. In: ECOOP'93—Object-Oriented Programming: 7th European Conference Kaiserslautern, Germany, July 26–30, 1993 Proceedings 7 (Vol. 1, pp. 406–431). Springer Berlin Heidelberg.
40. Gatziu, S., & Dittrich, K. R., (1992). SAMOS: An active object-oriented database system. IEEE Data Eng. Bull., 15(1–4), 23–26.
41. Gottlob, G., Schrefl, M., & Röck, B., (1996). Extending object-oriented systems with roles. ACM Transactions on Information Systems (TOIS), 14(3), 268–296.
42. Guidec, F., Jézéquel, J. M., & Pacherie, J. L., (1996). An object-oriented framework for supercomputing. Journal of Systems and Software, 33(3), 239–251.
43. Hadjerrouit, S., (1999). A constructivist approach to object-oriented design and programming. ACM SIGCSE Bulletin, 31(3), 171–174.
44. Halbert, D. C., & O'Brien, P. D., (1987). Using types and inheritance in object-oriented programming. IEEE Software, 4(5), pp. 70, 71.
45. Halbert, D. C., & O'Brien, P. D., (2000). Using types and inheritance in object-oriented languages. In: ECOOP'87 European Conference on Object-Oriented Programming: Paris, France, June 15–17, 1987 Proceedings (Vol. 1, pp. 20–31). Berlin, Heidelberg: Springer Berlin Heidelberg.
46. Hibbard, W., Rueden, C., Emmerson, S., Rink, T., Glowacki, D., Whittaker, T., & Anderson, J., (2002). Java distributed objects for numerical visualization in VisAD. Communications of the ACM, 45(4), 160–170.
47. Hirshfield, S., & Ege, R. K., (1996). Object-oriented programming. ACM Computing Surveys (CSUR), 28(1), 253–255.
48. Hogg, J., (1991). Islands: Aliasing protection in object-oriented languages. In: Conference Proceedings on Object-Oriented Programming Systems, Languages, and Applications (Vol. 1, pp. 271–285).
49. Holmes, B. J., & Joyce, D. T., (2001). Object-Oriented Programming with Java (Vol. 1, pp. 2–9). Jones & Bartlett Learning.
50. Howard, G. S., (1988). Object oriented programming explained. Journal of Systems Management, 39(7), 13.
51. Hyde, R. L., & Fleisch, B. D., (1998). A case for virtual distributed objects. Int'l. Journal on Parallel and Distributed Computing, 1(3), 1–11.
52. Jacobson, I., (1993). Object-Oriented Software Engineering: A Use Case Driven Approach (Vol. 1, pp. 5–10). Pearson Education India.
53. Joines, J. A., & Roberts, S. D., (1999). Simulation in an object-oriented world. In: Proceedings of the 31st Conference on Winter Simulation: Simulation—A Bridge to the Future (Vol. 1, pp. 132–140).

54. Kanaki, K., & Kalogiannakis, M., (2018). Introducing fundamental object-oriented programming concepts in preschool education within the context of physical science courses. Education and Information Technologies, 23(6), 2673–2698.

55. Kienzle, J., (2000). Exception handling in open multithreaded transactions. In: Workshop on Exception Handling in Object-Oriented Systems at ECOOP 2000, Sophia Antipolis, Cannes, France, June 12–16 (No. CONF) (2nd edn., pp. 3–6).

56. Kifer, M., Lausen, G., & Wu, J., (1995). Logical foundations of object-oriented and frame-based languages. Journal of the ACM (JACM), 42(4), 741–843.

57. Kniesel, G., & Theisen, D., (2001). JAC—Access right based encapsulation for java. Software: Practice and Experience, 31(6), 555–576.

58. Kölling, M., (1999). The problem of teaching object-oriented programming, Part 1: Languages. Journal of Object-Oriented Programming, 11(8), 8–15.

59. Kölling, M., (1999). The problem of teaching object-oriented programming, Part 2: Environments. Journal of Object-Oriented Programming, 11(9), 6–12.

60. Korson, T., & McGregor, J. D., (1990). Understanding object-oriented: A unifying paradigm. Communications of the ACM, 33(9), 40–60.

61. Kosbar, K., & Schneider, K., (1992). Object-oriented modeling of communication systems. In: MILCOM 92 Conference Record (Vol. 1, pp. 68–72). IEEE.

62. Lange, D. B., & Nakamura, Y., (1997). Object-oriented program tracing and visualization. Computer, 30(5), 63–70.

63. Lau, K. K., & Taweel, F. M., (2007). Data encapsulation in software components. In: Component-Based Software Engineering: 10th International Symposium, CBSE 2007, Medford, MA, USA, July 9–11, 2007. Proceedings 10 (Vol. 1, pp. 1–16). Springer Berlin Heidelberg.

64. Lieberman, H., (1986). Using prototypical objects to implement shared behavior in object-oriented systems. In: Conference Proceedings on Object-Oriented Programming Systems, Languages and Applications (Vol. 1, pp. 214–223).

65. Lu, Y., & Potter, J., (2006). Protecting representation with effect encapsulation. ACM SIGPLAN Notices, 41(1), 359–371.

66. Menzies, T., & Haynes, P., (1996). Empirical Observations of Class-Level Encapsulation and Inheritance (Vol. 1, pp. 6–9). Technical report, Department of Software Development, Monash University.

67. Meyer, B., (1997). Object-Oriented Software Construction (Vol. 2, pp. 331–410). Englewood Cliffs: Prentice Hall.

68. Miller, D. J., & Lennox, R. C., (1991). An object-oriented environment for robot system architectures. IEEE Control Systems Magazine, 11(2), 14–23.

69. Muntean, P., Wuerl, S., Grossklags, J., & Eckert, C., (2018). CastSan: Efficient detection of polymorphic C++ object type confusions with LLVM. In: Computer Security: 23rd European Symposium on Research in Computer Security, ESORICS 2018, Barcelona, Spain, September 3–7, 2018, Proceedings, Part I 23 (Vol. 1, pp.

3–25). Springer International Publishing.

70. Mylopoulos, J., Chung, L., & Yu, E., (1999). From object-oriented to goal-oriented requirements analysis. Communications of the ACM, 42(1), 31–37.
71. Narayanan, S., Bodner, D. A., Sreekanth, U., Govindaraj, T., McGinnis, L. F., & Mitchell, C. M., (1998). Research in object-oriented manufacturing simulations: An assessment of the state of the art. IIE Transactions, 30(9), 795–810.
72. Nordlander, J., (2002). Polymorphic subtyping in O'Haskell. Science of Computer Programming, 43(2, 3), 93–127.
73. Nygaard, K., (1986). Basic concepts in object oriented programming. In: Proceedings of the 1986 SIGPLAN Workshop on Object-oriented Programming (Vol. 1, pp. 128–132).
74. O'Grady, P., & Seshadri, R., (1991). X-cell—Intelligent cell control using object-oriented programming (part I). Computer Integrated Manufacturing Systems, 4(3), 157–163.
75. Oren, E., Delbru, R., Gerke, S., Haller, A., & Decker, S., (2007). ActiveRDF: Object-oriented semantic web programming. In: Proceedings of the 16th International Conference on World Wide Web (Vol. 1, pp. 817–824).
76. Plášil, F., & Stal, M., (1998). An architectural view of distributed objects and components in CORBA, Java RMI and COM/DCOM. Software-Concepts & Tools, 19(1), 14–28.
77. Poo, D., Kiong, D., & Ashok, S., (2007). Object-Oriented Programming and Java (2nd edn., pp. 1–7). Springer Science & Business Media.
78. Rahnev, A., Pavlov, N., Valchanov, N., & Terzieva, T., (2014). Object oriented programming (Vol. 2, No. 1, pp. 7–9). Lightning Source UK Ltd., London.
79. Raptis, K., Spinellis, D., & Katsikas, S., (2001). Multi-technology distributed objects and their integration. Computer Standards & Interfaces, 23(3), 157–168.
80. Rentsch, T., (1982). Object oriented programming. ACM Sigplan Notices, 17(9), 51–57.
81. Romanovsky, A., Dony, C., Knudsen, J. L., & Tripathi, A., (2003). Advances in Exception Handling Techniques (Vol. 1, pp. 4–8). Springer.
82. Saleh, K., Probert, R., & Khanafer, H., (1999). The distributed object computing paradigm: Concepts and applications. Journal of Systems and Software, 47(2, 3), 125–131.
83. Salvaneschi, G., Hintz, G., & Mezini, M., (2014). REScala: Bridging between object-oriented and functional style in reactive applications. In: Proceedings of the 13th International Conference on Modularity (Vol. 1, pp. 25–36).
84. Sanders, D., & Dorn, B., (2003). Jeroo: A tool for introducing object-oriented programming. In: Proceedings of the 34th SIGCSE Technical Symposium on Computer Science Education (Vol. 1, pp. 201–204).
85. Sanders, K., Boustedt, J., Eckerdal, A., McCartney, R., Moström, J. E., Thomas, L., & Zander, C., (2008). Student understanding of object-oriented programming as expressed in concept maps. In: Proceedings of the 39th SIGCSE Technical Symposium on Computer Science Education (Vol. 1, pp. 332–336).

86. Sandhu, P. S., & Singh, G., (2008). Dynamic metrics for polymorphism in object-oriented systems. International Journal of Computer and Information Engineering, 2(3), 697–700.
87. Santos, A. L., (2014). Novel interaction metaphors for object-oriented programming concepts. In: Proceedings of the 14th Koli Calling International Conference on Computing Education Research (Vol. 1, pp. 117–126).
88. Sarcar, V., (2022). Encapsulation using properties and indexers. In: Test Your Skills in C# Programming: Review and Analyze Important Features of C# (Vol. 1, pp. 183–211). Berkeley, CA: Apress.
89. Schäfer, J., & Rauch, D. I. N., (2004). Encapsulation and Specification of Object-Oriented Runtime Components (2nd edn., p. 89).
90. Schultz, U. P., & Axelsen, H. B., (2016). Elements of a reversible object-oriented language: Work-in-progress report. In: Reversible Computation: 8th International Conference, RC 2016, Bologna, Italy, July 7–8, 2016, Proceedings (Vol. 1, pp. 153–159). Cham: Springer International Publishing.
91. Shalloway, A., & Trott, J. R., (2005). Design Patterns Explained: A New Perspective on Object-Oriented Design, 2/E (Viol. 4, No. 1, pp. 6–10). Pearson Education India.
92. Singh, G. B., (1994). Single versus multiple inheritance in object-oriented programming. ACM SIGPLAN OOPS Messenger, 5(1), 34–43.
93. Singh, G. B., (1995). Single versus multiple inheritance in object-oriented programming. ACM SIGPLAN Oops Messenger, 6(1), 30–39.
94. Singh, S., & Kahlon, K. S., (2011). Effectiveness of encapsulation and object-oriented metrics to refactor code and identify error prone classes using bad smells. ACM SIGSOFT Software Engineering Notes, 36(5), 1–10.
95. Skoglund, M., (2003). Practical use of encapsulation in object-oriented programming. In: Software Engineering Research and Practice (Vol. 1, pp. 554–560).
96. Smith, M. D., & Robson, D. J., (1990). Object-oriented programming-the problems of validation. In: Proceedings, Conference on Software Maintenance 1990 (Vol. 1, pp. 272–281). IEEE.
97. Sridharan, M., Chandra, S., Dolby, J., Fink, S. J., & Yahav, E., (2013). Alias analysis for object-oriented programs. Aliasing in Object-Oriented Programming: Types, Analysis and Verification (2nd edn., pp. 196–232).
98. Srinath, K. R., (2017). Python–the fastest growing programming language. International Research Journal of Engineering and Technology, 4(12), 354–357.
99. Stal, M., (1999). Distributed objects from a patterns perspective. In: Proceedings of Technology of Object-Oriented Languages and Systems-TOOLS 30 (Cat. No. PR00278) (Vol. 1, pp. 445). IEEE Computer Society.
100. Stroustrup, B., (1995). Why C++ is not just an object-oriented programming language. In: Addendum to the Proceedings of the 10th Annual Conference on Object-Oriented Programming Systems, Languages, and Applications (Addendum) (Vol. 1, pp. 1–13).
101. Sutcliffe, A. G., (1991). Object-oriented systems development: Survey of structured

methods. Information and Software Technology, 33(6), 433–442.

102. Sventek, J., (1998). Guest editor's introduction: Selected papers from the 4th USENIX conference on object-oriented technologies and systems. Distributed Systems Engineering, 5(4), 139–140.
103. Uzakov, Z., Mamatov, F., & Begulov, O., (2019). Implementation of object-oriented programming technology in the one-dimensional oil displacement problem. In: 2019 International Conference on Information Science and Communications Technologies (ICISCT) (Vol. 1, pp. 1–5). IEEE.
104. Voigt, J., (2009). Characterizing the Use of Encapsulation in Object Oriented Systems (2nd edn., pp. 2, 3).
105. Voigt, J., Irwin, W., & Churcher, N., (2010). Class Encapsulation and Object Encapsulation: An Empirical Study, 1, 2–6.
106. Weimer, W., & Necula, G. C., (2004). Finding and preventing run-time error handling mistakes. In: Proceedings of the 19th Annual ACM SIGPLAN Conference on Object-Oriented Programming, Systems, Languages, and Applications (Vol. 1, pp. 419–431).
107. Wiedenbeck, S., Ramalingam, V., Sarasamma, S., & Corritore, C. L., (1999). A comparison of the comprehension of object-oriented and procedural programs by novice programmers. Interacting with Computers, 11(3), 255–282.
108. Wiener, R. S., & Pinson, L. J., (1988). An Introduction to Object-Oriented Programming and C++ (Vol. 1, pp. 2–7). Addison-Wesley Longman Publishing Co., Inc.
109. Wilde, N., & Huitt, R., (1992). Maintenance support for object-oriented programs. IEEE Transactions on Software Engineering, 18(12), 1038.
110. Wilde, N., Matthews, P., & Huitt, R., (1993). Maintaining object-oriented software. IEEE Software, 10(1), 75–80.
111. Wirfs-Brock, R. J., & Johnson, R. E., (1990). Surveying current research in object-oriented design. Communications of the ACM, 33(9), 104–124.
112. Wirfs-Brock, R., & Wilkerson, B., (1989). Object-oriented design: A responsibility-driven approach. ACM Sigplan Notices, 24(10), 71–75.
113. Wong, Y. S., Hayati, M., Yatim, M., & Hoe, T. W., (2017). A propriety game based learning mobile game to learn object-oriented programming—Odyssey of phoenix. In: 2017 IEEE 6th International Conference on Teaching, Assessment, and Learning for Engineering (TALE) (Vol. 1, pp. 426–431). IEEE.
114. Wu, C. T., (2006). An Introduction to Object-Oriented Programming with Java TM (Vol. 1, pp. 2–7). McGraw-Hill Incorporated.
115. Xianzhong, L., & Zhenyu, W., (1991). Ada-based support for abstraction, encapsulation and unit hierarchy. In: Proceedings of the Conference on TRI-Ada'91: Today's Accomplishments; Tomorrow's Expectations (Vol. 1, pp. 116–126).
116. Xinogalos, S., Satratzemi, M., & Dagdilelis, V., (2006). An introduction to object-oriented programming with a didactic microworld: ObjectKarel. Computers & Education, 47(2), 148–171.

117. Xu, G., (2013). Resurrector: A tunable object lifetime profiling technique for optimizing real-world programs. In: Proceedings of the 2013 ACM SIGPLAN International Conference on Object Oriented Programming Systems Languages & Applications (Vol. 1, pp. 111–130).

118. Yan, L., (2009). Teaching object-oriented programming with games. In: 2009 Sixth International Conference on Information Technology: New Generations (Vol. 1, pp. 969–974). IEEE.

119. Zimmermann, T., Dubois-Pelerin, Y., & Bomme, P., (1992). Object-oriented finite element programming: I. Governing principles. Computer Methods in Applied Mechanics and Engineering, 98(2), 291–303.

CHAPTER 6

DATABASE INTEGRATION: SQL AND NOSQL

UNIT INTRODUCTION

Database integration is a critical component of web development, allowing for efficient data storage, retrieval, and manipulation within web applications. Two popular types of databases used in internet programming are SQL and NoSQL databases. SQL databases, with their rigid structure and querying language, have been the go-to choice for traditional web applications. However, with the rise of more complex web applications and the need for faster, more scalable databases, NoSQL databases have gained popularity due to their flexible structure and ability to handle large amounts of unstructured data. This chapter will explore the integration of both SQL and NoSQL databases in internet programming, comparing their advantages, disadvantages, and best practices for implementation in web frameworks (Lawrence, 2014).

In the past, SQL databases were the only option for web developers as they provided a reliable, structured, and easy-to-use DBMS. SQL databases use a table-based data model and the Structured Query Language (SQL) to manage and manipulate data. These databases are designed for applications that require a high level of consistency and reliability in their data, such as financial systems and customer relationship management (CRM) systems. However, as web applications became more complex and required handling larger amounts of unstructured data, SQL databases proved to be less effective due to their rigid data structure. This led to the rise of NoSQL databases, which offer a flexible and scalable data model to handle the ever-increasing amounts of unstructured data generated by modern web applications. NoSQL databases are designed to handle unstructured, semi-structured, and polymorphic data, and have become popular for use in applications such as e-commerce platforms, social networks, and big data analytics (Liao et al., 2016).

Database integration is crucial in internet programming, as it enables web applications to interact with databases to store, retrieve, and manipulate data. By integrating databases in web applications, developers can build more efficient, scalable, and responsive web applications. Database integration is made possible through web frameworks such as Django, Ruby on Rails, and Express.js, which provide built-in features and libraries for connecting web applications to databases (Bjeladinovic et al., 2020).

Learning Objectives

At the end of this chapter, readers will be able to:

- Understand the differences between SQL and NoSQL databases and their respective strengths and weaknesses.
- Gain knowledge of the popular SQL databases such as MySQL, Oracle, and SQL Server.
- Learn the syntax and commands of SQL and how to integrate it into web applications.
- Explore the querying capabilities of NoSQL databases such as MongoDB, Cassandra, and Redis.
- Understand the advantages and disadvantages of NoSQL databases compared to SQL databases.
- Explore the integration of NoSQL databases into web applications.
- Discover best practices for database integration in web frameworks.
- Understand the common challenges associated with database integration in web programming.
- Gain a deeper understanding of the importance of database integration in internet programming.

Key Terms

- Cassandra
- Database Integration
- MongoDB
- MySQL
- NoSQL

- Oracle
- Querying Data
- Redis
- SQL
- SQL Commands
- SQL Server
- Web Applications

6.1. DEFINITION OF SQL AND NOSQL

SQL and NoSQL are two types of database management systems (DBMSs) used in internet programming. SQL stands for Structured Query Language (SQL), and is a traditional, relational DBMS that uses a structured data model to store and manage data. SQL databases are based on the concept of tables, where data is stored in rows and columns. SQL databases enforce a rigid structure, with predefined data types and relationships between tables, and use SQL queries to manipulate and retrieve data (Cattell, 2011) (Figure 6.1).

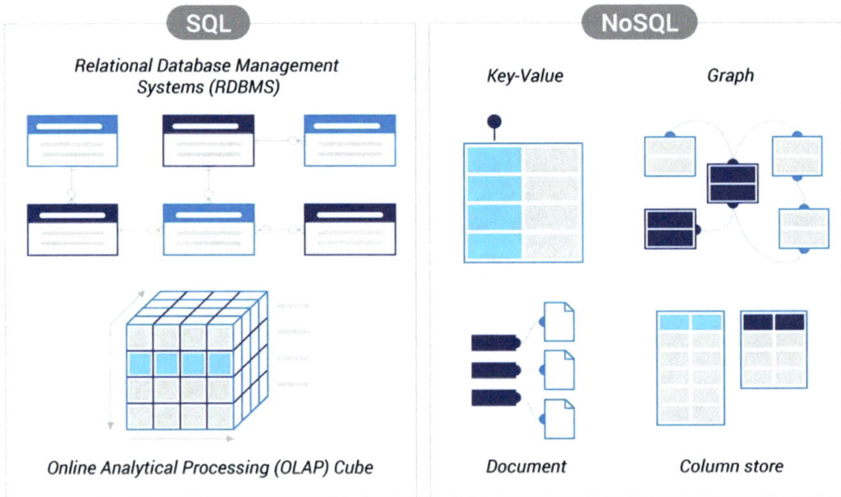

Figure 6.1. Difference between SQL and NoSQL.

Source: Scylla, creative commons license.

On the other hand, NoSQL databases, as the name suggests, are non-relational and provide a flexible, schema-less data model. NoSQL databases can handle large amounts of unstructured and semi-structured data, such as documents, graphs, and key-value pairs. Unlike SQL databases, NoSQL databases do not have a predefined schema, and do not enforce rigid data types or relationships between data. NoSQL databases provide a more scalable and flexible data model, and are designed to handle data that changes frequently or is not well-defined (Liu et al., 2016).

The choice between SQL and NoSQL databases depends on the specific requirements of the application. SQL databases are typically used for applications that require high levels of data consistency, such as financial systems or inventory management systems, where data must be stored in a structured, consistent manner. NoSQL databases are better suited for applications that require the ability to store and query unstructured data, such as social networks, e-commerce platforms, and big data analytics (Binani et al., 2016).

6.2. IMPORTANCE OF DATABASE INTEGRATION IN INTERNET PROGRAMMING

Database integration is an essential aspect of internet programming that allows web applications to store, retrieve, and manipulate data efficiently. In today's digital age, where data is generated at an unprecedented scale, it is crucial to have a robust DBMS in place that can handle large volumes of data and provide quick access to it (Huang et al., 2001) (Figure 6.2).

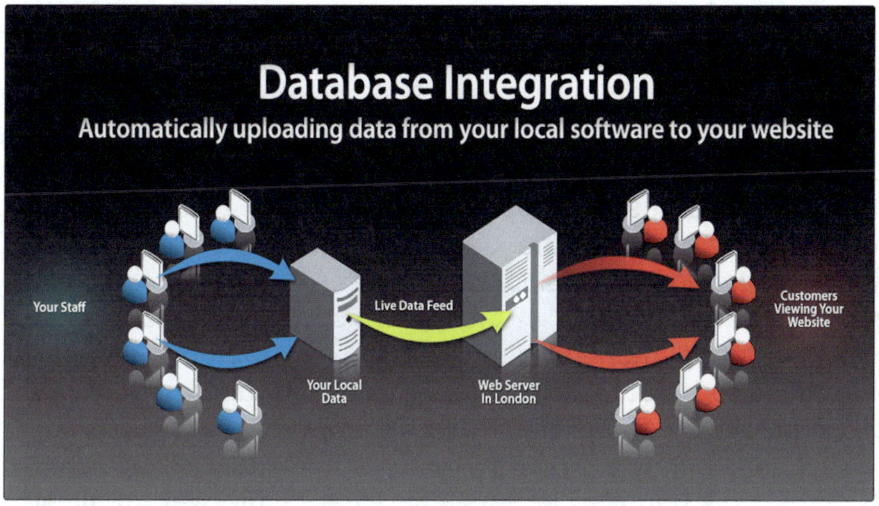

Figure 6.2. Schematic of the database integration.

Source: Tech-FAQ, creative commons license.

Web applications that lack proper database integration may struggle with slow response times, inconsistent data, and an inability to scale. Proper database integration enables developers to create web applications that are highly responsive, scalable, and efficient. By integrating a database into a web application, developers can store and retrieve data in real-time, provide users with a personalized experience, and analyze user data to make informed business decisions. In addition, database integration is critical in ensuring data security and data privacy. By implementing proper database security protocols, web applications can ensure that sensitive user data is protected against unauthorized access or data breaches (Ahmed et al., 2017).

Overall, database integration is essential in internet programming as it enables developers to create web applications that are fast, responsive, and scalable, while also ensuring the security and privacy of user data. It allows businesses to provide a better user experience, gain valuable insights from user data, and make informed business decisions (Khodadadi et al., 2016).

6.3. SQL DATABASES

SQL databases are a type of DBMS that use a structured data model to store and manage data. The acronym "SQL" stands for Structured Query Language, which is the language used to interact with the database.

SQL databases are based on the concept of tables, where data is stored in rows and columns. Each table represents a collection of related data and has a unique name. SQL databases are organized into multiple tables, and each table has a unique primary key, which identifies each row in the table. SQL databases enforce a rigid structure, with predefined data types and relationships between tables. SQL databases use SQL queries to manipulate and retrieve data, which enables developers to easily and efficiently manage and retrieve data from the database (Stonebraker, 2010). SQL databases are ideal for applications that require a high level of consistency and reliability in their data, such as financial systems, inventory management systems, and other systems that require transactions to be atomic, consistent, isolated, and durable (ACID). SQL databases ensure that data is stored in a structured and consistent manner, which makes it easy to query and manipulate data. SQL databases can also be easily integrated into web frameworks, allowing developers to build efficient, scalable web applications that can handle a high volume of transactions (Figure 6.3).

Figure 6.3. Illustration of the database in SQL.

Source: Educba, Creative Commons License.

Some popular SQL databases include MySQL, Oracle, SQL Server, and PostgreSQL. Each database has its own unique features and capabilities, but all use the SQL language to manage and retrieve data (Silva et al., 2016).

6.3.1. Examples of SQL Databases

Here are some examples of popular SQL databases (Figure 6.4):

1. **MySQL:** MySQL is an open-source relational DBMS that is widely used in web development. It is known for its scalability, speed, and ease of use. MySQL is often used in conjunction with PHP, which is a popular programming language for web development.

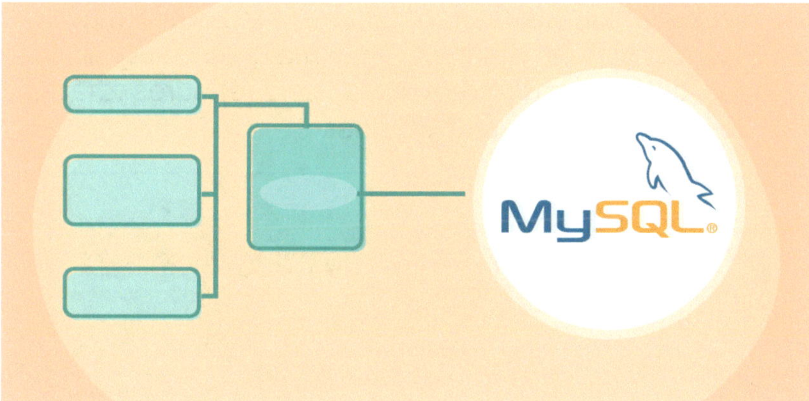

Figure 6.4. Schematic of the MySQL usage.

Source: Ryan Thelin, creative commons license.

2. **Oracle**: Oracle is a commercial relational DBMS that is widely used in enterprise applications. It is known for its scalability, reliability, and security. Oracle is often used in mission-critical applications, such as financial systems and CRM systems.
3. **SQL Server:** SQL Server is a relational DBMS developed by Microsoft. It is designed to work with Microsoft's. NET framework and is often used in enterprise applications. SQL Server is known for its scalability, performance, and security (Sequeda et al., 2011).
4. **PostgreSQL:** PostgreSQL is an open-source relational DBMS that is known for its robustness, reliability, and extensibility. It is often used in web applications and enterprise applications, and supports a wide range of programming languages.

Each of these SQL databases has its own unique features, strengths, and weaknesses. The choice of database depends on the specific requirements of the application and the resources available to the developer (Netz et al., 2001).

6.3.2. Advantages and Disadvantages of SQL Databases

SQL databases have several advantages and disadvantages that developers should consider when selecting a DBMS for their web application (Figure 6.5).

Following are the advantages of SQL databases:

1. **Structured Data:** SQL databases use a structured data model, which makes it easy to organize and manage data in a consistent manner. This makes it easy to retrieve, manipulate, and query data, and ensures that data is stored in a consistent manner.

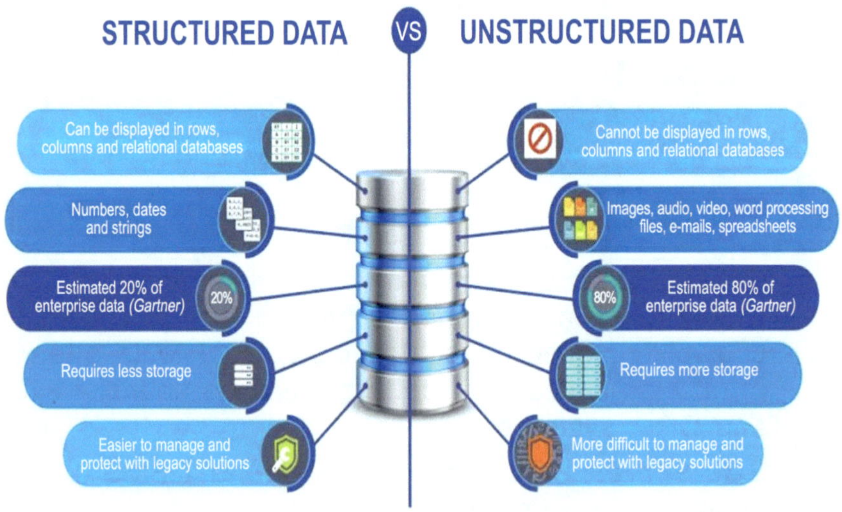

Figure **6.5.** Illustration of structured vs. unstructured data.

Source: Xpresso, creative commons license.

2. **ACID Compliance:** SQL databases are designed to support transactions that are ACID. This ensures that transactions are reliable and consistent, even in the event of a system failure.

3. **Wide Adoption:** SQL databases have been around for several decades, and have been widely adopted by developers and businesses. This means that there is a large community of developers who are familiar with SQL databases, and there are many resources available for developers to learn how to use them (Parker et al., 2013).
4. **Scalability:** SQL databases can be easily scaled up or down to handle a high volume of transactions. This makes them ideal for applications that require high availability and scalability.

Following are the disadvantages of SQL databases:

1. **Rigid Structure:** The rigid structure of SQL databases can make it difficult to store and retrieve unstructured data, such as images or videos. This can make SQL databases less suitable for applications that require a lot of unstructured data.
2. **Complexity:** SQL databases can be complex to manage and administer, especially for large-scale applications. This can result in increased maintenance costs and slower performance.
3. **Cost:** Some SQL databases, such as Oracle, can be expensive to license and use. This can make them less suitable for small businesses or startups that have limited resources.
4. **Limited Scalability:** While SQL databases can be scaled up or down, they may have limitations on scalability compared to NoSQL databases. This is because SQL databases are designed to maintain strict data consistency, which can limit their ability to scale horizontally across multiple servers (Deari et al., 2018).

Overall, SQL databases are a reliable and widely adopted choice for web applications that require structured data management and ACID compliance. However, they may not be suitable for applications that require storing and retrieving a lot of unstructured data or require unlimited horizontal scalability.

Did you Know?

The Structured Query Language (SQL) was first developed in the 1970s by IBM researchers, and it has since become one of the most widely used languages for managing relational databases.

6.3.3. SQL Commands and Syntax

SQL commands and syntax are used to interact with SQL databases and perform operations such as querying, inserting, updating, and deleting data (Figure 6.6).

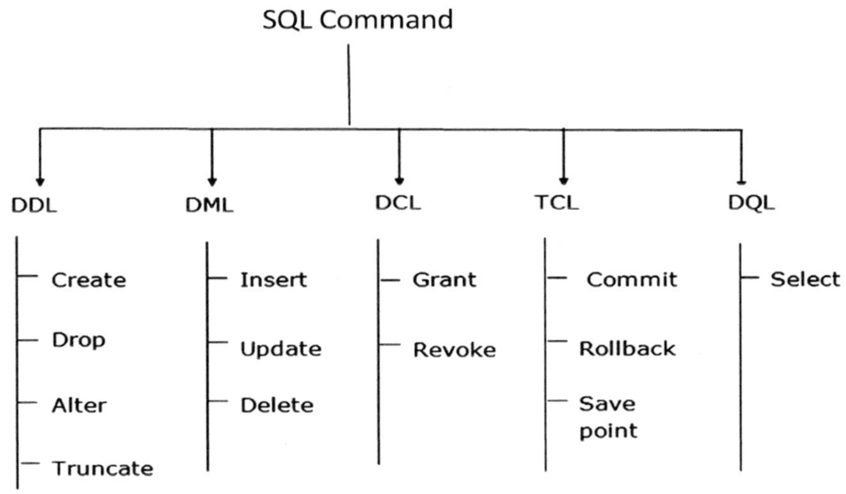

Figure 6.6. Schematic of the SQL commands.

Source: Java T point, creative commons license.

Here are some commonly used SQL commands and their syntax:

SELECT: SELECT is used to retrieve data from a database. The basic syntax for SELECT is as follows:

sql

SELECT column1, column2, ... FROM table_name;

This command will retrieve data from the specified columns in the table_name table.

INSERT: INSERT is used to add data to a database. The basic syntax for INSERT is as follows:

sql

INSERT INTO table_name (column1, column2, ...) VALUES (value1, value2, .);

This command will add a new row to the table_name table with the specified values.

UPDATE: UPDATE is used to modify existing data in a database. The basic syntax for UPDATE is as follows:

sql

UPDATE table_name SET column1 = value1, column2 = value2, ... WHERE condition;

This command will modify the values in the specified columns in the table_name table that match the specified condition (Halfond et al., 2006).

DELETE: DELETE is used to remove data from a database. The basic syntax for DELETE is as follows:

```
sql

DELETE FROM table_name WHERE condition;
```

This command will remove rows from the table_name table that match the specified condition.

CREATE TABLE: CREATE TABLE is used to create a new table in a database. The basic syntax for CREATE TABLE is as follows:

```
sql

CREATE TABLE table_name (

column1 datatype,

column2 datatype,

.

);
```

This command will create a new table with the specified columns and data types (Sallam et al., 2016).

These are just a few examples of commonly used SQL commands and syntax. SQL has many more commands and syntax for performing advanced operations, such as JOINs, subqueries, and aggregations. Developers must have a good understanding of SQL syntax and commands to effectively work with SQL databases (Jamison, 2003).

Remember

The integration of SQL databases in web applications is a powerful and popular approach for managing and storing large amounts of structured data.

6.3.4. Integration of SQL Databases in Web Applications

Integration of SQL databases in web applications involves connecting the web application to a SQL database and using SQL queries to retrieve, modify, and delete data.

Here are some key steps to integrate SQL databases in web applications:

1. **Choose a SQL Database:** Select a SQL DBMS that meets the requirements of the web application. Popular SQL databases include MySQL, Oracle, SQL Server, and PostgreSQL.
2. **Configure the Database:** Configure the SQL database by setting up user accounts, creating a database, and defining the table schema.
3. **Connect to the Database:** Connect the web application to the SQL database using a database connector. Most web frameworks provide built-in database connectors or libraries for connecting to SQL databases.
4. **Write SQL Queries:** Use SQL queries to retrieve, modify, and delete data from the SQL database. SQL queries can be embedded directly into the web application code or stored in separate files (Sharma et al., 2012).
5. **Use an Object-Relational Mapping (ORM) Tool:** An ORM tool can be used to map objects in the web application code to tables in the SQL database. This can simplify the integration process and reduce the amount of SQL code that needs to be written.
6. **Implement Security Measures:** Implement security measures, such as parameterized queries and input validation, to prevent SQL injection attacks and other security vulnerabilities.
7. **Test and Optimize:** Test the integration of the SQL database in the web application and optimize the database queries for better performance.

By integrating SQL databases in web applications, developers can build scalable, reliable, and efficient web applications that can handle a high volume of transactions. SQL databases are a popular choice for web applications that require structured data management and ACID compliance (Tuya et al., 2006).

6.3.5. Examples of Web Applications Using SQL Databases

SQL databases are widely used in web applications, especially for applications that require structured data management and ACID compliance. Here are some examples of popular web applications that use SQL databases (Figure 6.7):

1. **WordPress:** WordPress is a popular content management system that uses a MySQL database to store and manage website content. WordPress uses SQL queries to retrieve and modify data, and offers built-in features for managing database tables and optimizing database performance.
2. **Facebook:** Facebook uses a MySQL database to store user data, such as profiles, messages, and posts. Facebook also uses a custom query language called Facebook Query Language (FQL) to retrieve data from the database.

3. **LinkedIn:** LinkedIn uses a MySQL database to store user data, such as profiles, job postings, and company pages. LinkedIn also uses a custom query language called Galene to retrieve and modify data in the database (Eassa et al., 2018).
4. **GitHub:** GitHub uses a PostgreSQL database to store and manage code repositories. GitHub uses SQL queries to retrieve and modify data, and offers built-in features for managing database tables and optimizing database performance.
5. **Shopify:** Shopify uses a MySQL database to store and manage e-commerce data, such as product listings, orders, and customer information. Shopify uses SQL queries to retrieve and modify data, and offers built-in features for managing database tables and optimizing database performance.

Figure 6.7. Shopify to MS SQL server integration.

Source: Blendo, creative commons license.

These are just a few examples of popular web applications that use SQL databases. SQL databases are widely adopted by developers and businesses for their structured data management, ACID compliance, and scalability (Scott & Sharp, 2002).

6.4. NOSQL DATABASES

NoSQL databases are a type of DBMS that provides a flexible and scalable data model for storing and managing data. Unlike SQL databases, which use a structured data model based on tables,

NoSQL databases can handle unstructured, semi-structured, and polymorphic data, such as documents, graphs, and key-value pairs. NoSQL databases do not use the SQL language to interact with data, and instead use different query languages or APIs to interact with the database.

TIPS

NoSQL databases are ideal for managing large-scale and unstructured data sets, such as those found in social media and e-commerce applications.

NoSQL databases are designed to handle large volumes of data and support horizontal scaling, which means they can scale out to multiple servers to handle increased data volumes and traffic. NoSQL databases are often used in web applications that require storing and retrieving large amounts of unstructured data, such as social networks, e-commerce platforms, and big data analytics (Strauch et al., 2011) (Figure 6.8).

NoSQL databases can be categorized into several types based on their data models:

1. **Document Databases**: Document databases store data as JSON, BSON, or XML documents, and use document-based queries to retrieve and manipulate data. Examples of document databases include MongoDB and CouchDB.

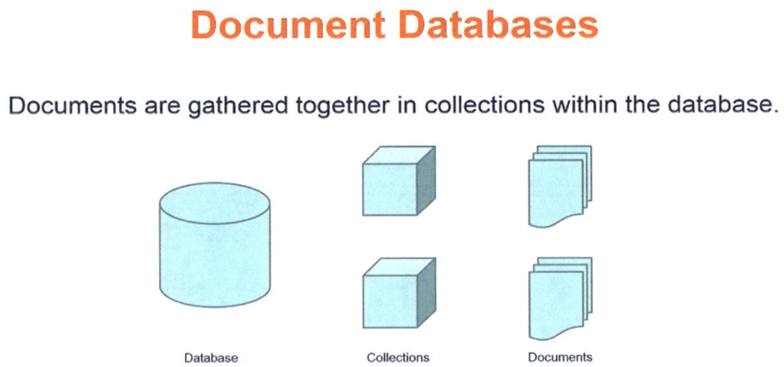

Figure 6.8. Document database as an example of NoSQL Database.

Source: CUNY school of professional studies, creative commons license.

2. **Key-Value Databases:** Key-value databases store data as key-value pairs, and use key-based queries to retrieve and manipulate data. Examples of key-value databases include Redis and Riak.

3. **Column-Family Databases:** Column-family databases store data as columns, and use column-family queries to retrieve and manipulate data. Examples of column-family databases include Cassandra and HBase.

4. **Graph Databases:** Graph databases store data as nodes and edges, and use graph-based queries to retrieve and manipulate data. Examples of graph databases include Neo4j and OrientDB.

NoSQL databases offer several advantages over SQL databases, including the ability to handle large amounts of unstructured data, support for horizontal scaling, and the ability to handle high traffic loads. However, NoSQL databases can be more complex to manage than SQL databases, and may require a different set of skills and expertise to use effectively (Han et al., 2011).

6.4.1. Examples of NoSQL Databases

Here are some examples of popular NoSQL databases (Figure 6.9):

Figure 6.9. NoSQL cloud platforms to store data.

Source: Aleksandra Budnik, creative commons license.

1. **MongoDB:** MongoDB is a popular document-oriented NoSQL database that uses JSON-like documents to store data. It is designed to scale horizontally across multiple servers and provides high availability and automatic sharding. MongoDB is widely used in web applications that require flexible data models, such as content management systems, e-commerce platforms, and social networks.
2. **Cassandra:** Cassandra is a popular column-family NoSQL database that is designed to handle large amounts of data across multiple servers. It provides high availability and automatic replication, and is often used in big data applications, such as analytics, IoT, and machine learning (Mason, 2015).
3. **Redis:** Redis is a popular key-value NoSQL database that is designed for fast read and write operations. It supports a wide range of data structures, such as strings, hashes, lists, and sets, and provides high availability and automatic failover. Redis is often used in applications that require fast caching and session management, such as e-commerce platforms and real-time messaging systems.
4. **Neo4j:** Neo4j is a popular graph NoSQL database that is designed to store and manage complex relationships between data. It uses graph-based queries to retrieve and manipulate data, and provides high

availability and automatic failover. Neo4j is often used in applications that require complex network analysis, such as recommendation engines and social networks.

Each NoSQL database has its own unique features, strengths, and weaknesses. The choice of database depends on the specific requirements of the application and the resources available to the developer (Bhogal & Choksi, 2015).

6.4.2. Advantages and Disadvantages of NoSQL Databases

NoSQL databases offer several advantages over SQL databases, but they also have some disadvantages. Here are some advantages and disadvantages of NoSQL databases:

Following are the advantages of NoSQL databases:

1. **Scalability:** NoSQL databases are designed to scale horizontally across multiple servers, which makes them ideal for applications that require high availability and scalability.
2. **Flexibility:** NoSQL databases can handle unstructured, semi-structured, and polymorphic data, such as documents, graphs, and key-value pairs. This makes them ideal for applications that require flexible data models.
3. **Performance:** NoSQL databases are designed for fast read and write operations, which makes them ideal for applications that require high performance, such as real-time analytics and real-time messaging.
4. **Availability:** NoSQL databases are designed for high availability and automatic failover, which ensures that the database is always available to handle requests (Leavitt, 2010).

Following are disadvantages of NoSQL databases:

1. **Limited Transaction Support:** NoSQL databases often sacrifice transaction support for scalability and performance. This means that they may not be suitable for applications that require strict transactional consistency.
2. **Complexity:** NoSQL databases can be more complex to manage and administer than SQL databases, especially for large-scale applications.
3. **Limited Query Capabilities:** NoSQL databases often have limited query capabilities compared to SQL databases, which can make it difficult to retrieve and manipulate data.
4. **Limited Community and Resources:** NoSQL databases are still relatively new compared to SQL databases, which means that there may be fewer resources and a smaller community of developers.

Overall, NoSQL databases are a good choice for web applications that require flexible data models, high scalability, and high performance. However, they may not be suitable for applications that require strict transactional consistency or complex queries. Developers should carefully consider the requirements of their application and choose a DBMS that meets their specific needs (Nayak et al., 2013).

6.4.3. Querying Data in NoSQL Databases

Querying data in NoSQL databases requires a different approach than querying data in SQL databases. NoSQL databases use different data models and query languages, such as document-based queries, key-based queries, or graph-based queries, to retrieve and manipulate data. In document-based NoSQL databases, such as MongoDB or CouchDB, data is stored as JSON, BSON, or XML documents, and document-based queries are used to retrieve and manipulate data. These queries are similar to SQL queries, but instead of joining tables, they join documents based on their structure and content. Document-based queries are designed to handle large amounts of unstructured data and can be used to perform complex searches and aggregations (Kaur & Rani,2013).

In key-value NoSQL databases, such as Redis or Riak, data is stored as key-value pairs, and key-based queries are used to retrieve and manipulate data. These queries are simple and fast, and can be used to perform basic operations, such as setting, getting, or deleting a key-value pair. Key-value databases are designed for high performance and scalability and can be used for caching and session management. In column-family NoSQL databases, such as Cassandra or HBase, data is stored as columns, and column-family queries are used to retrieve and manipulate data. These queries are similar to SQL queries, but instead of using tables, they use column families to organize and group data. Column-family databases are designed for large-scale applications and can handle high volumes of data and traffic (Guo & Onstein, 2020).

In graph NoSQL databases, such as Neo4j or OrientDB, data is stored as nodes and edges, and graph-based queries are used to retrieve and manipulate data. These queries are based on graph theory and can be used to perform complex network analysis and traversal operations. Graph databases are designed for applications that require complex relationship management, such as recommendation engines, social networks, or fraud detection systems.

Querying data in NoSQL databases requires a good understanding of the data model and query language used by the database. Developers must carefully design the data model and choose the right query language to ensure efficient and effective data retrieval and manipulation. While NoSQL databases offer many advantages over SQL databases, they also require a different approach to data modeling and querying, and may not be suitable for all types of applications (Oussous et al., 2013).

6.4.4. Integration of NoSQL Databases in Web Applications

Integration of NoSQL databases in web applications involves connecting the web application to a NoSQL database and using NoSQL query languages or APIs to retrieve, modify, and delete data. Here are some key steps to integrate NoSQL databases in web applications:

1. **Choose a NoSQL Database:** Select a NoSQL DBMS that meets the requirements of the web application. Popular NoSQL databases include MongoDB, Cassandra, Redis, and Neo4j.
2. **Configure the Database:** Configure the NoSQL database by setting up user accounts, creating a database, and defining the data model.
3. **Connect to the Database:** Connect the web application to the NoSQL database using a database connector or driver. Most web frameworks provide built-in connectors or libraries for connecting to NoSQL databases (Pokorny, 2019).
4. **Write NoSQL Queries:** Use NoSQL queries or APIs to retrieve, modify, and delete data from the NoSQL database. NoSQL queries can be embedded directly into the web application code or stored in separate files.
5. **Use an Object-Document Mapping (ODM) or Object-Graph Mapping (OGM) Tool:** An ODM or OGM tool can be used to map objects in the web application code to documents or graphs in the NoSQL database. This can simplify the integration process and reduce the amount of NoSQL code that needs to be written.
6. **Implement Security Measures:** Implement security measures, such as input validation and access control, to prevent security vulnerabilities and protect sensitive data.
7. **Test and Optimize:** Test the integration of the NoSQL database in the web application and optimize the database queries for better performance (Mehmood et al., 2017).

By integrating NoSQL databases in web applications, developers can build flexible, scalable, and efficient web applications that can handle large amounts of unstructured data. NoSQL databases are a popular choice for web applications that require flexible data models, high scalability, and high performance.

6.4.5. Examples of Web Applications Using NoSQL Databases

NoSQL databases are widely used in web applications, especially for applications that require flexible data models, high scalability, and high performance. Here are some examples of popular web applications that use NoSQL databases:

1. **Airbnb:** Airbnb uses a combination of MongoDB and Cassandra to store and manage user data, such as listings, reservations, and reviews. MongoDB is used for real-time data processing and querying, while Cassandra is used for high scalability and fault-tolerance.
2. **Twitter:** Twitter uses Cassandra to store and manage user data, such as tweets, followers, and timelines. Cassandra is used for its ability to handle high volumes of data and traffic, and provide high availability and scalability (Eassa et al., 2017).
3. **Netflix:** Netflix uses a combination of NoSQL databases, including Cassandra, Elasticsearch, and Neo4j, to store and manage user data, such as movie and TV show recommendations, ratings, and viewing history. Each NoSQL database is used for a specific purpose, such as Cassandra for high scalability, Elasticsearch for fast search and aggregation, and Neo4j for graph-based recommendations.
4. **Uber:** Uber uses a combination of NoSQL databases, including Cassandra, Elasticsearch, and MySQL, to store and manage user and ride data, such as trip history, user profiles, and payments. Cassandra is used for high scalability and availability, Elasticsearch is used for fast search and aggregation, and MySQL is used for transactional consistency.
5. **Amazon:** Amazon uses a combination of NoSQL databases, including DynamoDB, Elasticsearch, and Neptune, to store and manage user data, such as product listings, customer profiles, and search history. Each NoSQL database is used for a specific purpose, such as DynamoDB for high scalability and availability, Elasticsearch for fast search and aggregation, and Neptune for graph-based recommendations (Chen & Lee, 2019).

These are just a few examples of popular web applications that use NoSQL databases. NoSQL databases are widely adopted by developers and businesses for their flexibility, scalability, and performance, and are often used in applications that require managing large amounts of unstructured data, such as social networks, e-commerce platforms, and big data analytics.

6.5. DIFFERENCES BETWEEN SQL AND NOSQL DATABASSES

SQL and NoSQL databases have some key differences in their data model, query language, scalability, and performance characteristics.

Here are some of the main differences:

1. **Data Model:** SQL databases use a structured data model based on tables with a fixed schema, while NoSQL databases use a variety of

data models, such as documents, graphs, and key-value pairs, with a flexible schema.

2. **Query Language:** SQL databases use the SQL language to interact with data, which is a standard language for relational databases. NoSQL databases use different query languages or APIs, such as document-based queries, key-based queries, or graph-based queries, depending on the data model (Sharma & Dave, 2012).
3. **Scalability:** SQL databases typically scale vertically by adding more processing power and memory to a single server. NoSQL databases scale horizontally by adding more servers to handle increased data volumes and traffic.
4. **Performance:** SQL databases are designed for transactional consistency and ACID compliance, which can slow down performance for large-scale applications. NoSQL databases sacrifice transactional consistency for scalability and performance, which makes them ideal for large-scale applications that require fast read and write operations.
5. **Complexity:** SQL databases are generally easier to manage and administer than NoSQL databases, especially for small-scale applications. NoSQL databases can be more complex to manage and administer, especially for large-scale applications with multiple data models (Shataqija et al., 2018).
6. **Community and Resources:** SQL databases have a large community of developers and resources, which makes it easy to find help and support. NoSQL databases are still relatively new compared to SQL databases, which means that there may be fewer resources and a smaller community of developers.

Overall, SQL databases are a good choice for web applications that require strict transactional consistency and ACID compliance, while NoSQL databases are a good choice for web applications that require flexible data models, high scalability, and high performance. Developers should carefully consider the requirements of their application and choose a DBMS that meets their specific needs (Tudorica & Bucur, 2011).

6.6. BEST PRACTICES FOR DATABASE INTEGRATION

Here are some best practices for integrating databases in web frameworks:

6.6.1. Use Database Drivers or ORMs

Web frameworks typically provide database drivers or ORMs that allow developers to interact with databases using a programming language. These tools provide a simple and intuitive way to execute SQL statements and retrieve data, while also protecting against security vulnerabilities such as SQL injection. ORMs can also simplify database integration by providing object-oriented syntax and handling complex queries and relationships automatically (Lerner, 2013).

6.6.2. Follow Database Normalization Rules

To ensure data consistency and reduce redundancy, it is important to follow database normalization rules when designing the database schema. This includes organizing data into tables, avoiding duplicate data, and maintaining relationships between tables. Following normalization rules can improve the performance, scalability, and reliability of the application (Demba, 2013).

6.6.3. Use Database Migrations

Database migrations are changes to the database schema or structure over time. Using database migrations ensures that changes are made in a controlled and repeatable manner, without losing data or disrupting the application. Many web frameworks provide tools for generating migration scripts automatically, and some frameworks even provide built-in support for versioning and rollbacks (Elamparithi & Anuratha, 2015) (Figure 6.10).

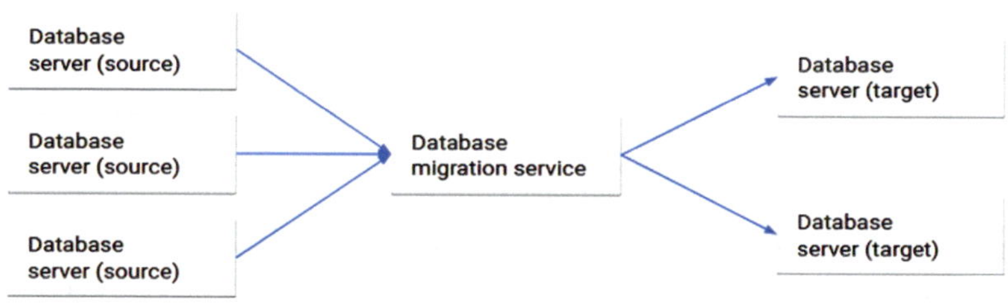

Figure 6.10. Illustration of the database migration concept.

Source: Google cloud, creative commons license.

6.6.4. Optimize Queries

Database queries can be a bottleneck for web application performance, so it is important to optimize them as much as possible. This includes using indexes, limiting the number of returned rows, and avoiding expensive operations such as joins and subqueries. Query optimization can improve the performance of the application and reduce the load on the database server (Haas et al., 1997).

6.6.5. Use Caching

Caching is a technique that stores frequently accessed data in memory, reducing the need for repeated database queries. Web frameworks provide built-in support for caching, and developers can also use external caching systems such as Redis or Memcached. Caching can improve the performance and scalability of the application, especially for read-heavy workloads (Barish & Obraczka, 2000).

6.6.6. Implement Security Measures

Web frameworks provide a range of security features to protect databases from security vulnerabilities and attacks, such as SQL injection or cross-site scripting. These features can include input validation, parameter binding, data sanitization, and access control. Web frameworks can also provide features such as encryption, hashing, and token-based authentication to further improve the security of database integration.

Overall, integrating databases in web frameworks requires careful planning, design, and implementation. Developers should follow best practices such as using database drivers or ORMs, following normalization rules, using database migrations, optimizing queries, using caching, and implementing security measures to ensure the performance, scalability, reliability, and security of the application (Merete et al., 2008).

6.7. COMMON CHALLENGES IN DATABASE INTEGRATION

Database integration is an essential part of modern web development, but it can also present several challenges that developers need to overcome. Here are some common challenges in database integration:

1. **Data Consistency:** Maintaining data consistency across multiple databases and applications can be challenging. Inconsistencies can arise due to differences in database schema, data types, and encoding. Developers need to ensure that data is synchronized and consistent across all systems.
2. **Performance:** Database queries can be a bottleneck for web application performance, especially for read-heavy workloads. Optimizing queries, using caching, and avoiding expensive operations such as joins and subqueries can improve performance, but these techniques require careful planning and implementation (Argelaguet et al., 2021).
3. **Security:** Databases are a frequent target of cyberattacks, such as SQL injection or cross-site scripting. Developers need to implement security measures such as input validation, parameter binding, data

sanitization, and access control to protect databases from security vulnerabilities and attacks.

4. **Scalability:** Databases need to be able to scale to meet the demands of growing web applications. Techniques such as sharding, replication, and load balancing can help increase database scalability, but these techniques also require careful planning and implementation.
5. **Complexity:** Database integration can increase the complexity of web application architecture, by requiring multiple DBMSs and integration layers. (Gligorijević & Przulj, 2015). Managing multiple databases and synchronization processes can be challenging, especially for large and complex applications.
6. **Cost:** Databases can be expensive to maintain and operate, especially for large and high-traffic web applications. Developers need to carefully consider the costs of database integration and choose the most appropriate DBMSs and hosting options based on the specific needs of their application

Overall, database integration presents several challenges that developers need to overcome, such as data consistency, performance, security, scalability, complexity, and cost. Developers need to carefully plan and implement database integration strategies that address these challenges, based on the specific needs of their application (Silvola et al., 2011).

ACTIVITY 6.1:

You are developing an e-commerce website that requires a database to store and manage customer information, product details, and transaction data. Compare and contrast the benefits and limitations of using SQL versus NoSQL databases for this project, and explain which one you would recommend and why.

SUMMARY

The chapter on "Database Integration: SQL and NoSQL in Internet Programming" covers the important aspects of integrating databases with web applications. The chapter starts with a definition and explanation of SQL and NoSQL databases, their differences, advantages, and disadvantages. It also covers the querying and integration of these databases into web applications, including examples of popular web frameworks such as Django, Ruby on Rails, Express.js, Flask, and Laravel. The chapter highlights the importance of database integration in internet programming and discusses the challenges that come with it, such as data consistency, performance, security, scalability, complexity, and cost. It also provides solutions to these challenges, including using appropriate tools, optimizing queries, implementing security measures, and following best practices for design and implementation. Finally, the chapter includes case studies and examples of successful database integration in web applications, including Airbnb, Netflix, Uber, LinkedIn, and Slack. These examples demonstrate the use of different database integration techniques, such as polyglot persistence, SQL and NoSQL databases, and machine learning algorithms, to achieve efficient, scalable, and secure database integration in large and complex web applications. Overall, the chapter provides a comprehensive overview of database integration in internet programming, including the benefits, challenges, solutions, and best practices. It highlights the importance of choosing the right tools and techniques to address the specific needs of the application and achieve efficient, scalable, and secure database integration.

REVIEW QUESTIONS

1. What is the difference between SQL and NoSQL databases?
2. What are some examples of popular SQL databases?
3. What are some examples of popular NoSQL databases?
4. What are the advantages and disadvantages of SQL databases?
5. What are the advantages and disadvantages of NoSQL databases?
6. What is the purpose of SQL commands?
7. How are SQL databases integrated in web applications?
8. How are NoSQL databases integrated in web applications?

MULTIPLE CHOICE QUESTIONS

1. What is the importance of database integration in internet programming?

a. It helps in reducing server load

b. It helps in improving website speed

c. It allows the use of structured data

d. All of the above

2. **Which of the following is an example of a popular SQL database?**
   a. MongoDB
   b. Cassandra
   c. Redis
   d. MySQL
3. **What are the advantages of using SQL databases?**
   a. They are easy to use
   b. They provide strong data consistency
   c. They have flexible schema design
   d. None of the above
4. **Which of the following is a SQL command?**
   a. FIND
   b. DELETE
   c. ADD
   d. UPDATE
5. **What is the purpose of querying data in NoSQL databases?**
   a. To manipulate the database schema
   b. To perform CRUD operations
   c. To retrieve specific data
   d. None of the above
6. **Which of the following is an example of a popular NoSQL database?**
   a. SQL Server
   b. Oracle
   c. Redis
   d. MongoDB
7. **What are the advantages of using NoSQL databases?**
   a. They have flexible schema design
   b. They provide strong data consistency
   c. They have a low cost of ownership
   d. None of the above
8. **What are the common challenges in database integration?**
   a. Inconsistent data across databases
   b. Security and access control

c. Integration with legacy systems
d. All of the above

Answers to Multiple Choice Questions

1. (a)	2. (c)	3. (d);	4. (b)
5. (a);	6. (c);	7. (b);	8. (d)

REFERENCES

1. Ahmed, E., Yaqoob, I., Hashem, I. A. T., Khan, I., Ahmed, A. I. A., Imran, M., & Vasilakos, A. V., (2017). The role of big data analytics in internet of things. Computer Networks, 129, 459–471.
2. Argelaguet, R., Cuomo, A. S., Stegle, O., & Marioni, J. C., (2021). Computational principles and challenges in single-cell data integration. Nature Biotechnology, 39(10), 1202–1215.
3. Barish, G., & Obraczka, K., (2000). World wide web caching: Trends and techniques. IEEE Communications Magazine, 38(5), 178–184.
4. Berger, B. J., Sohr, K., & Koschke, R., (2013). Extracting and analyzing the implemented security architecture of business applications. In: 2013 17th European Conference on Software Maintenance and Reengineering (Vol. 1, No. 1, pp. 285–294).
5. Bhogal, J., & Choksi, I., (2015). Handling big data using NoSQL. In: 2015 IEEE 29th International Conference on Advanced Information Networking and Applications Workshops, IEEE (Vol. 1, No. 1, pp. 393–398).
6. Binani, S., Gutti, A., & Upadhyay, S., (2016). SQL vs. NoSQL vs. NewSQL-a comparative study. Database, 6(1), 1–4.
7. Bjeladinovic, S., Marjanovic, Z., & Babarogic, S., (2020). A proposal of architecture for integration and uniform use of hybrid SQL/NoSQL database components. Journal of Systems and Software, 168, 110633.
8. Cattell, R., (2011). Scalable SQL and NoSQL data stores. ACM Sigmod Record, 39(4), 12–27.
9. Chen, J. K., & Lee, W. Z., (2019). An introduction of NoSQL databases based on their categories and application industries. Algorithms, 12(5), 106.
10. Culhane, D., Fantuzzo, J., Hill, M., & Burnett, T. C., (2018). Maximizing the use of integrated data systems: Understanding the challenges and advancing solutions. The Annals of the American Academy of Political and Social Science, 675(1), 221–239.
11. Deari, R., Zenuni, X., Ajdari, J., Ismaili, F., & Raufi, B., (2018). Analysis and comparison of document-based databases with SQL relational databases: MongoDB vs MySQL. In: Proceedings of the International Conference on Information (Vol. 1, No. 1, pp. 1–10).

12. Demba, M., (2013). Algorithm for relational database normalization up to 3NF. International Journal of Database Management Systems, 5(3), 39.
13. Eassa, A. M., Al-Tarawneh, O. H., El-Bakry, H. M., & Salama, A. S., (2017). NoSQL racket: A testing tool for detecting NoSQL injection attacks in web applications. International Journal of Advanced Computer Science and Applications, 8(11), 3-9.
14. Eassa, A. M., Elhoseny, M., El-Bakry, H. M., & Salama, A. S., (2018). NoSQL injection attack detection in web applications using RESTful service. Programming and Computer Software, 44, 435–444.
15. Elamparithi, M., & Anuratha, V., (2015). A review on database migration strategies, techniques and tools. World Journal of Computer Application and Technology, 3(3), 41–48.
16. Fegaras, L., & Maier, D., (2000). Optimizing object queries using an effective calculus. ACM Transactions on Database Systems (TODS), 25(4), 457–516.
17. Gligorijević, V., & Pržulj, N., (2015). Methods for biological data integration: Perspectives and challenges. Journal of the Royal Society Interface, 12(112), 20150571.
18. Guo, D., & Onstein, E., (2020). State-of-the-art geospatial information processing in NoSQL databases. ISPRS International Journal of Geo-Information, 9(5), 331.
19. Haas, L. M., Kossmann, D., Wimmers, E. L., & Yang, J., (1997). Optimizing queries across diverse data sources. In: VLDB (Vol. 97, pp. 25–29).
20. Halfond, W. G., Orso, A., & Manolios, P., (2006). Using positive tainting and syntax-aware evaluation to counter SQL injection attacks. In: Proceedings of the 14th ACM SIGSOFT International Symposium on Foundations of Software Engineering (Vol. 1, No. 1, pp. 175–185).
21. Han, J., Haihong, E., Le, G., & Du, J., (2011). Survey on NoSQL database. In: 2011 6th International Conference on Pervasive Computing and Applications (pp. 363–366). IEEE.
22. Huang, B., Jiang, B., & Li, H., (2001). An integration of GIS, virtual reality and the internet for visualization, analysis and exploration of spatial data. International Journal of Geographical Information Science, 15(5), 439–456.
23. Jagadish, H. V., Gehrke, J., Labrinidis, A., Papakonstantinou, Y., Patel, J. M., Ramakrishnan, R., & Shahabi, C., (2014). Big data and its technical challenges. Communications of the ACM, 57(7), 86–94.
24. Jamison, D. C., (2003). Structured query language (SQL) fundamentals. Current Protocols in Bioinformatics, (1), 2–9.
25. Kaur, K., & Rani, R., (2013). Modeling and querying data in NoSQL databases. In: 2013 IEEE International Conference on Big Data (Vol. 1, No. 1, pp. 1–7).
26. Khodadadi, F., Dastjerdi, A. V., & Buyya, R., (2016). Internet of things: An overview. Internet of Things, 1(1), 3–27.
27. Lawrence, R., (2014). Integration and virtualization of relational SQL and NoSQL systems including MySQL and MongoDB. In: 2014 International Conference on

Computational Science and Computational Intelligence (Vol. 1, pp. 285–290). IEEE.

28. Leavitt, N., (2010). Will NoSQL databases live up to their promise? Computer, 43(2), 12–14.
29. Lerner, R. M., (2013). At the forge: SQL alchemy. Linux Journal, 2013(226), 5.
30. Liao, Y. T., Zhou, J., Lu, C. H., Chen, S. C., Hsu, C. H., Chen, W., & Chung, Y. C., (2016). Data adapter for querying and transformation between SQL and NoSQL database. Future Generation Computer Systems, 65, 111–121.
31. Liu, Z. H., Hammerschmidt, B., McMahon, D., Liu, Y., & Chang, H. J., (2016). Closing the functional and performance gap between SQL and NoSQL. In: Proceedings of the 2016 International Conference on Management of Data (Vol. 1, No. 1, pp. 227–238).
32. Markatos, E. P., (2001). On caching search engine query results. Computer Communications, 24(2), 137–143.
33. Mason, R. T., (2015). NoSQL databases and data modeling techniques for a document-oriented NoSQL database. In: Proceedings of Informing Science & IT Education Conference (InSITE) (Vol. 3, No. 4, pp. 259–268).
34. Mehmood, N. Q., Culmone, R., & Mostarda, L., (2017). Modeling temporal aspects of sensor data for MongoDB NoSQL database. Journal of Big Data, 4(1), 8.
35. Merete, H. J., Albrechtsen, E., & Hovden, J., (2008). Implementation and effectiveness of organizational information security measures. Information Management & Computer Security, 16(4), 377–397.
36. Nayak, A., Poriya, A., & Poojary, D., (2013). Type of NOSQL databases and its comparison with relational databases. International Journal of Applied Information Systems, 5(4), 16–19.
37. Netz, A., Chaudhuri, S., Fayyad, U., & Bernhardt, J., (2001). Integrating data mining with SQL databases: OLE DB for data mining. In: Proceedings 17th International Conference on Data Engineering (Vol. 1, No. 1, 379–387). IEEE.
38. Oussous, A., Benjelloun, F. Z., Lahcen, A. A., & Belfkih, S., (2013). Comparison and classification of NoSQL databases for big data. International Journal of Database Theory and Application, 6(4), 1-5.
39. Parker, Z., Poe, S., & Vrbsky, S. V., (2013). Comparing NoSQL MongoDB to an SQL db. In: Proceedings of the 51st ACM Southeast Conference (Vol. 1, No. 1, pp. 1–6).
40. Pokorný, J., (2019). Integration of relational and NoSQL databases. Vietnam Journal of Computer Science, 6(04), 389–405.
41. Sahatqija, K., Ajdari, J., Zenuni, X., Raufi, B., & Ismaili, F., (2018). Comparison between relational and NOSQL databases. In: 2018 41st International Convention on Information and Communication Technology, Electronics and Microelectronics (MIPRO) (Vol. 1, No. 1, 0216–0221). IEEE.
42. Sallam, A., Fadolalkarim, D., Bertino, E., & Xiao, Q., (2016). Data and syntax centric anomaly detection for relational databases. Wiley Interdisciplinary Reviews: Data Mining and Knowledge Discovery, 6(6), 231–239.

43. Scott, D., & Sharp, R., (2002). Developing secure web applications. IEEE Internet Computing, 6(6), 38–45.
44. Sequeda, J. F., Tirmizi, S. H., Corcho, O., & Miranker, D. P., (2011). Survey of directly mapping SQL databases to the semantic web. The Knowledge Engineering Review, 26(4), 445–486.
45. Sharma, P., Johari, R., & Sarma, S. S., (2012). Integrated approach to prevent SQL injection attack and reflected cross site scripting attack. International Journal of System Assurance Engineering and Management, 3, 343–351.
46. Sharma, V., & Dave, M., (2012). SQL and NoSQL databases. International Journal of Advanced Research in Computer Science and Software Engineering, 2(8), 1–20.
47. Silva, Y. N., Almeida, I., & Queiroz, M., (2016). SQL: From traditional databases to big data. In: Proceedings of the 47th ACM Technical Symposium on Computing Science Education (Vol. 1, No. 1, pp. 413–418).
48. Silvola, R., Jaaskelainen, O., Kropsu□Vehkapera, H., & Haapasalo, H., (2011). Managing one master data–challenges and preconditions. Industrial Management & Data Systems, 111(1), 146–162.
49. Stonebraker, M., (2010). SQL databases v. NoSQL databases. Communications of the ACM, 53(4), 10, 11.
50. Strauch, C., Sites, U. L. S., & Kriha, W., (2011). NoSQL databases. Lecture Notes, Stuttgart Media University, 20(24), 79.
51. Tatbul, N., (2010). Streaming data integration: Challenges and opportunities. In: 2010 IEEE 26th International Conference on Data Engineering Workshops (ICDEW 2010) (pp. 155–158). IEEE.
52. Tudorica, B. G., & Bucur, C., (2011). A comparison between several NoSQL databases with comments and notes. In: 2011 RoEduNet International Conference 10th Edition: Networking in Education and Research (Vol. 1, No. 1, pp. 1–5).
53. Tuya, J., Suarez-Cabal, M. J., & De La Riva, C., (2006). SQLMutation: A tool to generate mutants of SQL database queries. In: Second Workshop on Mutation Analysis (Mutation 2006-ISSRE Workshops 2006) (Vol. 1, No. 1, pp. 1). IEEE.

CHAPTER 7

WEB APPLICATION SECURITY

UNIT INTRODUCTION

Web security for applications is unquestionably a hot-button issue nowadays. The stakes are enormous for everyone involved: companies that depend increasingly on online sales, consumers who give sensitive information to web applications, and criminals who can profit greatly by stealing payment information or hacking bank accounts. A crucial factor is a reputation.

Few companies like to reveal information about their security weaknesses or breaches since few consumers want to conduct business with an unsecured website. Finding accurate information regarding the current state of security for web apps is, therefore, not an easy process (Li & Xue, 2011).

This chapter briefly examines the development of web apps and their numerous advantages. Based on the author's knowledge, some stats on current web application vulnerabilities show that most apps are insecure.

Outline the main security issue web apps face—that users can provide arbitrary input—and the different aspects that make up their lax security posture. Finally, discuss the most recent security developments for web applications and how they may change shortly (Curphey & Arawo, 2006).

Learning Objectives

- At the end of this chapter, readers will be able to:
- Understand the concept of web application security
- Identify the core security problem in web applications
- Recognize the key problem factors that make web application security challenging
- Understand the concept of underdeveloped security awareness
- Understand the concept of custom development and its impact on web application security
- Recognize the challenges posed by deceptive simplicity in web application security
- Understand the impact of a rapidly evolving threat profile on web application security
- Recognize the impact of resource and time constraints on web application security
- Understand the impact of overextended technologies and increasing demands on functionality on web application security

Key Terms

- Custom Development
- Deceptive Simplicity
- Increasing Demands on Functionality
- Overextended Technologies
- Rapidly Evolving Threat Profile
- Resource and Time Constraints
- Security Perimeter
- Security Problem
- Underdeveloped Security Awareness
- Web Application Security

7.1. OVERVIEW OF WEB APPLICATION SECURITY

Web apps bring new security vulnerabilities, as with every new technology class. The list of problems that are most frequently found has changed throughout time.

Existing apps have been subject to new threats not considered when created. Some issues have decreased in frequency as public knowledge has grown. New technologies have emerged, opening up new opportunities for exploitation. Changes to internet browser software have made several categories of bugs mostly obsolete (Figure 7.1).

Figure 7.1. Illustration of the web application security and its components.

Source: Adam Murray, creative commons license.

Attacks on web apps that reveal sensitive information or get no limitation to the servers that the program is running on are the most dangerous. Such high-profile concessions continue to happen frequently.

However, any attack resulting in system downtime is critical for many firms. Application-level denial-of-service (DoS) attacks may accomplish the same goals as conventional infrastructure resource exhaustion assaults.

However, they are frequently employed in conjunction with subtler methods and goals. They may be employed to obstruct a specific user or service to outperform rivals in the markets related to financial trading, playing games, online bidding, & ticketing (Huang et al., 2017) (Figure 7.2).

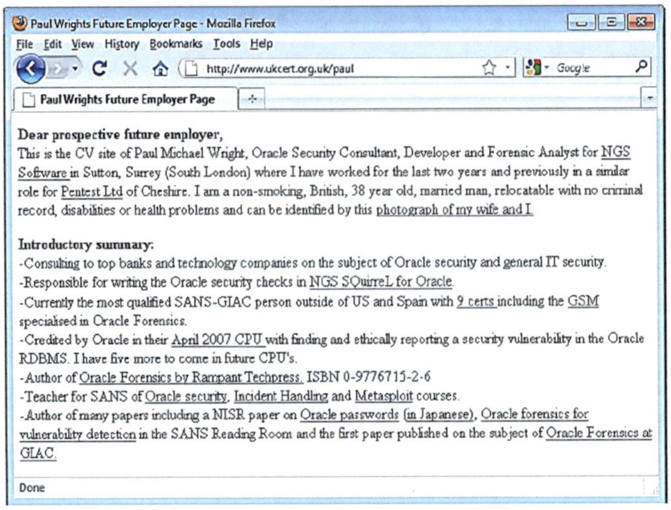

Figure 7.2. A traditional website containing static information.

Compromises of well-known web applications have continued to make headlines during this progression. There is no indication that a turning point has been reached or that these security issues are abating. With a decrease in certain measures, security for web applications is currently the most important front in the conflict between attackers and people who need to protect their computer resources and data, which is expected to continue for the foreseeable future.

Many people are aware that online applications' security is a problem. One can find reassurance that an application is secure by consulting its FAQ page (Huang et al., 2003).

The majority of programs claim to be secure since they employ SSL. For instance:

- This website is 100 percent secure. It has been created to utilize 128-bit SSL (Secure Sockets Layer) encryption to shield the information from unwanted users. Knowing the staff is protecting the data, one can confidently use this website.

Users are frequently advised to check the website's certificate, commend the sophisticated cryptographic protocols in utilize, and, as a result, trust it when providing their personal information.

To convince users that their data is secure, firms more frequently mention that services adhere to Payment Card Association (PCI) standards. An illustration:

We are very serious about security. The website is inspected daily to ensure PCI compliance remains secure from hackers. One may verify that this site is secure by looking at the emblem below, which displays the day of the most recent scan.

Despite the broad acceptance of PCI scanning and the extensive use of SSL technology, most web-based applications must be more secure (Meier, 2006). In recent years, the book's authors have evaluated hundreds of online apps. Figure 7.3 displays the percentage of applications assessed between 2007 and 2011 that were determined to be vulnerable to various common vulnerability types:

1. **Broken Authentication (62%):** This group of vulnerabilities includes several flaws in the application's login process that could let an attacker guess weak passwords, conduct an attack using brute force, or get around the login process altogether.
2. **Broken Access Controls (71%):** This pertains to situations where the program neglects to adequately secure access to its information and functionality, potentially allowing an attacker to read sensitive information stored on the server that belongs to other users or perform privileged operations.
3. **SQL Injection (32%):** An attacker can prevent the application from communicating with back-end databases using specially constructed input. An attacker might be able to access the application, retrieve any data they want, mess with its logic, or run instructions directly on the database server.
4. **Cross-site Scripting (94%):** This flaw allows an attacker to target other application users, perhaps getting access to their data, acting on their behalf without their knowledge, or engaging in other attacks against them (Musa et al., 2015).
5. **Information Leakage (78%):** This refers to situations where an application discloses private information that an attacker can use to create an attack against the program due to poor error handling or other actions.
6. **Cross-site Request Forgery (92%):** This flaw indicates that, depending on their user context & privilege level, application users may be persuaded to take undesired actions on the application. Due to the flaw, a malicious website the target user visited could communicate with the application and carry out tasks that the individual did not want (Huang et al., 2005).

Did you Know?

According to a 2021 report by Positive Technologies, over 70% of web applications contain at least one high-severity vulnerability, highlighting the importance of implementing strong web application security measures?

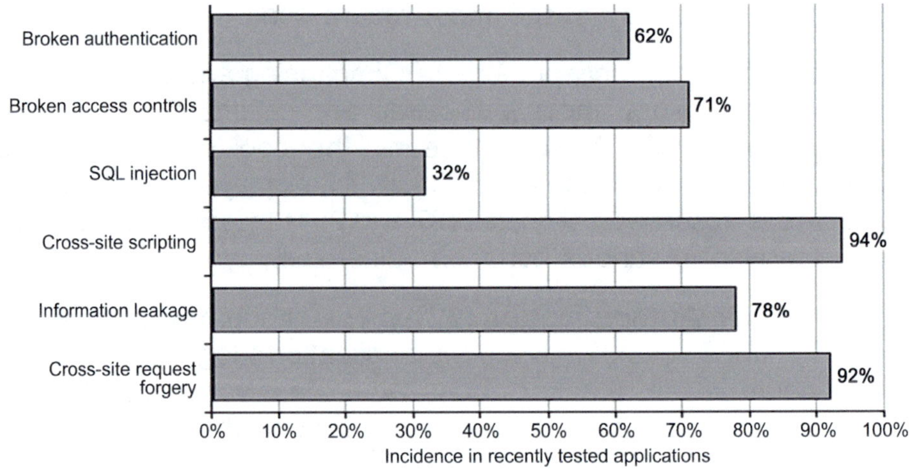

Figure 7.3. The incidence of some common web application vulnerabilities in applications recently tested by the authors (based on a sample of more than 100).

A great solution for ensuring the secrecy & integrity of data while it is being transmitted between a user's browser and a web server is SSL. It aids in preventing listen-ins and guarantees the user that the server he is communicating with is who it claims to be. However, unlike the majority of successful assaults, it does not prevent attacks that focus on the server and client aspects of an application. In particular, it does not guard against most of the vulnerabilities that were just mentioned or many others that might leave an application extremely vulnerable to attack. Despite using SSL, the majority of web applications still have security issues (Noman et al., 2020).

7.2. THE CORE SECURITY PROBLEM

Web apps have a basic issue that needs to be solved to be secure, just like most distributed programs. Users can provide any input to a server-side application because the client is not under the program's control. The application must regard all input as potentially harmful. It must therefore take precautions to guarantee that attackers cannot compromise the program by tampering with its logic or behavior, getting unapproved access to its data, and functioning using crafted input.

This fundamental issue appears in several ways: Users can alter any data sent between a client and a server, including cookies, HTTP headers, and request parameters. Input validation checks and other client-side security measures can be readily gotten through (Jing et al., 2014). Users can submit requests in any order and parameters anytime, including later than the application anticipates. Developers may breach any assumptions regarding how users will use the product. n Users cannot access the program simply through a web browser. Many widely accessible tools may be used with or without a browser to attack web applications. These programs can generate many queries quickly and make requests that a browser wouldn't typically make to detect and exploit issues.

Most web application attacks involve delivering specially designed information to the server, generating an outcome that the application's creator neither intended nor anticipated. Here are a few carefully designed input submissions that accomplish this goal:

1. Modifying a product's pricing and sending it through a secret HTML form field to fraudulently purchase it for less money.
2. Altering a session token sent in an HTTP cookie to steal another authenticated user's session
3. Eliminating some parameters that are typically given to take advantage of a processing flaw in the application
4. Modifying some input that would be used to access sensitive data via a back-end database to insert a malicious data query.

SSL does not affect an attacker's ability to trick the server into accepting their input (Suo et al., 2012). If the application employs SSL, it simply implies that the attacker's data cannot be viewed or altered while other users transmit it across the network. Since she controls her portion of the SSL tunnel, the attacker can send whatever she wants to the servers through this tunnel. Despite what its FAQ may claim, the application is categorically weak if any of the above are effective (Gollmann, 2010).

7.3. KEY PROBLEM FACTORS

Any time a web application needs to accept and process potentially harmful data that is untrustworthy, a security issue develops. However, some elements have come together in the context of web apps to worsen the issue and explain why the number of applications available on the web today is so ineffective at solving it (Nabil et al., 2011).

7.3.1. Underdeveloped Security Awareness

Although there has been an increase in web application security awareness in recent years, it still needs to be more advanced than in more established fields like networks and computing systems. Although most professionals understand the fundamentals of hardening hosts and safeguarding networks, there still needs to be more understanding and certainty regarding many main ideas related to web application security. The task of a developer of web applications increasingly entails combining dozens, possibly many hundreds of third-party packages, all of which are intended to shield the developer from the technologies that underlie the app. It is typical to encounter seasoned developers of web applications who hold unfounded beliefs about the security offered by their coding framework and are shocked to learn that many common defects exist (Prokhorenko et al., 2016) (Figure 7.4).

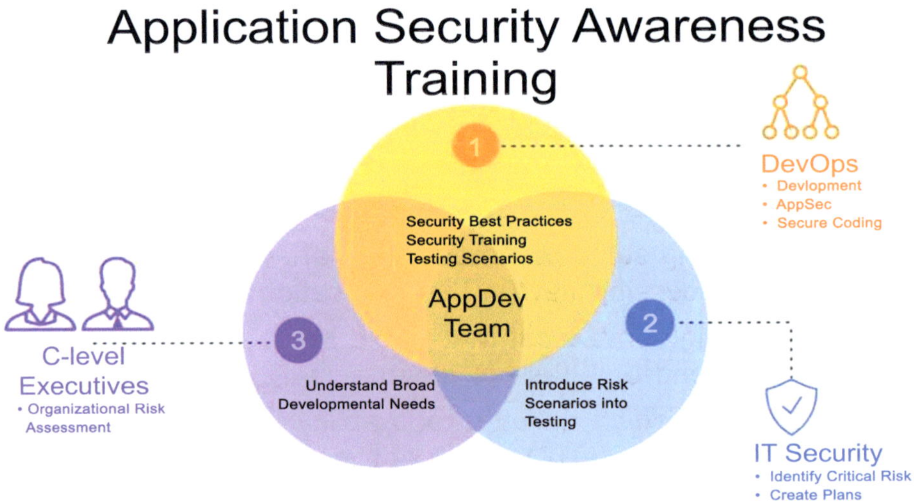

Figure 7.4. Awareness training on security of applications.

Source: The siliconreview, creative commons license.

7.3.2. Custom Development

The majority of web apps are created internally by employees of an organization or by outside contractors. Even though an application uses tried-and-true parts, these are usually modified or welded with new code. Every application is distinct in this case and can have different flaws. This contrasts with a traditional infrastructure deployment when a company can buy the best product available and install it by best practices (Antunes et al., 2022).

7.3.3. Deceptive Simplicity

With the web app platforms and development tools available today, even a non-programmer may quickly build a robust application from scratch. But writing useful code and writing secure code are two very different things. Many online applications are developed by well-intentioned people who lack the expertise and experience to recognize potential security issues. Application frameworks, which offer ready-made code elements to handle a variety of common functional areas, including authentication, page templates, forums, or interaction with standard back-end infrastructure components, have become a popular trend in recent years. Liferay and Appfuse are a couple of these frameworks as examples. Without understanding how the apps function or the possible hazards they might include, these products enable the quick and simple creation of functional applications. This implies that numerous businesses employ the same frameworks. As a result, once a vulnerability is found, it impacts other unrelated applications (Shahid et al., 2022).

Remember

Web application security can often be deceptively simple, leading to vulnerabilities that can be exploited by attackers.

7.3.4. Rapidly Evolving Threat Profile

Web application attack and defense research is still a thriving field where new ideas and dangers are developed more quickly than is currently the case for earlier technologies.

Research that reveals a novel attack technique frequently undermines the established protections against a specific assault, especially on the client side. By the time the program is finished and launched, the team of developers that starts a project with full knowledge of current dangers might have lost this status (Watson, 2007).

7.3.5. Resource and Time Constraints

Due to the economics of internal, one-off development, the majority of the development of web application projects is bound by stringent time and resource limitations. Employing specialized security knowledge in designing or developing teams is frequently impractical in most firms.

Additionally, because of project slippage, testing for security by experts is frequently postponed until the end of the project's life cycle. The necessity to create a stable & functional program before a deadline typically takes precedence over less obvious security considerations when weighing conflicting goals. A couple of person-days of assistance may be acceptable compensation for a typical small firm to test a new application. Quick penetration tests frequently locate the easy targets, but they could miss more subtle weaknesses that take time and persistence (Wang et al., 2016).

7.3.6. Overextended Technologies

Many fundamental technologies were developed in web apps when the World Wide Web's (WWWs) environment significantly differed. Since then, they have been used for much more than initially intended, as evidenced by using JavaScript as a data transmission method in many AJAX-based apps. The technologies utilized to provide this capability have trailed behind the curve. Expectations for web application capabilities have grown quickly, with outdated technology being stretched and modified to match new requirements. Unexpected side effects have, naturally, led to security problems (Jazayeri, 2007).

7.3.7. Increasing Demands on Functionality

Applications are primarily created with usability and usefulness in mind. Since user profiles used to be static, social networking capabilities like picture uploads and wiki-style page editing are available. When creating the login capability, a password and username challenge would have sufficed for an application creator just a few decades ago. A password recovery option, username recovery, password clues, and the option to remember the password and username for subsequent visits are all common features of modern websites. Such a website would tout its many security measures, but each is a self-service feature that increases its attack surface (Urbieta et al., 2012).

7.4. THE NEW SECURITY PERIMETER

Before the emergence of web applications, businesses' defenses against outside assault mainly revolved around the network perimeter. Hardening or upgrading the services it wanted to expose or firewalling access for others were required to defend this perimeter.

This has all changed thanks to web applications. The perimeter firewall has to permit inbound connections to reach the server via HTTP or HTTPS for the users of an application to access it. In addition, the server's ability to connect to necessary back-end systems, including databases, mainframes, and accounting and logistics systems, is required for the application to work. These systems, frequently at the heart of an organization's activities, are hidden behind several network-level security measures (Walden, 2008) (Figure 7.5).

Let's assume a web application has a weakness. In such instances, a hacker using the open Internet might be able to corrupt a company's main back-end systems just by sending specially designed information through his web browser. The organization's network defenses are completely bypassed by this data, just like regular, benign web application traffic.

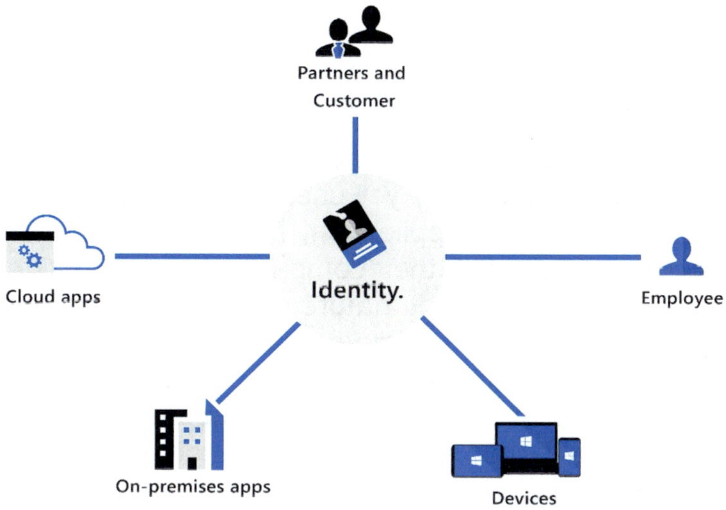

Figure 7.5. Schematic of identity as new security perimeter.

Source: Test prep training, creative commons license.

The result of the widespread use of web applications is a change in the location of a typical organization's security perimeter. Firewalls & bastion hosts still function as a portion of that perimeter. However, the company's web applications currently occupy a considerable portion. Web applications are vulnerable to various assaults because of the various ways they collect user input and transmit it to crucial back-end services. As a result, defenses over such assaults must be included in the apps themselves. A company's internal systems can become vulnerable due to just one line of incorrect code in one web application (Perera et al., 2016).

Furthermore, the server-side security barrier frequently goes much beyond the boundaries of the company itself with the development of mash-up programs, third-party widgets, and additional methods for cross-domain integration. The capabilities of external programs and services are implicitly trusted. Every firm should pause for reflection after reading the facts on the prevalence of vulnerabilities inside this new security perimeter.

The dangers that users encounter when using an insecure application are the cause of a second manner that web apps have shifted the security perimeter. A malicious attacker can use a harmless but susceptible online application to target every person who views it. The attacker may utilize the user's browser to attack the nearby network from the user's trusted position if the user is on an internal business network. The target might be able to accomplish any action the user could if she acted maliciously without the user's assistance. The size of the client-side attacking surface has significantly expanded due to the widespread use of browser extension technologies and plug-ins (Davidson & Yoran, 2007).

The prevention of users visiting harmful websites is a practice known to network managers, yet users are growing conscious of this danger. An insecure application, however, may pose just as much of a risk to its users & their company as an openly malevolent website due to the inherent nature of its vulnerabilities. As a result, the updated safety perimeter mandates that all application owners defend their clients from attacks launched through the application (Lebeau et al., 2013). The widespread usage of email as an additional authentication method is another way the security boundary has partially shifted to the client side. Many modern programs have a "forgotten password" feature that lets an attacker create and send an account restoration e-mail to any known address without additional user-specific data. This makes it simple for an attacker to escalate the attack and compromise the victim's accounts on most web apps with which the victim has registered after taking over the user's webmail account (Subashini & Kavitha, 2011).

TIPS

Keeping up-to-date with the latest security trends and implementing strong security measures is crucial for protecting web applications from potential cyberattacks.

7.5. THE FUTURE OF WEB APPLICATION SECURITY

Web applications are still plagued with flaws on the Internet today, more than ten years after they were widely used. The industry currently needs a thorough understanding of the security vulnerabilities that online applications face and practical solutions to these problems. There are currently few signs that the issue factors mentioned in this section will disappear anytime soon.

However, the specifics of the internet application security landscape are always changing. Even though well-known and dated vulnerabilities like SQL injection keep popping up, their frequency is rapidly declining. Additionally, locating and taking advantage of the instances still around is getting harder. Most recent work in these fields has been directed at creating sophisticated methods for tackling vulnerabilities that, until recently, could be easily spotted and exploited using merely a browser (Clincy & Shahriar, 2018).

The gradual change in focus from attacks on the application's server side to those aimed at application users is a second notable trend. The latter attack still takes advantage of flaws in the susceptible program, but it typically includes interacting with another user to compromise that person's interactions with the application (Rafique et al., 2015). This pattern has been observed in other software security domains. The client-side remains a crucial battleground when the learning process progresses because server-side issues are the first to be properly understood and fixed as knowledge of security dangers grows. The attacks covered in this book that target other users are the ones that are advancing the fastest and have received the majority of academic attention in recent years.

The landscape of web-based applications has changed due to recent technological advances (Xie et al., 2011). The most common and incorrect buzzwords used to describe these changes in public perception are these:

1. **Web 2.0:** This term describes the increased usage of technologies that facilitate user-generated material and knowledge sharing, such as asynchronous requests via HTTP and cross-domain interaction.
2. **Cloud Computing:** This phrase describes an increasing reliance on outside service providers for many components of the technological stack, such as software for apps, applications platforms, web server programs, databases, including hardware. Additionally, it alludes to a rise in the use of virtualization technologies in hosting environments (Seh at al., 2022).

As with technological advancements, these trends have produced new attacks and modifications to previous attacks. Despite the hoopla, the concerns are not as ground-breaking as they might first appear to be. Throughout this book, we shall discuss the security effects of such and other current trends at the proper places.

Despite all the modifications to web programs, several "classic" vulnerability types continue to exist. They still appear in the same manner as in the web's early years. These include errors in the application of access controls, faulty business logic, and other design flaws. These enduring difficulties will likely be pervasive even in an age of bolted-together application parts and everything-as-a-service (Dalai & Jena, 2011).

ACTIVITY 7.1:

You are working on a team that is responsible for maintaining the security of a web application that stores sensitive user data. Describe the steps you would take to assess and mitigate potential security risks, such as SQL injection, cross-site scripting, and authentication vulnerabilities.

SUMMARY

The WWW has developed over a decade from static information warehouses to highly functional apps that process sensitive information and take decisive actions with lasting effects. The bulk of modern online apps has a weak security posture due to several factors combined during their development. The main security issue that most programs deal with is that users can enter arbitrary data. Unless proven otherwise, every part of a user's interaction using the application has the potential to be malevolent. Applications may become exposed to attacks in various ways if this issue is not addressed effectively. All available information on the present state of security for web applications shows that, despite some security-related improvements, completely new risks have emerged to take their place. No appreciable progress has been made toward solving the issue overall. Web application attacks continue to pose an important danger to both the businesses that utilize them and the users that access them.

REVIEW QUESTIONS

1. What is web application security and why is it important?
2. What are the key problem factors in web application security?
3. How does custom development contribute to the security problem in web application security?
4. What is the new security perimeter in web application security and how does it affect security measures?
5. What are the future implications of web application security?
6. How can increasing demands on functionality contribute to the security problem in web application security?
7. What are some best practices for addressing the security problem in web application security?

MULTIPLE CHOICE QUESTIONS

1. What is the core security problem in web application security?

a. Underdeveloped security awareness
b. Custom development
c. Deceptive simplicity
d. Rapidly evolving threat profile

2. Which factor contributes to the new security perimeter in web application security?

a. Resource and time constraints
b. Overextended technologies

c. Increasing demands on functionality

d. All of the above

3. What is the future of web application security?

a. Uncertain

b. Secure

c. Vulnerable

d. None of the above

4. What is the most common factor contributing to the security problem in web application security?

a. Resource and time constraints

b. Increasing demands on functionality

c. Rapidly evolving threat profile

d. Custom development

5. What is the importance of security awareness in web application security?

a. It helps in custom development

b. It helps in identifying overextended technologies

c. It helps in identifying and addressing security threats

d. It helps in meeting increasing demands on functionality

6. What is the significance of the new security perimeter in web application security?

a. It expands the scope of security from traditional network boundaries to application boundaries

b. It reduces the scope of security to traditional network boundaries only

c. It eliminates the need for security measures in web applications

d. None of the above

Answers to Multiple Choice Questions

1. (d) 2. (d) 3. (a) 4. (d) 5. (c) 6. (a)

REFERENCES

1. Ami, P. V., & Malav, S. C., (2013). Top five dangerous security risks over web application. International Journal of Emerging Trends & Technology in Computer Science, 2(1), 41–43.

2. Antunes, M., Maximiano, M., & Gomes, R., (2022). A customizable web platform to manage standards compliance of information security and cybersecurity auditing.

Procedia Computer Science, 196, 36–43.

3. Auronen, L., (2002). Tool-Based Approach to Assessing Web Application Security (Vol. 11, pp. 12, 13). Helsinki University of Technology.
4. Aydos, M., Aldan, Ç., Coşkun, E., & Soydan, A., (2022). Security testing of web applications: A systematic mapping of the literature. Journal of King Saud University-Computer and Information Sciences, 34(9), 6775–6792.
5. Clincy, V., & Shahriar, H., (2018). Web application firewall: Network security models and configuration. In: 2018 IEEE 42nd Annual Computer Software and Applications Conference (COMPSAC) (Vol. 1, pp. 835, 836).
6. Curphey, M., & Arawo, R., (2006). Web application security assessment tools. IEEE Security & Privacy, 4(4), 32–41.
7. Dalai, A. K., & Jena, S. K., (2011). Evaluation of web application security risks and secure design patterns. In: Proceedings of the 2011 International Conference on Communication, Computing & Security (Vol. 1, No. 1, pp. 565–568).
8. Davidson, M. A., & Yoran, E., (2007). Enterprise security for web 2.0. Computer, 40(11), 117–119.
9. Gollmann, D., (2010). Computer security. Wiley Interdisciplinary Reviews: Computational Statistics, 2(5), 544–554.
10. Huang, H. C., Zhang, Z. K., Cheng, H. W., & Shieh, S. W., (2017). Web application security: Threats, countermeasures, and pitfalls. Computer, 50(6), 81–85.
11. Huang, Y. W., Huang, S. K., Lin, T. P., & Tsai, C. H., (2003). Web application security assessment by fault injection and behavior monitoring. In: Proceedings of the 12th International Conference on World Wide Web (Vol. 1, No. 1, pp. 148–159).
12. Huang, Y. W., Tsai, C. H., Lin, T. P., Huang, S. K., Lee, D. T., & Kuo, S. Y., (2005). A testing framework for web application security assessment. Computer Networks, 48(5), 739–761.
13. Jazayeri, M., (2007). Some trends in web application development. In: Future of Software Engineering (FOSE'07) (Vol. 1, No. 1, 199–213).
14. Jing, Q., Vasilakos, A. V., Wan, J., Lu, J., & Qiu, D., (2014). Security of the internet of things: perspectives and challenges. Wireless Networks, 20, 2481–2501.
15. Lebeau, F., Legeard, B., Peureux, F., & Vernotte, A., (2013). Model-based vulnerability testing for web applications. In: 2013 IEEE Sixth International Conference on Software Testing, Verification and Validation Workshops (Vol. 1, No. 1, pp. 445–452).
16. Li, X., & Xue, Y., (2011). A survey on web application security (Vol. 25, No. 5, pp. 1–14). Nashville, TN USA.
17. Meier, J. D., (2006). Web application security engineering. IEEE Security & Privacy, 4(4), 16–24.
18. Musa, S. B., Md Norwawi, N., Selamat, M. H., & Al-Alwani, A., (2015). Systematic review of web application security development model. Artificial Intelligence Review, 43, 259–276.

19. Nabil, D., Mosad, A., & Hefny, H. A., (2011). Web-based applications quality factors: A survey and a proposed conceptual model. Egyptian Informatics Journal, 12(3), 211–217.
20. Noman, M., Iqbal, M., & Manzoor, A., (2020). A survey on detection and prevention of web vulnerabilities. International Journal of Advanced Computer Science and Applications, 11(6), 1–20.
21. Perera, A. C., Kesavan, K., Bannakkotuwa, S. V., Liyanapathirana, C., & Rupasinghe, L., (2016). E-commerce (WEB) application security: Defense against reconnaissance. In: 2016 IEEE International Conference on Computer and Information Technology (CIT) (Vol. 1, No. 1, pp. 732–742).
22. Prokhorenko, V., Choo, K. K. R., & Ashman, H., (2016). Web application protection techniques: A taxonomy. Journal of Network and Computer Applications, 60, 95–112.
23. Rafique, S., Humayun, M., Gul, Z., Abbas, A., & Javed, H., (2015). Systematic review of web application security vulnerabilities detection methods. Journal of Computer and Communications, 3(9), 28.
24. Seh, A. H., Al-Amri, J. F., Subahi, A. F., Ansari, M. T. J., Kumar, R., Bokhari, M. U., & Khan, R. A., (2022). Hybrid computational modeling for web application security assessment. CMC-Comput., Mater. Continua, 70(1), 469–489.
25. Shahid, W. B., Aslam, B., Abbas, H., Afzal, H., & Khalid, S. B., (2022). A deep learning assisted personalized deception system for countering web application attacks. Journal of Information Security and Applications, 67, 103169.
26. Subashini, S., & Kavitha, V., (2011). A survey on security issues in service delivery models of cloud computing. Journal of Network and Computer Applications, 34(1), 1–11.
27. Suo, H., Wan, J., Zou, C., & Liu, J., (2012). Security in the internet of things: A review. In: 2012 International Conference on Computer Science and Electronics Engineering (Vol. 3, pp. 648–651). IEEE.
28. Urbieta, M., Rossi, G., Distante, D., & Ginzburg, J., (2012). Modeling, deploying, and controlling volatile functionalities in web applications. International Journal of Software Engineering and Knowledge Engineering, 22(01), 129–155.
29. Walden, J., (2008). Integrating web application security into the IT curriculum. In: Proceedings of the 9th ACM SIGITE Conference on Information Technology Education (Vol. 1, No. 1, pp. 187–192).
30. Wang, D., Wang, Z., Shen, B., Alsaadi, F. E., & Hayat, T., (2016). Recent advances on filtering and control for cyber-physical systems under security and resource constraints. Journal of the Franklin Institute, 353(11), 2451–2466.
31. Watson, D., (2007). The evolution of web application attacks. Network Security, 2007(11), 7–12.
32. Weissman, C. D., & Bobrowski, S., (2009). The design of the force. com multitenant internet application development platform. In: Proceedings of the 2009 ACM SIGMOD

International Conference on Management of Data (Vol. 1, No. 1, pp. 889–896).

33. Xie, J., Chu, B., Lipford, H. R., & Melton, J. T., (2011). ASIDE: IDE support for web application security. In: Proceedings of the 27th Annual Computer Security Applications Conference (Vol. 1, No. 1, pp. 267–276).

CHAPTER 8

PERFORMANCE METHODOLOGIES OF INTERNET PROGRAMMING

UNIT INTRODUCTION

Regardless of its use, internet technologies have been identified as a critical component in computing systems that affect performance. Since systems continue to creep further into our personal lives and sense, process and save various forms of data, data protection is the primary research area of Internet technology. This circumstance presents several security and privacy-related concerns, particularly for applications running on resource-constrained systems. The appraiser chose tried-and-true data protection measures to ensure data confidentiality and integrity. The effectiveness of various cryptographic block and flow ciphers, hashing algorithms, message authentication codes, signature techniques, and critical exchange protocols on the most sophisticated resource limiter systems is examined. Their results make it easier to compute performance/data protection thresholds and to design and construct secure Internet technology systems by providing restriction and data throughput values.

Millions of machines are expected to be connected with other devices using Internet technology. Numerous aspects of Internet technologies, such as cyber security, have received extensive academic attention. Nonetheless, the study focused on how to identify and secure Internet technology. They believe it is too significant to investigate how Web technology's integer arithmetic would respond whenever Internet technology platforms generate vast amounts of information. They also want to ensure that the existing network additions won't cause any issues since the current services could stop working.

Furthermore, security and confidentiality are significant concerns for Internet technologies. Safety and privacy played a dual role in this chapter. Initially, they investigated the performance topics of Internet technologies and network deductions for metrics such as latency, stress, and bandwidth, among others. Researchers then examined the operating costs incurred from implementing security in Internet technology.

Learning Objectives

At the end of this chapter, readers will be able to learn the following:

- Abilities, aspects, and management of internet technologies.
- Effective communication as a performance indicator of internet technologies.
- Energy efficiency as performance methodology of internet technologies.
- Media access control of internet technologies.
- Reliability as a performance indicator of internet technologies.
- Security of internet technologies.
- Various performance methodologies of internet technologies.

Key Terms

- Abilities
- Blockchain
- Effective Communication
- Energy Efficiency
- Media Access Control
- Reliability
- Security

8.1. SECURITY OF INTERNET TECHNOLOGIES

The most important concern about Web technologies networks is the integrity of the interconnections between Web innovations units and the Transmission Control Protocol. Whereas the overwhelming bulk of Internet technology endpoints is obliged to use massive amounts of bandwidth and computer complexity, the confidentiality of these interconnections is typically overlooked (Solic et al., 2017). As a result, modern Internet innovations incorporating embedded systems address this security issue by incorporating hardware-enhanced cryptography capability. An opportunity will come to use exceptional security techniques such as Transport Layer Security (TLS) (Table 8.1).

Table 8.1. A Summarized Table for Security

Internet Technologies Performance Criteria	Problem	Methods	Parameters	References
Interface effectiveness of Internet technologies under network conditions,	Glitch and insufficient bandwidth	Examining the effectiveness of Internet Technologies shared content	wireless communication access	(Tang et al., 2019) (Nimawat & Nagar, 2019)
Information systems use microdata block transmission mechanisms.	The Hypertext transfer protocol has a significant latency.	Transmission protocols based on names	Typical Search Engine	(Shafik et al., 2020) (Mostafavi & Shafik, 2019)
Connectivity with Blockchain	Techniques that do not require the involvement of a third party	Installation of the ability To translate Nodes	time, delay, and real-time	(Sobral et al., 2019) (Ray et al., 2019)
Taking The advantage	IEEE 802.15.4 standards for signal strength	Remedy based on fuzzy reasoning	core network safety	(Li & Huang, 2017) (Martinez et al., 2019)
Taking advantage of Blockchain-Enabled Applications	High power is required for protection.	Internet technologies powered by blockchain	Depression of resources	(Fathy & Mekhail, 2019) (Li et al., 2017)
Innovations for the Industrial Internet	Techniques with no outside interference	technique of analysis	use of bandwidth	(Dimitrov & Haas, 2012)
Connectivity with Blockchain	Harmonies	Method for estimating efficiency	Charge	(Ismail & Materwala, 2018)

Source: Wasswa Shafik et al., creative commons license.

Using an Internet technology node with ESP32 System-on-Chip (SoC), resource limitations are compared to two TLS verification algorithms, ECDSA and RSA. The studies have been directed by the idea of security level, which makes it feasible to compare all cryptographic algorithms fairly in terms of the computational power required to divide them into a range of security levels, from 80 to 192. A 512-byte JSON file downloads for 100 consecutive periods while adding the energy consumption and the median transaction time. While real-world scenario experimenting is required to determine which secp256r1 curve increases due to optimizations in ECC security configuration is the best choice for hardware operation libraries. Platform, Suárez-Albela et al. (2018) demonstrate a higher level of security than secp224r1. However, ECDSA surpasses all RSA testing (Figure 8.1).

Figure 8.1. Image of security of internet technologies.

Source: Dreams time, creative commons license.

Massive amounts of data are produced due to the rapid development of Internet technologies. This material contains a sizable portion of sensitive information. Al-Hasnawi et al. (2018) describe the Policy Enforcement Fog Module as a method for protecting sensitive Internet technology data (PEFM). One of the main tasks of the PEFM solution is the forced application of different policies for sensitive data related to Internet technologies, wherever this data is available throughout their lives. The positioning of PEFM within the fog computing substructure ensures that PEFM operates as closely as practical to edge data sources. A Self-safe method based on creating and broadcasting active data bundles is made possible by PEFM for Remote Applications (ADBs). In contrast, PEFM immediately applies the Internet technologies policy to local applications. Demonstrates the outcomes of the simulation, which even used one to five additional privacy standards to improve data privacy. Penalties are realistic regarding runtime and latency (around 12–15% and 19–13%). Surveys show that PEFM is comparable to real-time Internet technology applications, given the amount of real-time restrictions.

Energy harvesting (EH) from radio by Nhan Vo et al. In Internet technologies, sensor networks with numerous non-core relays pay attention to waves and safety issues. Mainly there are two steps to the communication protocol. In the first stage, which is used for EH, the electricity from the energy transmission stations is transmitted by the Internet technology sensor nodes (SNs). Data is sent using the second stage in two steps: 1) The selected SN uses the energy obtained to send data to the controller and relays. Additionally, to improve the quality of communication between the SN and the controller, the chosen relay uses the onward-and-reinforce protocol to convey data to the controller.

While transmitting data, the microcontroller becomes vulnerable to data failure due to the relay's potential activity as eavesdropping (an unreliable relay). To improve the confidentiality efficacy of the suggested mechanism, they proposed the Best Sensor-Best-untrusted Relay (BSBR). They compared it to random-sensor-random untrustworthy relays and cutoff point designs. The Sealed formulations for the secrecy outage probability (SOP) and secrecy throughput (ST) are produced and validated by Monte Carlo simulation to validate their approach's first demonstration. Additionally provided are EH time optimization and subjective confidentiality frequency optimization algorithms. In addition, the impacts of EH time, EH Productivity factor, the number of SNs and Undependable relays, and the level of target concealment are explored in SOP and ST. According to their findings, the BSBR performed better than the two basic models in SOP and ST (Yokotani et al., 2017). Blockchain is being considered as a potential solution to store, analyze, and share data safely and efficiently with a focus on the performance and safety challenges of massive Internet technology data. For blockchain-enabled Internet technologies systems, Liu et al. (2019) propose a deep reinforcement learning (DRL) performance-based optimization framework with three goals: 1) Offering a means of gauging the system's scalability, decentralization, security, and delay, 2) Increasing the infrastructure blockchain's scalability without compromising the system's decentralization, speed, or security; Additionally, a blockchain for Internet technology systems is being conceptualized in step three, with the ability to customize the block manufacturers, integration algorithms, block sizes, and block spacing utilizing the DRL approach. The simulation results demonstrate that their proposed framework can improve the returns of blockchain-enabled Internet technology systems and be well-congruent with the dynamics of Internet technology.

Current advances in data-driven technology have substantially simplified software-defined networking (SDN) capabilities for various cloud-enabled optimized applications. SDN also utilizes the operating cost of Internet technology funded by internet platforms for different and changing user needs. When operating using SDN, its combination of numerous network communication technologies has rendered Internet technologies vulnerable to multiple security risks. Foundation for Internet Technologies Security, shortened as RF-Internet technologies, has been implemented in the Internet technologies network infrastructure to tackle vulnerabilities (Ali et al., 2019) (Figure 8.2).

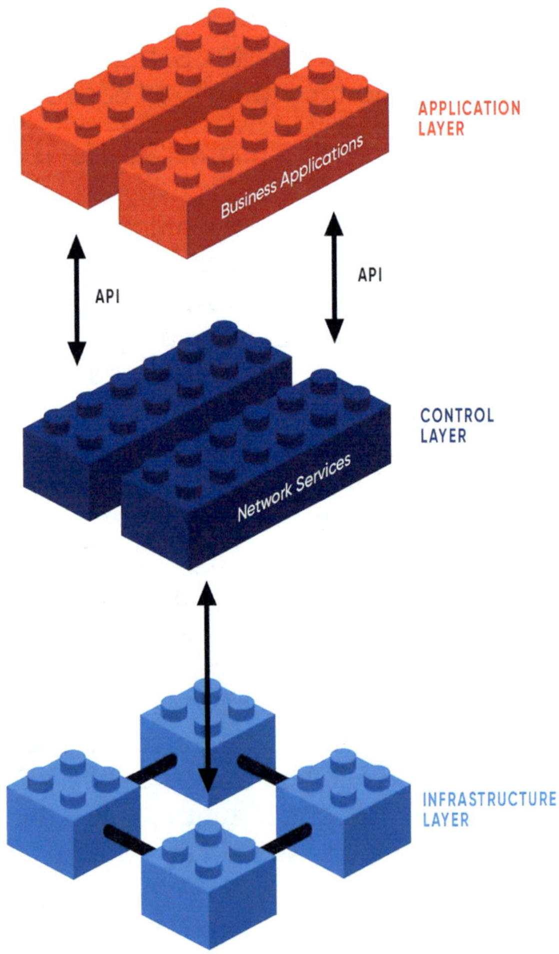

Figure 8.2. Image of Software-defined networking (SDN).

Source: Open networking foundation, creative commons license.

This paper proposes the necessary evaluations using SDR technology to assess the impact and identify pertinent research issues in the RFID domain, claiming that the PHY and MAC layers should be examined. To increase DFSA productivity (the number of tags reads per unit of time) and accelerate tag recognition, simple calculations indicate that the number of labels must equal the screen size (Kiran et al., 2017). In dynamic RFID environments, such as sophisticated stores or automated environments, it is essential to identify every item with a used RFID tag before it leaves the inspection area. Nowadays, commercial reader implementations use the DFSA standard as a light MAC to manage the communication between a reading and numerous labels. Despite this, the research discussing RFID effectiveness states that tags sensitivity is unpredictable, but this is typically disregarded when calculating bandwidth. In assessment campaigns, the tagged response probability (TRP) metric is utilized, which can be used to represent the MAC layer thoroughly (Yoo et al., 2017).

How to provide unsettling boundaries (with enough data) reported on the performance of the best-unbiased algorithms that need a parameter from the attacked data and communications after an anticipated statistical model reading whence the sensor data depends on the parameter before the attack. In terms of the boundaries careless of the algorithms, the impartial opinion system uses, these assaults offer a validated attack performance. By supporting new digital relationships, signal processing, and widespread sensor dispersion, internet technologies established pervasive sensing and inspection capabilities without posing significant security risks. The choices are made regardless of the unbiased estimating approach, which could use statistical signal processing, machine learning, deep learning, or any other method. Attackers can alter the data that Internet technologies sensors register or broadcast, which can significantly impact each algorithm that uses these data for reasoning.

This chapter's remaining sections are organized as follows. In section 2, we provide research on Internet technologies focusing on flow control and controls. We give studies on energy consumption efficiency in section 3. Section 4 shows integrated applications for Internet technologies and media Access restrictions. Section 5 presents applications connected to blockchain, dependability assessments, and other Internet technologies. The article is then concluded in the same section.

8.2. ENERGY EFFICIENCY

Li et al. (2018) note that due to the advancement of LPWA technology, NB-Internet innovations have attracted increasing attention and given a broad range of applications.

8.2.1. NB-Internet Technologies

An NB-Internet Technologies connection is a downlink from a user (UE) to an access point (BS) (base station). Multiple access transfer is a crucial element of NB-Internet technology, serving as the sensing database for numerous applications. Internet connection performance degradation, such as delay, may damage several systems with stringent uplink performance standards; in this book, Li et al. provide a method for statistically evaluating the effectiveness of transmit power for NB-Internet technology systems in terms to t delay and transfer dependability (Figure 8.3).

Figure 8.3. Image of energy efficiency in internet technologies.

Source: ESA- automation, creative commons license.

Their approach is accurate, considering protocol specifics and contemporary characteristics of NB-Internet technology, such as signal strength, the number of packets, multiple access conflict, etc. They validate the research findings with exhaustive models. According to the findings, their scientific specimen can calculate delay with 83% precision and reliability with 96%. In addition, they demonstrate that the results found can aid in the protocol for optimization, such as repeat frequency adjustment for reducing communication delays (Rauniyar et al., 2019).

Andres-Maldonado et al. (2019) NB-Internet Technologies version 13 introduced innovation as one of the options for providing mobile Web Technologies connection. NB-Internet solutions provide improved inside penetration, compatibility for a wide range of low systems, lower latency demands, and reduced electricity consumption. The widespread use of NB-Internet technology, in particular, poses a significant issue. The goal is to cover smartphones in areas previously unreachable by cell towers because of impact limitations or isolated sites. The approach is NB-Internet Technologies, which uses speed to reduce and repeat.

Although the performance of the channel approximation may significantly limit the coverage increase caused by repeats for the specified low range of SNR. In the study, they offer a framework for an analytical review to assess the effectiveness of NB-Internet technologies. Their investigation explores the calculation of the SNR as well as the constraints imposed by realistic channel estimation (CE). Results also demonstrated the impact of cover development on NB-Internet technologies' performance in terms of UE's uplink packet transmission latency and battery life cycle. Particularly about the battery life cycle of the UE, actual CE evaluations assume a battery life cycle reduction of roughly 90% compared to the ideal CE for an maximum coupling loss (MCL) of 164 dB.

8.2.2. Ah IEEE 802.11

Ah IEEE 802.11 A new update to the Wi-Fi standard adapt Wi-Fi networks to the latest developments in Internet technology. The critical element of.11ah is the Restricted Access Window (RAW), a cutting-edge channel access technique that reduces interference when even millions of Internet technology devices operate in the same space by allocating them to distinct channel periods. This study shows that existing studies inaccurately predict the actual system throughput, especially during reserved RAW slots, by oversimplifying the modeling of RAW behavior.

Their study's essential contribution was a new exact model built on a distinct methodology that produces more precise results and, as a result, enables improved Internet technologies system sizing. The extended model is suitable for a variety of situations that are common with Internet technology. It allows the discovery of RAW factors that enhance the system's throughput, power use, and packet loss ratio. The suggested fix can be applied to various traffic patterns, including those where each device sends a single packet, a group of packages of variable sizes, or full-buffer traffic.

Li et al. (2019) Internet Technologies still confront several obstacles, among which is how to deploy the public cloud quickly, accurately, and economically to provide Internet innovations to customers and transmit the domain with a positive quality of service. This preparedness, as a first step in addressing the issues, a pricing strategy is aimed problem as a result of various scarce funds in Internet technology devices and demanding service needs. Then they present an optimization method that answers the issue of the allocation of resources.

The optimal solution seeks to maximize the price ratio of specified internet inside the constraints of available resources and demand. Then they determine that the problem might well have exhibited characteristics of a semi-optimal solution. They proved to be the required universal solution, which can reduce the fundamental flaw to a pseudo-concave maximization problem and identify a practical solution. Therefore, they provide a helpful guidance method and develop algorithms to achieve the required result. In conclusion, they illustrate the conceptual deductions of the allocation of resources and the based algorithms for Internet-based cloud computing. This study's theoretical results and methodology can serve as design standards for allocating resources, schedule calculation, and communication protocol modeling in the centralized internet cloud.

8.2.3. Multi-Hop Reiterating

Chen et al. (2018). Multihop reiterating is a fundamental technology that will allow interconnections in complex systems such as those found in Internet technological applications. When half-duplex (HD) relays are used, the edge conversion rate decreases dramatically as the number of steps increases. They investigate the active power losses and signal margin of error for both HD and comprehensive (FD) changeover architectures in cross-systems with randomly oriented third-party equipment. They use a Poisson point process to design the placements of the device types. They obtain a shuttered expression for the fading channels and estimate the signal frequency for HD and FD transfers using BPSK and QPSK (Jin et al., 2020) (Figure 8.4).

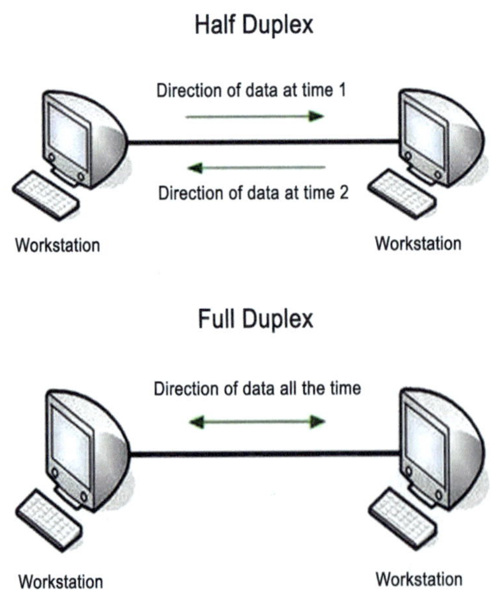

Figure 8.4. Illustration of full duplex vs. half duplex.

Source: Clustered networks, creative commons license.

The switching frequency demonstrates the benefits of utilizing a Markov chain approach for inter-down convert links. The example accurately depicts the channel's highly nonlinear paradigm, in which faulty symbolism interpretation may be "reformed" later in the system by a subsequent incorrect decode process. They validate that the paper seeks to analyze simulators and offer HD and FD solutions that reduce the phone's mistake rates and failure risk based on various attempts to interfere with density and residual self-interference degrees. The results recommend deploying HD and FD in cross-systems (Lachner & Dustdar, 2019).

8.2.4. Time Switch (TS) and Power Splitting (PS) Strategies

Time switch (TS) and PS strategies were used for UAV relays to implement EH transition, which was also chosen with signal-to-noise to noise ratio (SNR) maximization criteria as a result of which the study investigated the multiple Unmanned Aerial Vehicle (UAV) relays helped network in Internet technologies devices raised with energy out arriving until dominating the significant scale fading among source and sink also get the green-friendly communications.

Nevertheless, the conclusion revealed may become disorganized due to cumulative disturbance. Future 5G/B5G devices will have slight net signaling contact owing to small net signaling contact. Therefore, after employing and constructing TS and PS procedures, the shuttered expression of disconnection likelihood and the bit error rate (BER) for UAV relaying Internet Technologies equipment subjected to aggregation disturbance was determined. In addition, the latency and capacity limitations of UAV signal changeover were thoroughly examined. The study's findings and etymology indicated that the proposed inter general optimization of the multiplier, traversing energy, and UAV relaying choice could significantly minimize the network path loss and boost the gadget capacity and BER. The preliminary results' utility and the theoretical study's correctness were validated by simulated testing.

Li et al. (2015) Square lattice (SL), Triangle matrix (TL), and hexagonal lattice (HL) installation patterns are widely utilized for commercial Internet technologies. The efficacy of intellectual accessibility with these installation patterns, however, has yet to be verified. The paper first develops a transitional scheduling approach called cognition accessibility for standard architecture (CART) in radio resource sensing devices (CRSNs) with excellent transition efficiency and low channel saturation (Figure 8.5).

CART right sides channel-and-timeslot systems, cooperative spectrum-sensing design features, and design concepts for examining spectrum-sensing results (SSRs) in SL, TL, and HL. The research also examines acceptance frequency, CART's spectrum sharing effectiveness, coating schemas, and changeover latency for various transitional intervention areas.

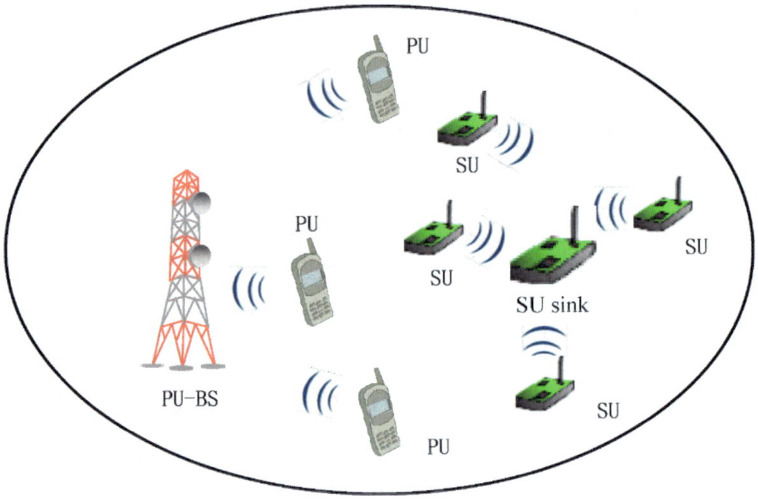

Figure 8.5. Image of system model of cognitive radio sensor networks (CRSNs).

Source: Jie Huang et al., creative commons license.

According to mathematical simulations and analysis, this paper compares CART and the neatest thing scheduling process for single-channel installation, in addition to another comparison across both implementation patterns (Ray et al., 2019). The accompanying experimental results demonstrate efficient CRSN implementation:

1. TL achieves a score of 3 out of 7 for best spectrum-sharing sensing properties among the three models using the information merging method.
2. SL calculated the optimum acceptance range under similar circumstances and installation regions.
3. For important complete areas, SL and TL cause the shortest transitional time.
4. For essential simultaneous insurance, SL results in less changeover time.
5. The likelihood of a solitary data type false report (FA) has minimal impact on changeover time; however, the chance of a principal patient's (PU) event has a discernible effect.
6. Transitions latencies can be reduced by increasing the ratios of the transfer period to the spectrally period.

Emphasize the projected reduced, solitary, and lengthy wireless communication for Internet technologies with battery-powered hubs. However, the efficiency of pure Aloha in LoRaWAN is disrupted by an increase in the number of end products and varying bandwidth needs. Due to this limitation, extensive calculations were conducted to evaluate the performance of Aloha in LoRaWAN. As standards, they utilized speed, packet drop rate (PER), energy usage, and latency of networks with varied numbers of edge devices and message lengths. In addition, the simulations show promising performance and PER improvements compared to Aloha. Despite this, delays have been reduced by a practical assessment. Finally, they validated aloha LoRaWAN for Green Internet Technologies.

Novo, the expansion of Internet technologies brings new issues, such as maintaining many different technology platforms (Novo, 2018). Due to the numerous safe managerial functions for Internet technologies, they have limits for many technology solutions applications. They suggested a distributed Internet technologies management solution using the blockchain to overcome these constraints. They calculated the rate of bandwidth and the percentage of delay associated with the gadgets in the articles and analyzed alternative setups of their system to maximize flexibility. They discovered that their approach might be extensible in the exact way current Internet technology methods are.

Zucchetto and Zanella (2017), an Internet information system, uses several procedures to interact with other networks, one of the most important of which is the multiple access technique. ALOHA-based accessibility or even some Listen to first Talk techniques is employed by many transitioning methods for the internet and some form of interaction. They compared Net innovations channel allocation approaches called ALOHA-based and Listen before Talk concepts in the book. They also offered a performance analysis of typically undergo versus fuel efficiency. According to the installation outcomes of Internet technologies, listening before Talk effectively lowers noise for transitioning; nevertheless, the energy efficiency would be less than that offered by ALOHA-based solutions. Furthermore, using specific methods saves energy across great distances from the recipient.

8.3. MEDIA ACCESS CONTROL

It has been illustrated that Internet-related content, User access, and linked apps. Individual IEEE protocols, such as the 802.11ah protocols, were created to allow networking connectivity to a large number of power and diverse service quality (quality of service) Internet infrastructure gadgets.

8.3.1. Disabled Access Windows Method (RAWM)

The disabled access windows method (RAWM) is a unique protocols element that aims to reduce multiple-access congestion by scheduling the beacon period and enabling an inadequate amount of nodes to compete for a specific slot (Sobral et al., 2019). In the IEEE 802.11ah RAWM, the performance measures of the medium access management level were examined concerning specific QoS Internet sites. Importance and acting as a buffer data can exist on

Internet-connected gadgets with compromising connection speeds, as determined by an experiment.

Following 3GPP TR 37.868, the efficiency study is conducted by considering the number of opening paragraphs and the total amount of preface broadcasts in the surrounding world. The arbitrary response (RAR) estimate methodology is proposed based on the results. Because there is a limitation when an actual LTE unit has a wide range of devices, unique components to imitate LTE's RA processes were created in terms of employee performance. A RA speed level simulator is required for LTE to support a wide range of devices (Martinez et al., 2019) (Figure 8.6).

Figure 8.6. Illustration of media access control.

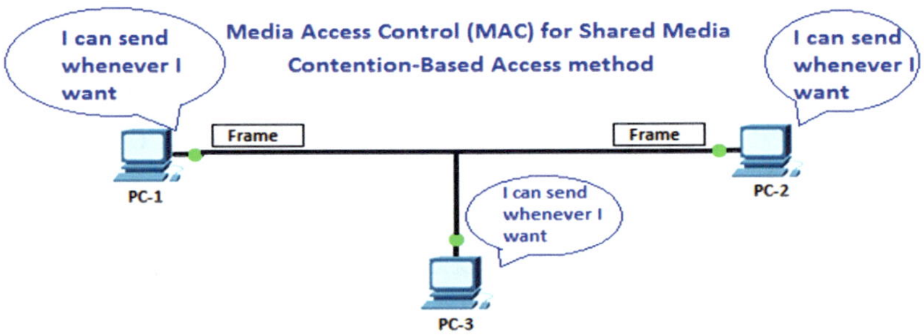

Source: Med Bouftira, creative commons license.

A revolutionary IEEE 802.15.4 media access (MAC) power management solution has been presented, which achieves the consumer level of station dependability while consuming the least amount of energy. The data type dependability, transmission buffer overflowing losses, latency, and energy user are clarified by calculating the packet arrival time. Successively, a three-dimensional Markov chain and M/G/1/K queuing have been used to mimic the IEEE 802.15.4 MAC and on-node traffic queued. In addition, they have created a mathematical model to describe the effects of confined on-node storage for sensing data storage on the efficiency of the MAC layer (Al-Hasnawi et al., 2018).

TIPS

The anticipated model has reached an accuracy of 97% and 94%, respectively, as measured by simulators and the real-time testing ground.

For many anticipated cellular Internet technologies applications, producing energy-efficient and delay-aware access is necessary. Before forwarding their data, devices in cellular networks use a random-access channel (RACH). This contention-based association technique introduces significant access delays and energy waste as the number of contending devices increases. Due to the complexity of uplink forwarding, which presents a wide range of interference elements, designing the RACH protocol's performance is difficult. A different mathematical framework based on stochastic geometry has been introduced to analyze the RACH protocol and understand its limitations in the context of cellular Internet technologies applications by many devices. The developed model considers device density, spatial network characteristics, power control strategies, and device mutual interference. Because of the rapid growth in online technology, it is projected that the number of short Internet technologies gadgets will rapidly increase in the following years. However, in the real world, such as with Internet technologies, networks or computers are subjected to an outside interfering actor, frequently resulting in systemic destruction. In this study, they did weigh forwarding the information of Internet relay node together with source node data using non-orthogonal multiple access (NOMA) procedures in the proximity of a trying to interfere transmitter to their different locations, which differs from a clichéd RF EH system where only a supplier base station message is transferred by transitional EH relay selection node (Ferrari et al., 2019). They have explored the integration of two prominent energy collecting transmitting optimization techniques shifting (TS) transmitting and energy division (PS) relay, via the NOMA method for Web technology relaying due to the proximity of interferences.

8.3.2. Wireless Sensor and Actuator Systems

Chinnalagi et al. (2017) Wireless sensor and actuator systems are other names for wireless sensor networks (WSN). Wireless sensors track physical or environmental conditions such as sound, humidity, etc. Internet technologies are networks of structures such as buildings, vehicles, and so on with embedded gadgets, applications, and detectors that are being used to send and receive data. A few subjects discussed in this research include media access control schemes, translation, implementation, core network, and quality of service. They may control the problems using the SSNI method (smart sensor network in Internet technologies) (Figure 8.7).

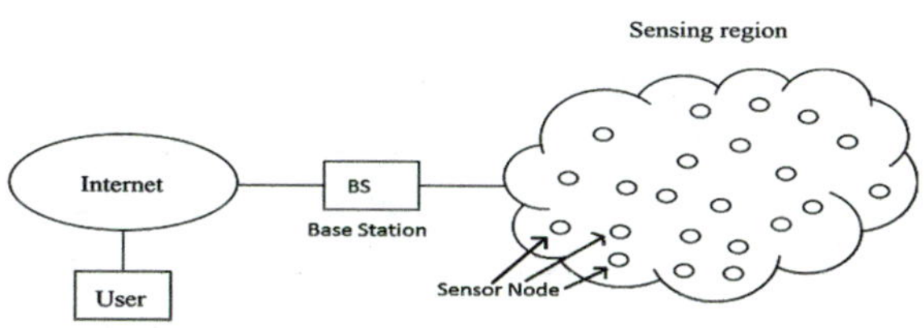

Source: Shivam Kumar, creative commons license.

Figure 8.7. Schematic of wireless sensor network (WSN).

8.3.3. Hazard Mitigation Program

Kim et al. (2017) newly, the hazard mitigation program that aids search and recovery victims in disaster areas utilizing robotics and toolkits rapidly expands as modern Internet technologies are created. The introduction of these new instruments will assist in enhancing time-sensitive relief efforts while also ensuring the security of firemen.

Even though the disaster area is difficult to access and goes through owing to tumble-offs, barricades, and the highest risks, they design and execute an individual's motivation performance review test-bed in the paper, which may occur in various unsafe working conditions that a robot and specific equipment may meet while traveling and bypassing them. In addition, the testing ground takes many Web technologies sensors to assess the ability objectively. The exam comprises slots, a stable slope, steps, sloped surfaces, a tube tunnel, a narrow channel, a liquid channel, and other features. The degree of difficulty for every route can be changed to give a foundation for evaluating the achievement of the target robot.

8.3.4. Monitoring Equipment

Kafhali et al. (2018) Monitoring equipment for client health is becoming commonplace due to the increased use of technological Web devices in the maintenance and development of overall fitness, mainly through the provision of health services through these gadgets. In a typical implementation, Medical Internet technologies) the device sends patient records to an Internet Technologies (medical database, where it is evaluated, stored, and made available to individuals. Nurses and physicians can demand health care stored information in these data sets, which are often housed in a public or private cloud (Banaie et al., 2018).

Did you Know?

In the event of an emergency, the performing agencies have access to data.

One of the most crucial performance criteria is quick response. It is critical to install health data on the internet to decrease response. Furthermore, the Cloud computing layer is employed for data storage and processing to reduce response. The project demonstrates and investigates methods to reduce resource costs while improving health information access reaction time in a fog or cloud-based. The paper recommends a queue mechanism to reduce reaction time while minimizing fog resources (Service Level Agreement). Their simulations demonstrate that the model can access the necessary resources for health data systems.

8.4. RELIABILITY

IEEE 802.15.4 In respect of dependability, connection integrity standards perform poorly in the medical setting. To maximize the effectiveness of these methods, a method fuzzy – based and extensive experimental questions about sustainability were given. They provide a remedy in four stages. 1) Understanding pertinent IEEE 802.15.4 standards and confirming their compliance with sick monitoring devices by simulations in Castalia 3.2 with the OMNet ++ platform. 2) Offering a thorough Evaluation and Evaluation of the Link Quality Procedures Employed. 3) Establishing a real-time testing ground for conducting experiments to identify genuine signal strength assessment in various medical situations (Leite et al., 2018).

A searcher recommends a fuzzy logic technique (FLS) for plotting the outcomes of test trials with the proposed FLS to attain optimum performance. For experimental purposes, medical connections are divided into four ecological sections: inside, corridor, ward to wards, and clinic to ward. Both static and moving situations are considered. Different channel quality criteria quantities for the Received Signal Strength Indicator (RSSI) and the Link Quality Indicator (LQI) are discovered for various medical circumstances. In most cases, LQI and package reception have a strong association, but RSSI and package acceptability have a weak point (Kim & Jung, 2019).

8.5. BLOCKCHAIN

Blockchain has demonstrated significant promise in Internet technology environments to develop confidence and broad consensus Methods even without the involvement of a third party. Understanding the relationship between communications and blockchain, as well as the performance restriction on peers, helps simplify the creation of a private blockchain Internet technologies platform. A created an analytical model for the mobile Broadband technology network utilizing blockchain. The spatial position of the nodes in the feature space and the quantity of deal input in the temporal domain are both elements plotted as a Poisson process (Lin & Matsumoto, 2018) (Figure 8.8).

The initial step is determining the transmission proportion, the winning percentage of blockchain transactions, and the overall throughput. Researchers create the algorithms based on the system model and the efficiency research to determine the ideal installation of the peak performance cluster for the blockchain network under the condition of employing optimum system throughput. Ultimately, the proposed systems are subjected to three standard security assaults. Techniques such as physical layer encryption are provided and considered for maintaining data security during these attacks. The numerical findings validate the soundness theoretic assessment and the best node placement algorithm (Anajemba et al., 2018).

Figure 8.8. Image of blockchain.

Source: Monica, creative commons license.

8.6. INTERNET TECHNOLOGIES MANAGEMENT

As Internet technologies advance, networks and system management will be necessary to force a few connecting devices to migrate and collect information. Internet technologies management demonstrates the difficulty in observing and controlling varied system components that accommodate many interfaces and quality of service needs, whether rational or physical.

The key management issues for Internet infrastructure settings are heterogeneous platforms and compatibility. Because multiplicity among systems & standards in Internet technologies network administration makes comparison difficult because greater standardization is required (Kiran & Rajalakshmi, 2018).

This research looked at internet Freedom technologies management solutions that used the very well Internet technologies managed services protocols in real-world scenarios. Actual surroundings of intelligent lighting systems are employed as a comparative. The research includes both qualitative and numerical measurements.

Based on the supplied statistics, the Open Daylight (ODL) architecture achieves the best performance using NETCONF and SNMP. It supports Internet technologies networking & Internet Technologies system administration interfaces remotely. It is deduced that such a flexible platform is an ODL platform that can create managed service techniques to meet every configuration, whether it be a situation with the shortest reaction speed as well as the highest transmission time or a set of circumstances that requires instant and energy savings (Li et al., 2019).

8.7. INTERNET TECHNOLOGIES ABILITIES AND ASPECTS

Internet technologies apps play a critical part in Internet technologies infrastructure, allowing end-users to expand their product offerings. The capabilities and features of Internet technology apps vary.

As a result, deciding between different programs can be stressful. This is particularly true because no baseline assessment exists to evaluate and examine various applications. The study attempts to reduce the obstacles in developing performance assessment instruments using open-source Internet technology (Badihi et al., 2019). The study explicitly evaluates sustainability in capacity and reaction time, as well as uniformity in resource usage and resilience.

8.8. EFFECTIVE COMMUNICATION

Because it facilitates the clear communication of Web technology applications, a large quantity of communication was developed. Internet technology companies are seen as having scarce funds. Internet Technologies equipment requires Wi-Fi connections, and most installations are distant. They must manage the relationship with connectivity that may be erratic, inconsistent, and of limited bandwidth (Liu et al., 2019). Therefore, the direct measurement for technological Web standards has not been examined in this scenario. The current effort aims to evaluate the effectiveness of Internet technologies message methods in constrained remote access networks (Figure 8.9).

Figure 8.9. Illustration of components of effective communication.

Source: Assignment point, creative commons license.

Aside from the growing popularity of Internet technologies solutions in numerous sectors of practical uses, efficiency has become a significant demand. While strategies for critical ideas, such as moving virtual machines and optimization, significantly impact edge throughput. They had planned an optimistic method of serviceability measuring performance for recovered Internet technological applications using generalized stochastic Petri net modeling approaches (GSPN) (Fathy & Mekhail, 2019). There have been published computational equations representing the behaviors of both facilities and Internet technological tools and numerical representations of performance characteristics.

Remember

The Web innovations environment is a set of devices, techniques, and entities that interact with one another via sourced local portals.

When customers rely on protocol-specific upward silos involved with the e-healthcare or consumers' wellness care domains inside an Internet technologies-based situation, this inquiry gets more sensitive, leading to a hazardous network collapse by generating questions for the customers (Shafik et al., 2020). To illustrate this issue, the best online technologies-gateway platform is planned that contains the heterogeneous view to ensure compatibility by employing network control broker solutions to assist in providing well-being customer services.They had practically constructed the Internet technology solutions with 3 Web-based technologies orbs to construct a solid evidence e-health messenger app while referring to real-life cardiac sensors, vital sign detectors, and skin conductance reaction detectors (Nimawat & Nagar, 2019). They construct the finest interoperability Web innovations doorway test-bed that includes 2.4 GHz commercial, science, and clinical radio signals, IEEE 802.11b/g/n, and Bluetooth technologies to be effortlessly switched in replaceable forms in their investigation. The researchers showed two extra intelligent virtual Internet technologies-motes. They implanted them in the best-selling Internet technologies-gateway physical device to replicate and test the potential for additional procedures to attach with the sophisticated online technologies access foundation. The modern Internet technologies gateway is evaluated based on various network quality variables and accessible gold standards to ensure optimal quality of care rendered to fictitious customers. Over-the-air (OTA) performance appraisals are desperately required because of the increasing number of Internet-based wireless apps for mobile devices (Jun Tang et al., 2019).

Nonetheless, the constraints posed by Internet-enabled electronic applications have necessitated the operation of OTA measures that are precise, rapid, and expensive (Li et al., 2017). This section provides several approaches for enhancing typical

OTA measurement to suit the OTA needs of Internet technologies. Three test procedures are presented for single-input single-output (SISO) endpoints to accelerate their overall isotropic sensitive testing and improve their accuracy results. The radiating two-stage (RTS) method is introduced for Internet technologies inter multi-output (MIMO) devices. Mathematical descriptions of the fundamental ideas include pattern measurement noise removal and inverted matrix auto-solving. The benefits of the RTS for MIMO system monitoring are discussed. In addition, smart test systems appropriate for ordinary office buildings were developed. These chambers can accommodate both SISO and MIMO, giving in significant cost savings.

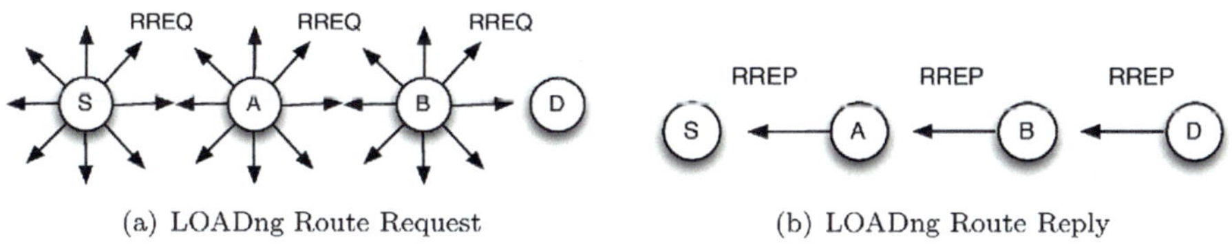

Figure 8.10. Schematic of LOADng path discovery.

Source: Clausen et al., creative commons license.

Thus, with advancements in technology and procedures, the Internet technologies business may tolerate and benefit from OTA reviews (Dimitrov & Haas, 2012). They are responsible for constructing pathways and transmitting packets of data between nodes in the network. Routing protocols are a crucial aspect of the Internet technology situations that follow. In this context, the Lightweight On-demand Ad hoc Distance vector Routing Protocol – Next Generation (LOADng) is a new solution for Internet technology networks that, despite being adequate for a dynamic environment due to their responsive operation, have performance problems. In circumstances involving mobile Internet technologies, the transit between networks creates topology changes that make the task of routing algorithms more challenging (Ismail & Materwala, 2018) (Figure 8.10). As a result, existing Internet technology's navigation methods tend to provide stronger circumstances and decreased efficiency in these settings, necessitating several extra modifications to greatly serve device movement (Li & Huang, 2017). Furthermore, a few controlling messages are included, allowing nodes to update their forwarding table while maintaining a typical control packet periodicity. Moreover, a novel navigation measure is intended for building routes based on the dependability of the connection and surrounding nodes' proximity.

ACTIVITY 8.1:

Enlist some performance measurement methodologies that are currently employed in internet technologies.

SUMMARY

We offered a complete comprehensive assessment of the massive performance of Internet technologies in this chapter. The critical Internet technologies have been researched and analyzed further, such as Internet technologies security, congestion control, flow control, and energy demand efficiency in various areas of computing. Investigators can employ the summary table of Internet technologies performance assessment to develop models that tackle current technical difficulties, according to research on numerous elements of Internet technologies technology, such as security concerns, access to media, vast quantities of dependable and consistent data transmission, traffic shaping, and more. A substantial study has been conducted, and practical solutions for increasing effectiveness and energy administration have been offered; however, new difficulties still require additional investigation due to new technologies, including such cellular networks.

REVIEW QUESTIONS

1. What security methodologies should be used when implementing internet technologies?
2. How can internet technologies be made more energy efficient?
3. What is the purpose of Media Access Control in performance methodologies of internet technologies?
4. What measures can be taken to ensure reliability in performance methodologies of internet technologies?
5. How can blockchain be used to enhance performance methodologies of internet technologies?
6. What abilities should be considered when designing performance methodologies of internet technologies?
7. What strategies can ensure effective communication between users and internet technologies?

MULTIPLE CHOICE QUESTIONS

1. Which of the following is a performance methodology of Internet Technologies?

a. Security
b. Energy Efficiency
c. Media Access Control
d. All of the above

2. What is the primary purpose of blockchain technology?

a. To increase reliability
b. To improve abilities

c. To provide effective communication

d. To provide a secure distributed ledger

3. What is the main difference between media access control and security?

a. Media access control is used to control access to resources, while security is used to protect resources from unauthorized access.

b. Media access control protects resources from unauthorized access, while security controls access to resources.

c. Media access control is used to protect resources from energy efficiency, while security is used to control access to resources.

d. Media access control is used to control access to resources, while security is used to protect resources from energy efficiency.

4. What is the primary purpose of effective communication in Internet Technologies?

a. To improve reliability

b. To improve abilities

c. To increase security

d. To provide fast and reliable communication

5. Which of the following is NOT a performance methodology of Internet Technologies?

a. Blockchain

b. Security

c. Energy Efficiency

d. Time Management

Answers to Multiple Choice Questions

1. (d); 2. (d); 3. (b); 4. (d); 5. (d)

REFERENCES

1. Al-Hasnawi, A., Mohammed, I., & Al-Gburi, A., (2018). Performance evaluation of the policy enforcement fog module for protecting the privacy of IoT data. In: 2018 IEEE International Conference on Electro/Information Technology (EIT) (Vol. 1, pp. 0951–0957). IEEE.

2. Ali, M. Z., Mišić, J., & Mišić, V. B., (2019). Performance evaluation of heterogeneous IoT nodes with differentiated quality of service in IEEE 802.11 ah RAW mechanism. IEEE Transactions on Vehicular Technology, 68(4), 3905–3918.

3. Anajemba, J. H., Tang, Y., Ansere, J. A., & Iwendi, C., (2018). Performance analysis of D2D energy-efficient IoT networks with relay-assisted underlying technique. In: IECON 2018–44th Annual Conference of the IEEE Industrial Electronics Society (Vol. 1, pp. 3864–3869). IEEE.
4. Andres-Maldonado, P., Ameigeiras, P., Prados-Garzon, J., Navarro-Ortiz, J., & Lopez-Soler, J. M., (2019). An analytical performance evaluation framework for NB-IoT. IEEE Internet of Things Journal, 6(4), 7232–7240.
5. Badihi, B., Ghavimi, F., & Jäntti, R., (2019). On the system-level performance evaluation of Bluetooth 5 in IoT: Open office case study. In: 2019 16th International Symposium on Wireless Communication Systems (ISWCS) (Vol. 1, pp. 485–489). IEEE.
6. Banaie, F., Misic, J., Misic, V. B., Moghaddam, M. H. Y., & Seno, S. A. H., (2018). Performance analysis of multithreaded IoT gateway. IEEE Internet of Things Journal, 6(2), 3143–3155.
7. Belloch, J. A., Badía, J. M., Igual, F. D., & Cobos, M., (2019). Practical considerations for acoustic source localization in the IoT era: Platforms, energy efficiency, and performance. IEEE Internet of Things Journal, 6(3), 5068–5079.
8. Chen, G., Coon, J. P., Mondal, A., Allen, B., & Chambers, J. A., (2018). Performance analysis for multihop full-duplex IoT networks subject to Poisson distributed interferers. IEEE Internet of Things Journal, 6(2), 3467–3479.
9. Chinnalagi, V., Murugeswari, R., Priyadharshni, T., Rajalakshmi, K., & Ananthi, J. V., (2017). Dynamic performance of smart sensor network using IoT. In: 2017 International Conference on I-SMAC (IoT in Social, Mobile, Analytics, and Cloud) (I-SMAC) (Vol. 1, pp. 49–53). IEEE.
10. Da Cruz, M. A., Marcondes, G. A., Rodrigues, J. J., Lorenz, P., & Pinheiro, P. R., (2018). Performance evaluation of iot middleware through multicriteria decision-making. In: 2018 IEEE Global Communications Conference (GLOBECOM) (Vol. 1, pp. 1–5). IEEE.
11. Dimitrov, S., & Haas, H., (2012). Information rate of OFDM-based optical wireless communication systems with nonlinear distortion. Journal of Lightwave Technology, 31(6), 918–929.
12. El Kafhali, S., Salah, K., & Alla, S. B., (2018). Performance evaluation of IoT-fog-cloud deployment for healthcare services. In: 2018 4th International Conference on Cloud Computing Technologies and Applications (Cloudtech) (Vol. 1, pp. 1–6). IEEE.
13. Fathy, C. E. M., & Mekhail, T., (2019). Investigations of the instantaneous performance of a solar chimney power plant installed in Aswan using IoT. IET Renewable Power Generation, 13(12), 2261–2266.
14. Ferrari, P., Rinaldi, S., Sisinni, E., Colombo, F., Ghelfi, F., Maffei, D., & Malara, M., (2019). Performance evaluation of full-cloud and edge-cloud architectures for industrial IoT anomaly detection based on deep learning. In: 2019 II Workshop on Metrology for Industry 4.0 and IoT (MetroInd4. 0&IoT) (Vol. 1, pp. 420–425). IEEE.

15. Ismail, L., & Materwala, H., (2018). Energy-aware VM placement and task scheduling in cloud-IoT computing: Classification and performance evaluation. IEEE Internet of Things Journal, 5(6), 5166–5176.
16. Ji, B., Li, Y., Zhou, B., Li, C., Song, K., & Wen, H., (2019). Performance analysis of UAV relay-assisted IoT communication network enhanced with energy harvesting. IEEE Access, 7(1), 38738–38747.
17. Jin, H. Y., Jung, E. S., & Lee, D., (2020). High-performance IoT streaming data prediction system using Spark: A case study of air pollution. Neural Computing and Applications, 32(17), 13147–13154.
18. Jun, T. Z., Guo, Y., & Liu, Q., (2019). Research on an improved fusion RFID collision avoidance algorithm. Journal of Communications Technology, Electronics, and Computer Science, 22(1), 6–19.
19. Kaur, N., & Sood, S. K., (2015). A game theoretic approach for an IoT-based automated employee performance evaluation. IEEE Systems Journal, 11(3), 1385–1394.
20. Khorov, E., Krotov, A., Lyakhov, A., Yusupov, R., Condoluci, M., Dohler, M., & Akyildiz, I., (2019). Enabling the internet of things with Wi-Fi halow—Performance evaluation of the restricted access window. IEEE Access, 7, 127402–127415.
21. Kim, T., & Jung, B. C., (2019). Performance analysis of grant-free multiple access for supporting sporadic traffic in massive IoT networks. IEEE Access, 7(1), 166648–166656.
22. Kim, Y. D., Jung, S. H., Gu, D. Y., Kim, H. K., & Song, C. H., (2017). IoT sensor-based mobility performance test-bed for disaster response robots. In: 2017 6th IIAI International Congress on Advanced Applied Informatics (IIAI-AAI) (Vol. 1, pp. 990, 991). IEEE.
23. Kiran, M. S., & Rajalakshmi, P., (2018). Performance analysis of CSMA/CA and PCA for time-critical industrial IoT applications. IEEE Transactions on Industrial Informatics, 14(5), 2281–2293.
24. Kiran, M. S., Subrahmanyam, V., & Rajalakshmi, P., (2017). Novel power management scheme and effects of constrained on-node storage on the performance of MAC layer for industrial IoT networks. IEEE Transactions on Industrial Informatics, 14(5), 2146–2158.
25. Lachner, C., & Dustdar, S., (2019). A performance evaluation of data protection mechanisms for resource-constrained IoT devices. In: 2019 IEEE International Conference on Fog Computing (ICFC) (Vol. 1, pp. 47–52). IEEE.
26. Leite, J. R., Ursini, E. L., & Martins, P. S., (2018). Performance analysis of IoT networks with mobility via modeling and simulation. In: 2018 International Symposium on Performance Evaluation of Computer and Telecommunication Systems (SPECTS) (Vol. 1, pp. 1–13). IEEE.
27. Li, F., Zheng, K., Long, H., & Guan, D., (2019). Performance analysis of complementary GFDM in IoT communications. In: 2019 IEEE 89th Vehicular Technology Conference (VTC2019-Spring) (Vol. 1, pp. 1–5). IEEE.

28. Li, H., Chen, G., Wang, Y., Gao, Y., & Dong, W., (2018). Accurate performance modeling of uplink transmission in NB-IoT. In: 2018 IEEE 24th International Conference on Parallel and Distributed Systems (ICPADS) (Vol. 1, pp. 910–917). IEEE.
29. Li, J., Liu, Y., Zhang, Z., Ren, J., & Zhao, N., (2017). Towards green IoT networking: Performance optimization of network coding based communication and reliable storage. IEEE Access, 5(1), 8780–8791.
30. Li, S., & Huang, J., (2017). GSPN-based reliability-aware performance evaluation of IoT services. In: 2017 IEEE International Conference on Services Computing (SCC) (Vol. 1, pp. 483–486). IEEE.
31. Li, W., Zhu, C., Leung, V. C., Yang, L. T., & Ma, Y., (2015). Performance comparison of cognitive radio sensor networks for industrial IoT with different deployment patterns. IEEE Systems Journal, 11(3), 1456–1466.
32. Li, X., Tan, L., & Li, F., (2019). Optimal cloud resource allocation with cost performance tradeoff based on the internet of things. IEEE Internet of Things Journal, 6(4), 6876–6886.
33. Lin, W., & Matsumoto, T., (2018). Performance analysis of distortion-acceptable cooperative communications in wireless sensor networks for the internet of things. IEEE Sensors Journal, 19(5), 1979–1989.
34. Liu, M., Yu, F. R., Teng, Y., Leung, V. C., & Song, M., (2019). Performance optimization for blockchain-enabled industrial internet of things (IIoT) systems: A deep reinforcement learning approach. IEEE Transactions on Industrial Informatics, 15(6), 3559–3570.
35. Liu, S., Liu, Y., Wu, F., & Fan, W., (2019). Feature data selection for improving the performance of entity similarity searches in the internet of things. IEEE Access, 7, 49938–49944.
36. Martinez, B., Adelantado, F., Bartoli, A., & Vilajosana, X., (2019). Exploring the performance boundaries of NB-IoT. IEEE Internet of Things Journal, 6(3), 5702–5712.
37. Mostafavi, S., & Shafik, W., (2019). Fog computing architectures, privacy, and security solutions. Journal of Communications Technology, Electronics, and Computer Science, 24(1), 1–14.
38. Moussa, H. G., & Zhuang, W., (2018). RACH performance analysis for large-scale cellular IoT applications. IEEE Internet of Things Journal, 6(2), 3364–3372.
39. Nimawat, D., & Nagar, N., (2019). Self-tuning fuzzy PID controllers application on industrial hydraulic actuator using unique system identification approach. Journal of Communications Technology, Electronics, and Computer Science, 22(1), 1–6.
40. Novo, O., (2018). Scalable access management in IoT using blockchain: A performance evaluation. IEEE Internet of Things Journal, 6(3), 4694–4701.
41. Rahman, W. U., Choi, Y. S., & Chung, K., (2019). Performance evaluation of video streaming application over CoAP in IoT. IEEE Access, 7(1), 39852–39861.
42. Rauniyar, A., Engelstad, P. E., & Østerbø, O. N., (2019). Performance analysis of RF energy harvesting and information transmission based on NOMA with interfering

signal for IoT relay systems. IEEE Sensors Journal, 19(17), 7668–7682.

43. Ray, P. P., Thapa, N., & Dash, D., (2019). Implementation and performance analysis of interoperable and heterogeneous IoT-edge gateway for pervasive wellness care. IEEE Transactions on Consumer Electronics, 65(4), 464–473.
44. Shafik, W., Matinkhah, M., Asadi, M., Ahmadi, Z., & Hadiyan, Z., (2020). A study on the internet of things performance evaluation. Journal of Communications Technology, Electronics, and Computer Science, 1, 1–19.
45. Shafik, W., Matinkhah, S. M., & Ghasemzadeh, M., (2020). Internet of things-based energy management, challenges, and solutions in smart cities. Journal of Communications Technology, Electronics, and Computer Science, 27(1), 1–11.
46. Sobral, J. V., Rodrigues, J. J. P., Rabêlo, R. A., Saleem, K., & Kozlov, S. A., (2019). Improving the performance of LOADng routing protocol in mobile IoT scenarios. IEEE Access, 7(1), 107032–107046.
47. Solic, P., Blazevic, Z., Skiljo, M., Patrono, L., Colella, R., & Rodrigues, J. J., (2017). Gen2 RFID as IoT enabler: Characterization and performance improvement. IEEE Wireless Communications, 24(3), 33–39.
48. Suárez-Albela, M., Fernández-Caramés, T. M., Fraga-Lamas, P., & Castedo, L., (2018). Practical performance comparison of ECC and RSA for resource-constrained IoT devices. In: 2018 Global Internet of Things Summit (GIoTS) (Vol. 1, pp. 1–6). IEEE.
49. Yokotani, T., Shimuzu, A., Sasaki, Y., & Mukai, H., (2017). Proposals for packet processing and performance evaluation of IoT devices. In: 2017 Japan-Africa Conference on Electronics, Communications, and Computers (JAC-ECC) (Vol. 1, pp. 5–8). IEEE.
50. Yoo, S. S., Lee, S. H., Jung, S. Y., & Kim, J. H., (2017). Performance evaluation of random access response estimation scheme for IoT communications. In: 2017 IEEE International Conference on Communications (ICC) (Vol. 1, pp. 1–6). IEEE.
51. Zhang, J., Blum, R. S., & Poor, H. V., (2018). Approaches to secure inference in the internet of things: Performance bounds, algorithms, and effective attacks on IoT sensor networks. IEEE Signal Processing Magazine, 35(5), 50–63.
52. Zucchetto, D., & Zanella, A., (2017). Uncoordinated access schemes for the IoT: Approaches, regulations, and performance. IEEE Communications Magazine, 55(9), 48–54.

INDEX

D

E

F

W

Printed in the United States
by Baker & Taylor Publisher Services